Reflections from an Engineer
for His Grandchildren

Jim I. Jones

Copyright © 2024 by Jim I. Jones

All rights reserved. No part of this book may be reproduced or transmitted in any form or by any means, electronic or mechanical, including photocopying, recording, or by any information storage or retrieval system without written permission from Jim I. Jones, except for the inclusion of a quotation in a review.

Printed in the United States of America

ISBN-13: 978-0-9672159-2-1

Library of Congress Control Number: 2023923974

Publisher: Jim I. Jones

Other Books by Jim I. Jones

The Document Methodology, Hardcover, 256 Pages, ISBN-13:978-0- 9672159-0-7, ISBN: 0-9672159-0-0, Published 1999 by Jim I. Jones, Priority Process Associates Inc

The Document Methodology for Enterprise Analysis, Second Edition, ISBN- 13:978-1-4259-9824-0, ISBN: 1-4259-9824-0, 224 Pages, Published 2007 AuthorHouse..

The Document Methodology for Enterprise Analysis and Healthcare Transformation Third Edition, ISBN-13:978-0- 9672159-0-7, ISBN: 0-9672159-1-4, 320 Pages, Published 2020 Ingram Spark

Reflections for My Grandchildren, Paperback, 160 Pages, ISBN-13: 978-1- 4196-7954-4, ISBN: 1-4196-7954-6, Published 2007 Createspace

Faith and Reason - The Universality of God and Fallacy of Atheism, Paperback, 130 Pages, ISBN-13: 978-1-970024-75-3, ISBN: 1-970024- 75-5, Published 2017 Lulu.

Preface

One of life's great gifts are grandchildren. The original Reflections book published in 2007 was dedicated and written to my nine grandchildren who sadly did not respond to it. Seven of them have finished at least four years of college and two will be Juniors this fall. I dedicate this to them again; maybe one of them will read it.

Reflections resulted from my granddaughter's question: "So why do I need to know anything about the "Theory of Relativity" (see Reflection 3). Grandchildren need to know a lot about a lot of things. The first Reflections look at past, present, and future to showcase specific areas. It discusses how one might educate him/herself to contribute to that area. Some reflections are fun, but others are difficult (please persevere). Reader, you are no less than the stars; you can make a difference; but you must persevere.

As you read this, remember that the first 30 Reflections were written in 2007. The remainder were finalized in 2023.

Albert Einstein once said: "I want to know (God's) thoughts; the rest are details." I'd like to know everything, but it seems the more I know, the more I know I don't know.

"It takes considerable knowledge just to realize the extent of your own ignorance." - Thomas Sowell

In the preface to the "Great Books," Robert Hutchins writes: "The reiteration of slogans, the distortion of the news, the great storm of propaganda that beats upon the citizen twenty-four hours a day all his life long mean either democracy must fall prey to the loudest and most persistent propagandists or that people must save themselves by strengthening their minds so that they can appraise the issues themselves" (and that's 50 years before Internet nonsense). Education cannot help form an intelligent opinion if facts are not available, but it can provide habits of mind to demand the information necessary to form one. Unfortunately, although billions of facts are available on the Internet, they are embedded in trillions of points of misinformation (noise).

After many years as an engineer/mathematician (geek^2), I was able to discern which kinds of complex mathematics applied to a problem. Not having the benefit of a liberal education, I had not read history or philosophy and distained written communication. In the last sixty years, I've read philosophy, theology, history, and theoretical physics. After writing three versions of a process analysis book, I acquired minimal writing skills. It is unfortunate that liberally educated people take little mathematics and no engineering and engineers study nothing else. Political vision requires love of country and the political process but also requires extensive planning and problem-solving skills.

Forty-seven years of Christmas letters provide some idea of the angst and joys of parenting three sons with only occasional visits to see nine grandchildren. Some readers of those letters encouraged me to publish them; so, this book is partially their fault while a few said to stop writing them. Several reviewers suggested that they would like to reflect on other topics or expand on my limited viewpoints for their grandchildren. If so, see Appendix C.

It might have been better to wait until I had fifty Christmas letters but since many of our lifelong friends are debilitated, dying, or dead, I am not sure I'll make it to the 50th letter. There are five extra Reflections in Appendix A.

Appendix B contains six reflections based on Coffee House Conferences that ended each chapter of my process analysis book, *The Document Methodology for Enterprise Analysis and Healthcare Transformation* (TDM), that proposed how to provide higher quality healthcare (and manufacturing) at lower cost. Directors of a manufacturer and healthcare facility discuss critical ideas associated with analysis methods. The coffee house waitress is a philosophy graduate who argues that philosophy provides critical insight into the solution of their business problems.

Sons, family, and work provided plenty of experiences to reflect upon: creative negative feedback for children, distorted views of relationships, wine tasting, evolution, mathematics, philosophy, theology, environmentalism, science, engineering, and a bunch of other stuff. The reflections after the publication of the first version have a heavy engineering, philosophy and theology influence extracted from a not yet published Philosophy of Engineering book.

Everyone should know what engineers are up to and what they might think of next. I would argue that engineers have inflicted more change on societies and the planet in the last 100 years than any other group; some good and some really bad. Whereas the change inflicted by other groups, politicians, lawyers, NGOs, and activists, were mostly bad.

There are lots of folks writing books that tell you how to live your life, build relationships, raise your children, watch your diet, make money, buy light bulbs and many other tiny details. Reflections are not intended as advice but are ideas that I have spent some time reflecting upon. On the more controversial topics, do your own research, and come to an informed conclusion.

I would also like to give you some idea about how to think about solving a problem that you have no idea how to solve. The philosopher Carl Sanders Peirce concluded that deduction and induction were inadequate to explain the entirety of the scientific/philosophical process. He named a third activity, abduction, which formulates something from nothing to create something novel and never thought of before. I call it muddling (Reflection 45). It starts like this: if no one in group knows how to solve a problem, you give it to the best muddler. In a room full of people smarter than me, I was the best muddler. An important characteristic of muddlers is not being intimidated by the breadth and depth of their ignorance. It also requires system and theological engineering skills (Reflection 37 and 42).

I thank Judy Banyai, Helen Haglund, LeRoy Haynes, Carl Hurty, Mike Sterling for critiquing the first book. Their efforts resulted in significant improvements and made some reflections almost readable in version I of this book.

I would also like to thank Jeff Jones, Mike Sterling, Bob Anderson, Bob Higel and Joanne Sloan for their critique of this book.

I thank my sons, Jeff, John, and Jamison for providing much to think about and reflect upon.

Most important, I would like to thank Judy (BA, RN, WIFE) who was my partner in comedy and provided our lives' greatest gifts by giving birth to our sons. She taught our sons how to behave despite my bad example. I would especially like to thank for her editing and critiquing ALL of the drafts of ALL six of my books.

jimijones@aol.com

Table of Contents

INTRODUCTION 1
CHRISTMAS 1977 4
    REFLECTION 1: STRESS/HEALTH 6
CHRISTMAS 1978 8
    REFLECTION 2: WINE 10
CHRISTMAS 1979 13
    REFLECTION 3: CAD AND THE SCIENTIFIC METHOD 15
CHRISTMAS 1980 18
    REFLECTION 4: CULTURE SHOCK 20
CHRISTMAS 1981 22
    REFLECTION 5: FAMILY – CHILD PSYCHOLOGY 24
CHRISTMAS 1982 27
    REFLECTION 6: BUREAUCRACY 29
CHRISTMAS 1983 31
    REFLECTION 7: LIBERAL EDUCATION AND USMA 33
CHRISTMAS 1984 35
    REFLECTION 8: INTERNATIONAL BUSINESS 37
CHRISTMAS 1985 39
    REFLECTION 9: GOD, MORTALITY, MORALITY AND LAW 41
CHRISTMAS 1986 44
    REFLECTION 10: COMMUNICATION AND MEMES 46
CHRISTMAS 1987 48
    REFLECTION 11: MOBILITY AND ENERGY 50
CHRISTMAS 1988 53
    REFLECTION 12: ENVIRONMENT AND SUN 55
CHRISTMAS 1989 57
    REFLECTION 13: NURSING AND MEDICINE 59
CHRISTMAS 1990 61
    REFLECTION 14: EDUCATION 63
CHRISTMAS 1991 65
    REFLECTION 15: WAR – STRATEGY AND TACTICS 67
CHRISTMAS 1992 69
    REFLECTION 16: GENERATIONS AND GENES 72
CHRISTMAS 1993 74
    REFLECTION 17: GALAXIES 77
CHRISTMAS 1994 79
    REFLECTION 18: INTERNET 81
CHRISTMAS 1995 83
    REFLECTION 19: FINE ARTS 85
CHRISTMAS 1996 87
    REFLECTION 20: CHARTS IN 1421 89
CHRISTMAS 1997 91
    REFLECTION 21: REFLECTION AND PHILOSOPHY 93

CHRISTMAS 1998	**95**
REFLECTION 22: WIND AND NAVIGATION	97
CHRISTMAS 1999	**100**
REFLECTION 23: FLOW OF KNOWLEDGE	102
CHRISTMAS 2000	**104**
REFLECTION 24: COUNTING	106
CHRISTMAS 2001	**108**
REFLECTION 25: ISLAMIC TERRORISM AND PEACE	110
CHRISTMAS 2002	**112**
REFLECTION 26: SHIPS AND SEAS	114
CHRISTMAS 2003	**116**
REFLECTION 27: CHRISTIANITY AND REASON	118
CHRISTMAS 2004	**121**
REFLECTION 28: AUSTRALIA	123
CHRISTMAS 2005	**126**
REFLECTION 29: BEAVER ISLAND TO MANHATTAN	128
CHRISTMAS 2006	**130**
REFLECTION 30: ARCHITECTURE	132
CHRISTMAS 2007	**134**
REFLECTION 31: 1434	136
CHRISTMAS 2008	**138**
REFLECTION 32: BLACK HOLES	141
CHRISTMAS 2009	**143**
REFLECTION 33: QUANTUM PHYSICS	146
CHRISTMAS 2010	**149**
REFLECTION 34: PERMACULTURE	151
CHRISTMAS 2011	**155**
REFLECTION 35: KNOWLEDGE FROM NOISE	157
CHRISTMAS 2012	**160**
REFLECTION 36: VALUE FROM KNOWLEDGE FLOW	162
CHRISTMAS 2013	**164**
REFLECTION 37: ENGINEERING PHILOSOPHY	165
CHRISTMAS 2014	**168**
REFLECTION 38: LEGISLATIVE LUNACY	170
CHRISTMAS 2015	**173**
REFLECTION 39: PROCESS FLOW AND COMMUNITY	175
CHRISTMAS 2016	**178**
REFLECTION 40: PANENTHEISM	180
CHRISTMAS 2017	**183**
REFLECTION 41: NOT ATHEISM	185
CHRISTMAS 2018	**188**
REFLECTION 42: THEOLOGY OF ENGINEERING	190

CHRISTMAS 2019 .... **193**
   REFLECTION 43: TRANSFORMING HEALTHCARE 195
      Best Practice will *197*
CHRISTMAS 2020 .... **198**
   REFLECTION 44: A CURE FOR USA HEALTHCARE 200
CHRISTMAS 2021 .... **203**
   REFLECTION 45: MUDDLING 205
CHRISTMAS 2022 .... **207**
   REFLECTION 46: SCIENCE RANT 209
CHRISTMAS 2023 .... **211**
   REFLECTION 47: PURPOSE 213
   SUMMARY 215
BIBLIOGRAPHY **217**
APPENDIX A: ADDITIONAL REFLECTIONS **220**
   REFLECTION 48: THE INFORMATION 220
   REFLECTION 49: FIVE GENERATIONS OF DIGITAL COMPUTING 223
   REFLECTION 50: USA EPA MPGE 225
   REFLECTION 51: HOW TO GET OLD 227
   REFLECTION 52: HABITAT SUSTAINABILITY 230
   REFLECTION 53: DEMISE OF A DEMOCRACY 233
   REFLECTION 54: FINITE PLANET 235
APPENDIX B: COFFEE HOUSE CONFERENCES **239**
   THE EXAMPLE MANUFACTURING PROBLEM 242
   THE EXAMPLE HEALTHCARE PROBLEM 245
   REFLECTION 55: WEALTH (SMITH) 246
   HEALTH KNOWLEDGE OBSERVATION 251
   REFLECTION 56: KNOWLEDGE (SOCRATES) 253
   HEALTH PROCESS OBSERVATION 259
   REFLECTION 57: PROCESS (DESCARTES) 260
   HEALTHY PEOPLE OBSERVATION 265
   REFLECTION 58: PEOPLE (LOCKE) 266
   HEALTH SYSTEM OBSERVATION 272
   REFLECTION 59: SYSTEMS (KANT) 274
   BUILDING ENTERPRISE WEALTH 279
   HEALTH POLICY OBSERVATIONS 279
   HEALTH CHANGE OBSERVATION 280
   REFLECTION 60: CHANGE (LAO TZU) 281
APPENDIX C: COLLEGE CURRICULUM TO REFLECT **287**

INTRODUCTION

Epistle to Grandchildren

Who are you?
Where has the world evolved?
What do you intend to do about it?

Now is your time. My generation has left you with some very large opportunities, which is a polite way of saying huge problems:
1] Terrorism and War,   2] National Debt,   3] Crime,
4] Declining education,   5] Spiraling Healthcare costs,
6] Government ineptitude 7] Mindless Advocacy,
8] Population growth: 2 to 9 billion people in a century,
9] Mega pollution, consumption and oil usage,
10] Exported jobs and increasing illegal immigrants.

The good news is that we know and can do 100 times more in most areas of human endeavor than we could 100 years ago including: Mathematics, Biological Sciences, Physical Sciences, Engineering, Medicine, and Education. So, you must be ready to do something soon. Your job as a kid was to have fun and learn as much as you could so that you can save our planet. There are more than 500 areas of study identified. I was going to dump the whole thing on you up front, but I wanted you to read at least a little further.

One of this book's goals is to interest you in three questions:
1] Who am I? 2] Where does the world come from?
3] What do I intend to do about it?

To get through all of the areas of knowledge listed in the book would take several thousand years (which is about how old I feel). Not to worry, you just need to pick one or maybe two. Your parents worked hard and saved money to pay for four year$ of your higher education. Now it's your turn.

Reviewers told me that I overstate the case for Mathematics. Nope. Some people deprive themselves of participating in and fail to understand science because they think that proficiency in Mathematics is optional. I beg to differ. Many "unintended consequences" stem from mathematical and statistical ignorance.

Major areas of study follow. Mathematics is first because you won't become proficient in any future science without it. I will discuss a topic associated with many of the 75 disciplines.

General Areas of University Study

Mathematics	Social Sciences
1] Pure Mathematics	39] Anthropology
2] Applied Mathematics	40] Architecture
3] Statistics & Probability	41] Communication
Biological Sciences	42] Economics
4] Biology, General	43] Geography
5] Ecology & Evolutionary Biology	44] Linguistics
6] Public Health	45] Political Science
7] Genetics & Genomics	46] Psychology
8] Immunology/Infectious Disease	47] Sociology
9] Kinesiology	**Arts and Humanities**
10] Microbiology	48] American Studies
11] Neuroscience & Neurobiology	49] Classics
12] Environmental Health	50] Fine Arts
13] Physiology	51] Foreign Language Literature
14] Animal Sciences	52] Language & Literature
15] Entomology	53] Language & Societies
16] Food Science	54] History
17] Forestry & Forest Science	55] History of Art
18] Nutrition	56] Music
19] Plant Sciences	57] Philosophy
20] Bioinformatics/Biotechnology	58] Religion
Physical Sciences	59] Theatre & Performance
21] Astrophysics & Astronomy	60] Film Studies
22] Chemistry	**Medical Science**
23] Computer Sciences	61] Dentistry
24] Earth Sciences	62] Human Medicine
25] Climate Sciences	63] Nursing
26] Physics	64] Osteopathic Medicine
Engineering	65] Pharmacy
27] Aerospace Engineering	66] Public Health
28] Biomedical Engineering & Bioengineering	67] Veterinary Medicine
	Government, Law, Policy
29] Chemical Engineering	68] Government
30] Civil/Environ'tal Engineering	69] Law
31] Computer Engineering	70] Public Policy
32] Electrical Engineering	**71] Business**
33] Engineering Science	**72] Agriculture**
34] Materials Science	**73] Education**
35] Mechanical Engineering	**74] Military Officer Training**
36] Operations Research	**75] Seminary**

If you are bored, keep reading anyway. If you don't understand something, look it up. Talk about statements made by me that you disagree with. Make up your own mind.

I took many courses in Mechanical Engineering, Electrical Engineering, Computer Engineering, and Mathematics. I demonstrated a complete lack of competency for the practical aspects of Engineering. So, I escaped to Applied Mathematics where I wouldn't seriously injure myself operating mechanical or electrical equipment.

Some important and interesting topics like Art, Music and Theater receive not enough attention because I know little about them. I have no credentials on other topics but, like journalists and politicians, it did not keep me from writing about them. Even though I have spent a great deal of effort to verify the facts in this book, the theories, however well established, may eventually be proven wrong.

We'll discuss climate, evolution, galaxies, physics, sciences, philosophy, theology, and more. Some sciences are predictive like planetary travel and most areas of engineering. Some are well established, but not predictive like psychology, sociology, and ecology.

Even if you don't become a mathematician, engineer, or scientist, it is important that you understand the idea of being predictive in science. If you ask three physicists how long it will take to get to the moon, they will give you answers that will agree within minutes. If you ask three climate scientists, how many years it will take the oceans to rise three feet, you will get answers that vary by centuries.

However, unpredictive, climate science would be a way cool area to study; you could be the one that develops the theory that makes it predictive and provides the information to preserve the planet for your grandchildren.

You will notice as you read through this book that I encourage areas of work that make you think a lot, work hard and that probably won't make you rich. My personal investment strategies kept me working. If you want to get rich, marry someone who is rich. Being rich is fine; getting rich takes a lot of hard work and when you're all done with life, your kids get the money. So, encourage your parents to get rich so that you can think, work hard, and serve the world and yourself in the best and funnest possible way. Love, Grandpa.

CHRISTMAS 1977

1st Epistle of Jim

Frohliche Weihnachten und ein gluckliches Neues Jahr von Deutschland.

This has been our year for culture shock. Our geographic location, friends, language, recreational activities, school, job, food, and general lifestyle all changed at once. We all seem to have recovered our sanity, (those of us that had it) but still have relapses and by no means are completely adjusted. We can find the bathroom -"Wo ist die toilette", we can get fed- "Die Speisekarte, bitte" and can request numerous other items, which were simply taken for granted in the past.

But let us digress a moment to give you an idea of how we got here. We started our transfer from GM to Adam Opel in July rather hysterically by selling our last car and renting the house within FIVE DAYS before we left. We then flew to Miami with our fifteen pieces of luggage (a truck load was shipped ten days before) to see my parents in Key West. When planning our trip to Germany, we noticed that the connecting flight was in Nassau. So we spent five days in Key West and three days in Nassau. That was the last time we saw the sun for a significant period of time or a large body of water.

The sun struggles to come out from time to time and now that it's cold, the sun has shone for an entire day. But, let me reemphasize my previous point - THERE WASN'T A DAMN PLACE TO SAIL! I had taken to sucking my thumb, as a form of recreation, but am recovering since I found a small harbor on the Rhein near Frankfurt that has SAILBOATS!

The first two months after arriving in Frankfurt are kind of a blur. I know we stayed at the Holiday Inn for two weeks, moved into our house, got our furniture, wondered what the hell we were doing here, learned to drive 100 mph and spent weekends separating good from bad tourist attractions for future visits from our old friends.

It occurred to me that too much change and the resulting stress can be bad if you are not mentally and physically prepared. Maybe I should exercise, pork down and take vitamins.

We finally started to get settled in October which was none too soon. Judy's parents came for 22 days in November. We were glad to see them and really had a good time together. Judy took them to at least one tourist attraction per day. I think they were ready to go back home for a rest. We had six inches of snow while they were here which made our beautiful view even better.

We live in a very small town called Glashutten, in the Taunus mountains which is just northwest of Frankfurt. We must have thousands of acres of open land behind us comprised of farmland, forests, and mountains. Fortunately, it is pretty, even in the rain. However, my normal 35-minute drive to work can take as long as three hours when it snows. There are horses, one bit Jamison, and sheep (one used our kitchen for a toilet). The children have helped the farmer pick his potatoes in the field behind us.

As you can see, we may be having fun, but I'm not sure we can tell yet. In the sense that suffering brings strength, I'm sure this is a good experience. Assuming we get adjusted (hopefully we're not adjusted) this should be a very good experience.

We have all been to London and had a really great time. It was good to hear English and see some of the places of interest there. We are planning to go to Holland this Christmas, the Canary Islands in February and maybe Monaco in April. We'll struggle along and see as much of Europe as we can.

We miss you all and would like to hear from you. If you are planning a trip to Europe, make sure you stop to see us. We have plenty of room.

Reflection 1: Stress/Health

Stress can cause illness if you are not mentally and physically prepared.

Having a clear understanding of where you are going and what the issues and problems will be and then planning a "growth program" is the way educators and business think about professional growth. The kind of growth described here falls into the category "what doesn't kill me makes me stronger."

My objective was to immerse grandma, your dads and myself in the culture; thereby learning about culture through experience. We did learn through experience, but it felt like a child who learns that a burner is hot by putting his hand on it.

Like many Americans who live abroad for the first time, we were shocked to discover that Germans are NOT like Americans; and, they all speak a foreign language. I tried to point out that God speaks English and so should they, but the Germans retorted that truly great philosophical discourse requires German, and God is obviously a German philosopher. Who could argue with such a logical view of God, but he's really an English-speaking mathematician. These conversations were best reflected on with wine.

As many teenagers know, one of the defenses when in conflict with parents and others is sarcasm. It's tough being sarcastic in a language that you don't speak, and even when I learned to speak, Germans didn't understand my sarcasm.

Language, culture, work environment, food, church, absence of friends, schools, no English TV all contributed to elevating stress. After three months of exhibiting all the symptoms of a paranoid schizophrenic, I came upon a book called the "Body Maintenance Manual." Among the exercise and diet advice was a table that related points to stress topics like the ones described above. It stated that 100 stress points would cause some kind of emotional or physical problem. My stress points were in the neighborhood of 500, that suggested that paranoia was well deserved. I was ready for intellectual growth, but cultural growth was another matter and required maturity.

Intellectual and cultural growth, parenting and life require physical stamina. Supplemental vitamins and exercise were far more important for me than diet and sleep.

Because large agricultural firms are concerned with getting more crops from less land and then shipping those products to distant markets, we may not be getting all the nutrients that we need from our food. Hence, I discovered that vitamins and minerals along with exercise aided in my quest for wellness and sanity.

The effect of large doses of vitamin supplements was not well understood. Consequently, I was experimenting on myself. However, understanding how your body works and taking care of it is each person's responsibility. The medical profession can do amazing things to cure disease and injury, but wellness needs to be each person's focus.

My personal health evaluation was a study in Psychology, Kinesiology, Physiology and Nutrition. Psychology was used to determine that I was going nuts from stress. Physiology helped me assess what was happening to my chubby body and how it negatively impacted my response to stress. Kinesiology helped define the exercise required and assess the impact. Understanding nutrition helped me understand what foods impacted exercise performance. Statistics and Design of Experiments helped me determine the appropriate metrics and evaluate what conditions improved my physical condition and reaction to stress. Metrics were simple:
1] How fast did I complete a three-mile run?
2] How much weight could I lift and how many times?
3] Did the twitch in my eye and paranoia go away?
4] What was my weight and waist and hip circumference?

Data collected (listed in order of impact on metrics) included:
1] vitamins (especially B complex and E),
2] barometric pressure (surprise),
3] Food - meat (strength), sweets, carbohydrates (endurance),
4] liquids consumed,
5] alcoholic beverages consumed and
6] hours slept.

I discovered that exercise reduced the negative effects of stress. 45 minute runs and 45 minute weight work outs on alternate days along with a multiple vitamin and extra B and E helped me survive the ordeal. Most people exercise under the level at which their body pays attention. After exercising for the last 30 years, my reward is that I need to exercise harder if I want my body to pay attention.

In order to study how to keep bodies working, you need to study Medical or Biological Sciences and Statistics, Kinesiology, Physiology, and   Nutrition.

CHRISTMAS 1978
2nd Epistle of Jim

Merry Christmas and Happy New Year from Germany.

We now have spent 18 months here. Judging from the grumblings about no skateboard parks, three-hour drive to sail, crowded supermarkets, problems with speaking German and no sunshine, I think everybody is ready to return to the good old U.S.A.

All of Europe is full of beautiful castles, cathedrals, museums, and historical monuments. On every vacation and short trip we have tried to see as much as possible, but I think I have surpassed my limit for absorbing cultural experiences. This year we went to Paris, Luxembourg, Strasbourg, Berlin, skied in Austria and drove up and down the Rhine and Mosel Rivers a couple of times. We enjoyed our six weeks back in Miami and Detroit last summer most of all. We still must see Spain, Italy, Switzerland, Scandinavia, Ireland, Scotland, Greece, and a few other countries. However, two more big trips and a couple of long weekends are about all I'm going to be able to handle next year. Judy is much more capable of absorbing culture than I but finds me so intolerable when I drive that she has limited our excursions.

The boys are enduring their blessings better than their parents. All three are continuing to learn German and John is also taking French. They get a lot of attention in school since the average class is about 20.

Last year I comforted myself with the fact that a five-year-old could speak German. Now I'm told that many Germans don't speak "good" German. With six more months of study and practice, people won't know whether I can't speak German too well or I'm just a little slow. Judy is also working diligently to learn German and plans to study some French too. There doesn't seem to be an easy way for me to learn--just suffer with it.

Our initial problems with culture shock are wearing off. We have "adjusted" to some degree, but there are vast differences in behavior which we will never get used to. Dogs are preferred over children in restaurants and public places. There is very little violence, but the rate of injuries and deaths from auto accidents is at least 50% higher. People here love rules and make sure everyone else obeys them, as much as Americans love "freedom" from rules. Driving is madness; 60% of the drivers think that every road is part of a 24-hour Grand Prix.

On a positive note, Judy and I are continuing our study of German wines. I have read a few pages on the topic but am convinced that the only way to educate one's palate is by continued and unrelenting practice.

Judy and I are both running. We run because we can eat more and not gain weight. I run on a hilly route and a flat route. Although the latter involves less suffering, it was made less desirable by a large German Shepard who classifies me somewhere between a rubber bone and a fleeing thief.

We are "convinced" this is a good experience, but we can only stand so much improvement at one time. After living here, we have been able to put our own country in perspective and find it to be much more to our liking.

Frohe Weihnachten und ein Gluckliches Neues Jahr von Deutschland.

Reflection 2: Wine

Terroir - land, soil, slope, elevation, and climate - where the grape is grown bonds with the vintner's art and science to produce fine wines.

Wine making is an art and requires knowledge of plant science, statistics, agriculture, weather, and environment. Like me, most Americans don't know much about wine, but we talk about it endlessly.

Why talk about wine? Beer is usually associated with sports, liquor with aggressive cocktail parties and wine with reflection. These reflections required reflective, inductive, and deductive thought, but moderate wine drinking promoted reflective discussion that helped crystallize my ideas.

In 1748, Montesquieu published "The Spirit of Laws;" his estate also produced wine. The English bought many copies of the book and wine sales increased which led Montesquieu to quip: "The success of my book in that country contributed to the success of my wine, although I think the success of my wine has done still more for the success of my book."

A major benefit of living in the Frankfurt area was proximity to vineyards. We learned about wine by drinking it. When people came to visit, we drove along the Rhein River through to Koblenz, turned left and drove along the Mosel river stopping frequently at vineyards to taste and buy wine.

One might ask - "How could you drive and drink all day?" Sip, don't drink wine if you intend to buy cases of it. For my first wine tasting, I drank all of fifteen 0.1-liter glasses that significantly numbed my taste buds. As a result, I bought 50 bottles of wine that tasted like pee.

There are many grape varieties, but most red wines are made from Cabernet Sauvignon, Merlot, Pinot Noir, Syrah (Shiraz) and Zinfandel grapes; white wines are made from Riesling, Chardonnay, Sauvignon Blanc, Semillon, and Chenin Blanc grapes. In most countries, the grape used to make it describes the wine; except in France, where it is described by region: Bordeaux, Burgundy, Champagne, Beaujolais, etc.

Making wine is more complicated than stomping grapes into juice, letting it ferment and then bottling it. Fine wine is like most fine art: a combination of the best materials (grapes), the best technology, and well-defined processes that are used to create wine by the artist/vintner. The weather must help: too little or too much sun, too little or too much rain, too high or too low temperatures can result in bad grapes. Growing, harvesting, fermenting in a stainless-steel barrel, aging in oak barrels and bottling take more than a year.

The best wines in France grow in lousy soil. Rocky, chalky, and mineral poor soil force the vine roots to go deep and struggle to stay alive. The stress of this struggle sometimes produces the best grapes; other times they whither or rot. When problems make you struggle, you can grow to greatness like a fine wine; or you can just whine; your choice.

If we are going to give the appearance of knowing something about wine, we need a little more terminology:
- Varietal character - each grape has a specific smell and taste but reflects many flavors; some wine experts think Sauvignon Blanc should smell a little like cat piss (honest).
- Integration - components of the wine (acid, tannin, alcohol, sugar) are interwoven to balance the flavor.
- Expressiveness - wine's aroma and flavors are well defined.
- Complexity - multiplicity of flavors change with each taste.
- Connectedness- bond between wine and its terroir: land, soil slope, elevation, and climate where the grape is grown.

When you read a wine label, it describes how wonderful the wine is and lists a bunch of flavors which I always thought were artfully made up by an English major. They are not; there is actually a list. Here are a few for:
- Whites: apple, apricot, banana, coconut, fig, lemon, lime, orange, asparagus, olives, almond, hazelnut, yeast, cloves, cinnamon, ginger, white pepper, gardenia, geranium, honey suckle, rose, chalk, flint, hay, straw, oak, toast, vanilla, piss.
- Reds: blackberry, blueberry, raspberry, strawberry, prunes, asparagus, olives, truffle, all types of chocolate, coffee, mocha, espresso, black pepper, cinnamon, cloves, licorice, cedar, pine, geranium, rose, violet, oak, toast, vanilla, cola, game, tar, leather, manure.

Now we know five important words and a bunch of flavors; never mind that we don't know exactly what they mean, few do. It's like talking about politics, astrology, or abstract art; it's not the content of what you say but how you connect harmonious sounding adjectives. It helps to read the wine label to get this partly right.

Before we can describe the wine, we must first taste it. Swirling and sniffing the wine is an art form in itself. Swirling will tell you about the viscosity of the wine (how thick it is). The slower it runs down the glass the more viscous. You can say something like this wine has "nice legs." I don't know what this means, but it will make you sound sensuously knowledgeable.

You then need to tilt the glass 45 degrees, stick your nose inside the glass, and give it a good sniff. Be careful not to snort liquid; blowing boogers and wine on the wine steward is considered very bad form. After swirling and sniffing the wine, sip and slosh it around in your mouth, but don't gargle. You then nod to the steward or host who serves everyone else and fills your glass last.

You are now ready to say something incomprehensible about the wine, but peek at the label so you are not too far off. It might go something like this: This wine seems fairly well integrated, but with a touch too much acidity. It expresses itself with well-defined flavors of licorice, cedar, and mocha.

After another sip, say: The wine isn't too complex, but now I taste blackberry with hints of raspberry. This wine reflects the terroir (land, soil, climate) of its Napa Valley roots. If you taste flavors of cat piss or manure, it's probably not good to mention it. Your host might not understand. You may have no idea what you just said, but almost nobody else will either. If you learn to talk like this on a variety of subjects, it may even get you nominated for president.

Consider this a first lesson. We have not talked about acidity, tannins, sugar, aging, champagne, growing regions, varietal grapes, wine technology and methods, etc. But you can sound like an expert around people who know absolutely nothing about wine. Remember to start off by saying: I don't know much about wine but.... If you want to become a real expert, read Karen Mac Neil's 900-page book: "The Wine Bible." Unfortunately, you won't be drinking until you are 21.

To under-stand how to grow better grapes and make better wine, study: Statistics, Plant Science, and Agriculture.

CHRISTMAS 1979

3rd Epistle of Jim

MERRY CHRISTMAS. We're back from two years in Deutschland and are now officially certified semi-cultured. We satisfied our cathedral, museum and wine tasting requirements, but still sound very elementary speaking German.

Fortunately, we rented our house here while we were in Europe or we would have been able to buy about half of it. What have you people done to the cost of living while we were gone. You've all been buying and borrowing haven't you!

Judy certainly is glad to get back to the shopping centers. The first couple of weeks she was semi-paralyzed in disbelief at all the THINGS available. To my consternation, Judy has made a spectacular adjustment and is now making significant contributions to the economy.

The boys thought that one big improvement about American school would be the absence of German class. However, it turns out that their Junior High School is right next to the High School where they are fortunate enough to be in third year German. I can't tell you how pleased they are.

It's really good to see blue sky after 300 days per year of gray sky. Michigan weather is just wonderful: Whenever it rains you can be sure that the weather is going to change. In Frankfurt there was no change from the rain.

We managed to travel a little last year - - Prague, Bavaria, Switzerland, Italy, Spain and France. Prague was oppressive. I don't think I want to go to a communist country again. I kept thinking an agent was about to jump out, especially when one of our more "fearless" tour companions almost slugged a waiter.

We went skiing in Oberstdorf - a small town in southwest Germany. The boys were really impressed with my full-speed collision with a 5 foot snow drift. One expects to hear expressions of concern, not applause while lying there reviewing your skeletal structure. They claim I sprayed snow 10 feet in the air. I received even less sympathy from the Austrian ski patrol, who informed me that going straight down the mountain was dangerous, irresponsible and a bad example for my children. She did not think it was funny when I told her that I served that function regularly.

We took a car ferry from Italy to Spain and drove back up to Germany through France. The boys went swimming in the boat's 10 ft. swimming pool in 50 degrees and 6 ft. swells. Swimming the length of a ten foot pool with 3 ft. waves turned out to be a real workout.

Spain was really beautiful: incredible mountains rising up from volcanic beaches. Beautiful hotels were crowded together and half of them were closed because of strikes. It took us four hours of driving before we found a hotel for under $150 a night.

The weather in Spain was super, loved seeing the sunshine. The last day I'll never forget: We drove 1000 miles (not kilometers) from Peniscula, Spain to Frankfurt (19 hours). The food and accommodation prices in France kept us going.

On a business note, the project that I was sent to Germany to complete was successful. I finished managing 15 separate projects to install a transatlantic interactive graphics CAD/CAM system. Nobody had ever done this before. My boss said I was lucky: better lucky than smart. Maybe the fact that those 15 projects defined a theory about what would work and tested its validity had something to do with it as well.

We're back and we're glad!

Reflection 3: CAD and the Scientific Method

Great science does more than define a theory and test its validity; it predicts something that has not been observed.

My first four years of college started with Mechanical Engineering and ended with Electrical Engineering. My practical skills suggested that I would crush myself with a 20,000-pound press as a Mechanical Engineer and electrocute myself as an Electrical Engineer. Fortunately, I demonstrated an exceptional aptitude for mathematics. I was accepted into a Mathematics program at Michigan State where I ran into two 17-year-olds with IQs that could not be measured. It's very depressing to discover that I was a minor and not a major league thinker. I did, however, demonstrate enough capability to be the dumb guy in a development group at the General Motors Technical Center. Intellectual limitations notwithstanding, in order to be a part of that community, I still needed certain credentials, which resulted when I obtained advanced degrees in the course work below.

Mathematics

1] Pure Mathematics
Algebra
Algebraic Geometry
Analysis
Discrete Mathematics
Dynamics
Geometry & Topology
Harmonic Analysis
Logic & Foundations
Number Theory
Set Theory

2] Applied Mathematics
Control Theory
Dynamic Systems
Non-linear Dynamics
Numerical Analysis & Computation
Partial Differential Equations
Ordinary Differential Equations
Applied Dynamics

3] Statistics & Probability
Applied Statistics
Probability
Statistical Methodology
Statistical Theory

Engineering (partial)

35]Mechanical Engineering
Applied Mechanics
Computer-Aided Engineering & Design
Electro-Mechanical Systems
Energy Systems
Heat Transfer
Manufacturing

36] Operations Research, Systems Engineering & Industrial Engineering
Industrial Engineering
Operational Research
Systems Engineering

37] Emerging Fields:
Computational Engineering
Information Science

I spent my first 15 years of employment at General Motors as a Mathematician/Programmer developing Computer Aided Design and Computer Aided Manufacturing software (CAD/CAM).

GM, MIT, and Boeing Corporation were first to develop Computer Aided Design (CAD) software. GM then exported that system to Adam Opel in Germany to design automobiles for Europe. The work done to develop this system is an example of the scientific method which is crucial in developing solutions that work.

Science evolves when a scientist looks at a bunch of data or seemingly very different events and develops a theory that explains them all. She then submits her work to the scientific community (associated with her discipline) with suggestions as to how to prove her theory WRONG. If, after the entire community looks at her work and cannot prove it wrong and provides additional proofs, it is accepted and used by the community as CORRECT.

In his book: "The Structure of Scientific Revolutions," Thomas S. Kuhn says sciences progress in a way that other fields do not:
- there is a relative scarcity of competing schools,
- members of a given community provide its primary audience,
- members are the only judges of the community's work,
- the nature of scientific education is about puzzle solving,
- the value system of a scientific group deploys in crisis and decision making.

To be a member of GM's CAD/CAM community I met Kuhn's criteria:
- How does one become a member? Knowledge in Applied Mathematics and Engineering was required as demonstrated by my MS in Math and BS in Electrical Engineering.
- What is the process and what are the stages of socialization to the group? I had to develop software that demonstrated that I was proficient in programming and Mathematics.
- What does the group collectively see as its goals? Our goal was to design free form car surfaces and computer tool positions to machine dies that stamped out automobile surface parts (e.g. fender, hood, roof, outer door, bumper).
- What deviations, individual or collectively will it tolerate? I was considered almost normal in this group.
- How does it control the impermissible aberration? If one could defend his proposed solution before the team, the proposal was approved for further work. After approval, progress reports were submitted to management and the team to ensure the actual solution was reasonably close to the proposed solution.

Thomas Kuhn was working on his Ph.D. at MIT when he decided to look at the structure of science rather than become a member of the physics community. His study required a strong scientific background, but his subsequent work is considered to be social, cultural, archaeological, biological, physical, and linguistic anthropology.

Read Charles Wynn and Arthur Wiggins book where they describe what are arguably "The Five Biggest Ideas in Science:"
- Big Idea #1: Physics' Model of the Atom – Do basic building blocks exist, and if so what do they look like?
- Big Idea #2: Chemistry's Periodic Law – What relationships exist among different kinds of atoms?
- Big Idea #3: Astronomy's Big Bang Theory – Where did the atoms of the Universe come from, and what is their identity?
- Big Idea #4: Geology's Plate Tectonics Model – How is the matter of the Universe arranged on planet Earth?
- Big Idea #5: Biology's Theory of Evolution – How did life on planet Earth originate and develop?

Great science does more than validate ideas; it predicts something that has not been observed. For example, Einstein predicted that light would be bent by a large mass and space-time would be curved. He had not observed this. With his famous $E = mc^2$ he was just taking the old $E=mv^2$ and pushing the velocity to the speed of light thereby showing that Energy is nothing other than mass times a conversion factor. In the case of the atom, it happens to release fantastic energy. This had not been observed but was predicted by him.

To become part of one of these or other communities: study several of the Physical or Biological Sciences.

CHRISTMAS 1980
4th Epistle of Jim

Merry Christmas, again. Didn't we just have a Christmas two months ago. What happened to summer. With the New Year at hand, getting adjusted somehow seems important. I've finally decided to be permanently maladjusted. The world is out of adjustment, not me. Wouldn't it be terrifying if we all stopped to reflect on what we're doing and where we're going. I keep trying to think and plan, but my life seems to be constructed to keep me busy. I've read three interesting books lately all of which state that we don't become an adult until after 40. I wonder what I'm going to be when I grow up.

Speaking of growing, Judy is a student again. She's getting A's in Microbiology and Nutrition at a local college. She really does enjoy school. Keeping house and servanting children is enough to drive any mother to school. Have you noticed that teenagers think Mother and Servant are synonyms. Instead of school, I keep encouraging Judy to be "liberated" and get a high paying job so that I can retire and "reflect"; but she seems to have a different understanding of liberated. Judy did help out at her Dad's warehouse and earned some pocket money. We pay taxes on her money with our money.

All three boys are doing fine considering two of them are teenagers. Jeff specialized in goofing off last year. To barter his way out of incarceration, I decided that he must participate in any sport and any club. Wonder of wonders, Jeff picked swimming. He now swims four miles per day, five days a week. Not only is he building a strong, healthy body, but also on some days he goes to bed at 8 pm. Swimming is a special gift to fathers of fun loving, energetic teenagers.

Our 13-year-old, used to be our student but has developed other interests this year. He's into boy scouts, guitar, piano and TV. John has caught up with over two years of audio/video deprivation in Germany with 15 months of dedicated viewing. No program was too tasteless to escape his and his father's indiscriminating eyes.

In many cases he had to avoid practicing piano and doing homework. Needless to say, we have some adjustments to make.

Jamie studies hard, works hard, plays hard and never forgets to ask for his allowance. Jamison played on the 3rd place, fifth-sixth grade flag-football team this year. How his team finished isn't as interesting as his attitude. In his last game, he was ecstatic because his opponent was 20-30 lbs. heavier than he. It really gave him an opportunity to "make contact". It makes me feel like I got his two older brothers for practice so that I could be ready when he gets to be a teenager.

We have a dog -- our first dog. He's large, hairy, cute, understands quickly and listens to orders occasionally - fits right in. He's 60 lbs., half miniature sheep dog and half black setter, is gray and black and has hair that covers his eyes. His name is Rudy, but he answers to the names Rudith, Turkey, Wookie, dog, big nose, and fuzz face. He rarely barks, never bites and only jumps up or trips you when he wants attention.

I'm still running and lifting weights, but my body is still the same cylindrical shape. I'm growing older as gracelessly as possible and don't seem to be able to avoid birthdays which, like Christmas, seem to come every two months. I joined a spa where they have a track, pool, racquet ball courts and weight room. It's so fancy, that I asked permission to sweat. Hopefully, staying in shape will help me survive teenage sons and sailboat racing. I was the helmsman on a 34 foot sailboat in a bunch of races that tended toward extreme boredom (winds under 5 mph.) and terror (winds gusting above 40). For the record, I deal much better with boredom than terror.

Every American should experience the German culture; their rules and homogeneity afford them a cultural advantage in making a plan work, but those same rules and lack of diversity constrain them from developing an innovative plan. We are all glad to be back, and although we're not quite adjusted, we are settling down and celebrating diversity.

With the expense of fuel, food, and money, we really haven't had to worry much about how to manage our money. Like most Americans, the majority of our problems stem from too many 'Blessings.' However busy we are during the holiday season, we will take time to reflect on our blessings and our Friends.

Reflection 4: Culture Shock

Culture should balance diversity with homogeneity.

Our time in Germany had a significant impact on how we perceived our environment and other cultures. We learned the value of what we had and saw how Europeans consumed far less than Americans.

Culture is the acquired knowledge people use to interpret experience and generate behavior. Culture makes information meaningful. Culture gives a person the set of rules by which to behave. These rules are knowledge – actionable information that suggests how to interpret a situation and what to do next. Reusing and sharing knowledge is quicker and more effective than recreating it. Both individual and collective contributions of people benefit their community. The sum of contributions supports the community.

How much we can accomplish collectively is dependent upon how well people can create, capture, validate and share "know what, know how, know why and know when."

Germans celebrate homogeneity. Most Germans "know" what right behavior is and expect it from their neighbors. As a consequence, less energy is required to cope with and create laws to deal with diversity. But keep in mind that every 500 miles in Europe the language and government completely change. Europeans have created homogeneity by segregating their diversity into independent countries.

Culture shock for us revolved around German homogeneity. We were alternately amazed and frustrated by a German culture which produced some of the world's greatest philosophers, scientists, sausage, beer and two world wars.

Germans are publicly rude to each other by American standards and become friendly when they get to know you better. Americans are friendly to strangers and rude to their best friends. Amongst "us engineering guys" trading insults was a gesture of affection.

Americans celebrate diversity. Accepting immigrants from diverse cultures is credited with keeping America adaptive and innovative by constantly expanding our cultural perspective.

Let's celebrate a little homogeneity. A recent five-year study by Robert Putnam, Harvard political scientist, suggests that immigration and ethnic diversity have a devastating short and medium-term influence on the social capital, fabric of associations, and neighborliness that create and sustain communities.

Celebrating diversity views members as a group rather than individuals. We should not support ethnic behavior which does not agree with our constitution. We must expect certain behaviors as an established norm with no excuses for one's race, gender, or ethnic background. I am not Gaelic-American. I am an American.

The problem with celebrating diversity is that ethnic groups don't assimilate culturally and subsequently some contribute less or don't contribute at all to society. The effort to build a technologically advanced, innovative, trusting culture can come undone if we tolerate diverse subculture that continually doesn't contribute.

Too many of our illegal immigrants become part of a subculture that takes from our social programs like Medicare and unemployment compensation and gives little back. To fix this problem, we need to understand the elements of our culture that we consider important and insist that diverse groups adhere to these elements. When we determine this, we can define a LEGAL acceptance and assimilation process.

Also, the rich in Mexico exploit the poor. If we must nation build as in Iraq, we should direct half of that energy to Mexico while insisting on proper working and living conditions there. Why don't we? We want cheap Mexican labor here as well.

Remember, how much we can accomplish collectively is dependent upon how well people can create, capture, validate and share "know what, know how, know why and know when." This can not be accomplished in an atmosphere of distrust.

Having a general set of objectives to which everyone is expected to adhere is good depending on the objectives. Eugenics wasn't such a good idea, but it is a very good idea to require everyone to: speak English, graduate from high school, obey the law, respect their neighbors, pay their bills, etc....

Germans and Europeans consider attending university a privilege that must be earned. A good liberal education (Reflection 7) is our country's best opportunity for diverse groups to acquire knowledge that has evolved over thousands of years and can provide the continued foundation for a progressive, innovative society.

To learn how culture evolves, study: Anthropology, Language and Literature, Language and Societies.

CHRISTMAS 1981

5th Epistle of Jim

I have survived another year to pen my fifth Christmas epistle. Only five more years and I can enjoy the boys when they visit. Jamie will be 13 this February which means we will have THREE teenage sons. I must be getting tougher; I almost enjoy them but I'm with them only half as much as Judy.

Trying to civilize three sons that you brought up NOT to be intimidated by anyone, is a real challenge. I find creative, negative *feedback* can be an aid to helping them learn that freedom comes from appropriate constraint - not from doing what you feel like.

Judy is threatening to go to nursing school full time next fall (good for her). Unfortunately, that will mean that I won't be able to avoid some responsibility for taking care of the house. I'll have to get the boys mobilized. They can divert some of the energy that they're expending "to be free from parental tyranny" to do some work.

Judy is doing very well in her Physiology and Anatomy class this semester and continues to run with "little" Rudy our 60 pound puppy. He keeps her moving at a good speed until he trips her.

Jeff got it together and generated a semi-acceptable report card. This is particularly terrifying because I just ran out of negative feedback reasons for postponing his driver's license. He'll be out and about by the end of the year. He is diving again this year and continues to learn life's many lessons. Last week he learned that he could stay out late on Friday eat a huge lobster dinner, sleep three hours, deliver 52 morning papers, but he couldn't be competitive at his 8 a.m. diving meet on Saturday.

Our 15-year-old is enjoying his piano and plays anywhere he can find an audience. John really feels comfortable and in control of the keyboard. He does well in school which surprises me because he can never figure out how to do his chores and needs negative feedback to "clarify" instructions.

Jamie played defensive end this year in 7th grade football. He finally got to wear a football uniform and tackle someone after two years of flag football. He managed to get through the season without acquiring any noticeable tread marks on his anatomy.

Current courting rituals amaze me. Not to worry about rejection; our three guys have two or three girls calling them. With an average of 20 minutes per call, our phone is virtually useless in the afternoon and evening.

I continue to run and exercise in my struggle to deter the aging process. I am well over the hill, having had my 40th birthday this year. Since I planned ahead, I was depressed and had my mid-life crisis between 39 and 40. With that behind me, I now have to figure out what I am now that I'm grown up.

We had a fun (exhausting) vacation this year. We camped all the way down the east coast from St. John's, New Brunswick to North Carolina in three weeks. We had the greatest dinner of all time on the shores of Deer Island at a picnic table overlooking the Bay of Fundy. I cooked ten pounds of lobster, 5 pounds of clams, and ten potatoes on a Coleman stove. Everybody really enjoyed camping in our two back-packing tents especially since we stayed in motels when it rained.

Other than assembling a 24 foot sailboat, Jeff's tonsillectomy, Judy's automobile accident, Jamison's stitches, rising food costs, a declining Dow Jones average, several rounds of colds, my pulled leg muscles and John's foot problems, everything went along without a hitch.

We almost enjoyed ourselves last year coping with too many alternatives, participating in too many activities, and pulling each other in too many directions. I think we're overdoing it, but I'd rather be overdone than underdone. Enjoying the "good life" really takes stamina.

Reflection 5: Family – Child Psychology

Negative feedback can help teenagers learn that freedom comes from constraint - not from doing what they feel like.

The concept of spending "quality time" with children has been identified as a key component of family life and parenting. I have never quite understood how to create "quality time."

Family for us was about dragging sons everywhere we could. This included eating meals together, going on vacation together, going to their sports together, etc. It tires me out just thinking back on it. Spending quality moments took many forgettable hours and many moments that were an aggravating pain in the butt. Fortunately, I could be the biggest pain so we could keep things under control some of the time. The major exception was when grandma and I would drive all day from Michigan to Florida while the kids (your dads) mostly ate and slept. Trying to sleep in a motel after kids just slept for 14 hours in the car tended to bring out the worst in their father. Grandma and I were younger with more endurance back then.

Have you ever noticed the biggest, toughest kid tends to dictate what the peer group does? Until they were teenagers and because I haven't matured, I thought of myself as that kid. Unfortunately, our sons were never intimidated by size. We did, however, tend to maintain the illusion of control. The appropriate word was probably more like "contain."

Trying to contain a gaggle of energetic children is not like single people who delude themselves by repeating "I'm finally in control of my life." It's more like a surfer who maintains control while riding a twenty-foot wave; one misguided move and its chaos.

My sons are doing far better than I at parenting, but I must have done something right or maybe they just used my bad example and corrected from there. Whatever the case, here is a systems engineer's view of child rearing. A key point that many parents seem to miss is "negative feedback." I never viewed myself as an authority figure or a good example, but a negative feedback specialist. Most mechanical and electrical systems require negative feedback signals of some sort to keep them under control. Unchecked positive feedback will accelerate a system to a point where it burns out.

Creative negative feedback varies with the child. For example, being very calm and putting Jamison in his room would drive him absolutely crazy, PERFECT. If I put John in his room, he'd just read a book; whereas making him write something over and over again drove him nuts, PERFECT. Jeff drove me nuts - he wasn't allowed to drive, until he was 17; I should have waited until 21.

Most parents try to reason with children. Recent research indicates that development of judgment doesn't emerge in the brain until the early twenties and in some of us it doesn't develop at all. So, parent-child relationships are less about reason and more about POWER. Here are two things that I may have gotten right:

1] My anger didn't mean that they did something wrong, it just meant I was pissed off (anger is a form of insanity).

2] When I was done being angry, if appropriate, I would administer creative negative feedback for inappropriate behavior.

I've read that most teenagers are more afraid of what their peers think than what their parents think. But creative negative feedback, administered calmly and academically is an excellent tool to maintain the illusion of control with energetic sons. One of my sons told me that he HATED my lack of emotion (awesome).

Some teenagers' favorite trick is to make their parents angry so that they are free to scream that their parents don't care and that they are not understood. Calm, authoritative, academic response (usually not my first emotion) to inappropriate behavior frustrates the crap out of screaming teenagers. It also works with belligerent confrontational business associates.

Telling your children that you love them is important but taking time to care is much more important. Telling someone you care takes two seconds, showing them that you care takes a lifetime. That means showing up at events that are important to them and dragging them everywhere that's important to you.

The latter category included having three sons in a two-person sailboat when Grandma and I were racing. Imagine our competitors surprise when we would WIN while the kids played with their Superman and Batman. Our sons did pick up on that intensity in their view of life but are not particularly fond of being in a boat with me. Growing up in this family probably made life in the "real world" seem easy.

Loving children ferociously is a parent's job. But as children get older, a parent must develop the attitude that Sun Tzu in the "Art of War" calls characteristics of good generals: "action and inaction are a matter of strategy, and they cannot be pleased or angered."

Every parent wants their children to be able to function as an adult and a parent in a complex and confused society. Commands of a Household General are best phrased in terms of "thou shalt not," because freedom comes from identifying and administering appropriate constraints - not from doing what you feel like.

Now it's up to our sons and their wives to deal with the power struggle of what's right for their kids. Early on parents are overwhelmed with the first child, but then they are heavy into correcting mistakes that they think their parents made. We grandparents have to learn our role all over again.

Our family got considerably more complicated with the addition of five females. It is clear to me and others that I do not understand women, but granddaughters have given me some perverse insights.

With sons, the conflict was: get out of my way so that I can do what I feel like. With granddaughters, it becomes you must want to do what they feel like because it is the reasonable, sensible thing to do. So they make up rules, to which you must conform. This behavior evolves as most married males know. My ability to submit to arbitrary rules is extremely limited. I am sure Grandma would whole heartedly agree.

Granddaughters have given me much greater but still limited insight into the female psyche; partly because there is no attempt to justify the rules with obfuscating rhetoric. You are just supposed to do what she tells you, which I do. But, as I said before, my capacity is limited; so, I begin to insist that she abide by her own rules which of course results in a new set of rules. This continues for a while until we both get bored, and I buy ice cream or some other forbidden treat.

The Universal Law of Grandfathering states: Grandfathers ally with grandchildren to annoy parents. We, of course, endure the most severe scolding since we are the oldest child (guys never mature) and we buy or acquire the forbidden stuff (e.g., chocolate, soda, military toys, etc). It is way cool to be a grandfather because you are the biggest kid, and you can give them back to their parents if they really go bonkers on sugar.

To help people improve family relationships or to become a super nanny, study Social Sciences: Psychology, and Sociology.

CHRISTMAS 1982

6th Epistle of Jim

MERRY CHISTMAS. It took me until December 18 to get into the "spirit of Christmas" and another five days to summarize our ongoing comedy.

Judy's doing great in nursing School, but studies all the time or sleeps with a book open in front of her. Actually, she also manages to take care of us too, but the house is really taking a beating. Who knows MAYBE I'll try to help out next year (wonder of wonders). Judy keeps threatening to hire someone at $30/hour to do repairs as an incentive for me to do something, sometime, somehow.

I QUIT GENERAL MOTORS after 23 years of loving loyal dedicated service. I am sure everyone at GM needed to put out an extra 10% to overcome a loss of that magnitude. I now work in a small computer firm (65 people) that is growing fast. After being frustrated by GM's inept bureaucracy, it's really fun to work and see that you've had an impact on the company's progress. I always knew GM couldn't do without me but never understood why.

I continue to exercise to prevent feebleness and negate the accelerating defects of aging but have not prevented tubbiness. My sons point out, I may be in good shape for an old man, but I'm not shaped good.

Our baby is a large 13-year-old. He's about two inches shorter than the oldest but makes up for it in width. He'll need to grow into his feet because, in spite of my warning about senseless slaughter, he loves football. His specialty in addition to growth is number of consecutive days with over one hour phone conversations.

It really is a blessing to see your sons grow into healthy, strong young men, but it would make sense to own a grocery store. Ten bags of groceries don't last a week.

John's achievements are really too numerous to mention here. He started high school this year and is on the diving team with his older brother. It doesn't surprise me that both of them are into diving; it's a logical extension of the contortions they go through to avoid chores.

Jeff is a HS senior and is preparing to go to college. He's beginning to appreciate why he should have studied in the 9th and 10th grades now that he's distributing his past sins to colleges on his transcripts. He has developed a real skill for computing fuel usage. He holds the world record for miles driven with the fuel gauge on empty. No risk is too great to leave the car for me with fumes.

Survival drills were the highlight of our Georgian Bay camping, sailing vacation. Everyone wondered why "Mr. experienced sailor" wanted to sail in protected waters until we experienced the thrill of 35 mph winds with the windows in the water. Fortunately, I overcame my judgmental stupidity with brilliant helmsmanship and found refuge at some sympathetic people's private dock. When the going gets tough, I bail out.

Rudy, (alias Hairball, Bruno, dog breath, etc.) our two-year-old dog is not the most trainable of animals. I can't say he isn't bright, because he makes it perfectly clear what he expects of us. He also is kind enough to walk Judy six times a week.

We continue to struggle with each other's conflicting interests, needs and personalities. We still find time to laugh, share special moments and do some things as a family. We hope you find the strength to cope with your problems and enjoy your blessings.

Reflection 6: Bureaucracy

Inept bureaucracies underlie many of this century's problems.

General Motors 15 level hierarchy of management bureaucracy was a constant source of frustration for those of us who were chartered with changing the organization. Even though I was part of a group advising Roger Smith, the president of GM, I was told that my efforts were much like being a gnat on an elephant's butt trying to change its direction.

Smith tossed the pieces of organizations around so much that he disturbed the structure of the company. What he did not realize was that the giant 15 level organization chart of GM meant little or nothing relative to getting cars out. People knew each other over time. They knew people at Design Staff or Cadillac or Fisher Body who would help or do things out of the organization chart. Smith's constant and dramatic organization changes moved people around so much that they lost track of each other and could not respond quickly enough to make a difference.

Also, GM could no longer manage very good segments of its business, which were small by GM standards. GM got rid of GM Robotics and then found that they needed robotics. They got rid of Detroit Diesel and others, which were profitable under different and new management (Penske, Fanuc etc). They also got rid of the great cash cow, GM Parts Division, but kept the pension and the health care obligation! GM had groups for both CAD/CAM and computer security where I was a senior project manager. They became a whole industry and GM ignored that too. This folly was all caused by the distance between Smith and people who knew how to do things.

Like most big companies, GM added a level of hierarchy to the company every time it got bigger. Have you ever played that game where you whisper something in someone's ear, and they pass it on? After it gets passed on 15 times, the last person has no clue as to what was originally said. Shortly after I left GM, companies began to realize that these levels reduced competitiveness and prevented senior management from understanding what was going on in their company.

Much too late, GM started eliminating levels of middle management with no regard for who really understood the business - resulting in a series of disastrous losses in money and market share. No wonder Asia makes most of our stuff.

Had GM senior managers understood its information, engineering, manufacturing, distribution, and information systems, it may have successfully downsized and restructured. Once many management layers are eliminated, who looks after employees? The answer is: employees are self-directed.

Unlike me, you should learn to follow and lead in a bureaucracy since civilization is built on them. This is why the Liberal Education as defined in the next reflection is so important; every college graduate should have a foundation to become an effective leader or follower.

In his Nobel Prize winning book, "The Glass Bead Game," Herman Hesse concludes that organizations maintain themselves by rewarding obedience with privilege. Organizational bureaucracy "had been infected by the characteristic disease of elitehood -- hubris, conceit, class arrogance, self-righteousness, exploitive."

Since 1991, Carnegie Mellon has developed Capability Maturity Models for a myriad of disciplines. To minimize hierarchy and "elitehood" in bureaucracy, its People Capability Maturity Model identifies elements for a work force to manage itself:

- Workforce Planning coordinates workforce activities with current and future business needs.
- Workgroup Development organizes work around competency-based process abilities.
- Competency Development constantly enhances capability of the workforce to perform their assigned tasks.
- Career Development ensures that individuals develop workforce competencies that achieve career objectives.
- Participatory Culture ensures a flow of information within a firm to use the knowledge of individuals into the decision-making processes.
- Competency-Based Practices ensures that all workforce practices are based in part on developing competencies.

Underlying many of the problems of this century are inept bureaucracies in Federal, State, and local governments and our major companies. At the heart of inept bureaucracies are people who don't know what to do or how to do it or both.

To major in business or fix bureaucracy in government, review Carnegie Mellon's web site and read the next reflection to see if your university measures up.

CHRISTMAS 1983
7th Epistle of Jim

This has been our most hectic year, yet someone keeps turning up the treadmill. In the interest of keeping life simple (?), we are restoring a 1970 Beetle; which makes three partially functioning cars and one malfunctioning 1971 Opel GT with 300 lbs. of bondo. We are also making our auto mechanic independently wealthy.

Jeff went off to college this year, where he claims to be doing great at Central Michigan University getting a liberal education. We enjoy his weekend visits and doing his laundry. He has been so busy studying, playing racquetball, swimming, socializing, etc. that he didn't find work. Too bad I only pay tuition, room, and board, but don't make personal loans.

John, our star student, let his grades plummet to a B plus average. He seems to be majoring in extra-curricular activities: soccer, barbershop quartet, gymnastics, jazz band, acting, relentless TV viewing and chore avoidance. He accompanies the women's treble choir on the piano and is on the women's gymnastics team. In the summer, he sang barbershop quartet in the "Music Man."

Jamie is the Junior High heart throb. Last spring, he played drums in his band at the school talent show, with great showmanship and energy, but feminine squeals of delight drowned out his voice. He ran spring track and played fall football. Over the season, he did OK but maximized glory and recognition right at the end of the season. In track, after a slow 100-yard dash, he ran the anchor leg of the 440-relay winning the event and the city meet. In football, he ran 60 yards for a touchdown on the last play of the season immortalizing himself in 10-seconds.

Judy just finished the second-to-last and most difficult semester of her nursing program. After next August, she won't have to bore herself to sleep by reading 100 pages of medical text. It's amazing how quickly she could go to sleep sitting up holding a five-pound book. Judy's really doing well, but still winds herself up into a knot before each test. Since the semester is over, it's like she had a personality transplant just in time for Christmas.

I've been keeping busy at work. It looks like I'm going to play a role in the Company's entry into the European marketplace. Next year will bring terminal jet lag, but I should be able to find something to do in Tokyo, Stockholm, Frankfurt, and London. I'm still a rotund runner. I now run with five-pound dumbbells in each hand to maximize suffering at low speeds. I still run with Rudy's leash around my waist. That's one dumbbell on one end of the leash and three on the other.

Christmas gets more like a T.V. commercial every year, but it is a special season and without it most of us might never write. So, keep us in your thoughts and we promise to remember you with love.

Reflection 7: Liberal Education and USMA

Liberal education should teach problem solving and communication skills and love of Democracy.

I keep seeing ads for various trade schools and universities about how much more money one can earn by being educated at their illustrious institutions. They don't mean educated; they mean trained in a skill for which someone will pay. Being able to support oneself is not a bad idea.

Having been trained as an engineer was useful for muddling through life while making a little money. I had a fine education in problem solving in a fairly narrow subject area.

In engineering problem solving, you demonstrate whether or not a problem was solved. Either what you did worked, or it did not. An educational environment in which students must prove that their ideas work would benefit our society where rhetoric now predominates (e.g. government programs).

We have many people in leadership positions that have no clue about technology, engineering, science, and problem solving including those who govern (see Reflection 6).

We also have a large number of people who could solve many of the problems that face society (engineers and scientists) that can't be bothered. It would be nice to get more trained problem solvers focused on society's real problems. I spent 7 years taking Math, Physical Science and Engineering courses and NOTHING else.

In his book, "The Spirit of Laws," Montesquieu wrote: "Now a government is like everything else: to preserve it we must love it. ... Everything therefore depends on establishing this love of republic; and to inspire it ought to be the principal business of education." To make effective decisions in a democracy, citizens must be able to communicate and solve problems effectively and love democracy which requires an understanding of English, mathematics, history, political science and ethics.

To build a course index, I surveyed University curriculums, the National Academy of Sciences, the National Academy of Arts, and the State of New York Education program indices. After compiling this list, it occurred to me that I had not adequately covered Military Science. To my surprise, the United States Military Academy's web site defined an outstanding 21st century core curriculum in the form of learning models.

ALL college graduates should have USMA learning model skills, in addition to their chosen area of study whether that is poetry, art, theater or engineering.

Here is a simplified overview of those learning models:

Math, Science, and Technology	Graduates draw upon their knowledge and skills in mathematics and science to address issues pertaining to technology, decision-making, problem solving.
Engineering Thought Process	Graduates use the engineering thought process by which mathematical and scientific facts and principles are applied to leading a technologically complex organization.
Cultural Perspective	Graduates draw on an appreciation of culture to understand human behavior, achievement, and ideas and appreciate both the diversity of American culture and the challenges of performing in a global multicultural environment.
Historical Perspective	Graduates draw on an appreciation of history to understand in a global context human behavior, achievement and ideas; leaders are expected to have an historical perspective and to be sensitive to patterns of continuity and change of societies.
Human Behavior	Graduates understand patterns of human behavior, particularly how individuals, organizations, and societies pursue social, political, and economic goals and apply that understanding to effective leadership.
Communication	Graduates express their thoughts and communicate, especially in writing, in precise language, correct sentences, and concise, coherent paragraphs.
Moral Awareness	Graduates recognize moral issues and apply ethical considerations in decision making and can rationally analyze ethical responses to moral problems.
Continued Educational Development	Graduates have the foundation for continued educational development and capability and willingness to pursue additional learning on their own.
Creativity	Graduates confront ambiguous situations, apply their thinking skills and innovation to solve problems and can transfer what they know in one context or discipline to another.

Liberal education requires studying: Applied Math, Engineering Science, Anthropology, Communications, Political Science, Psychology, Sociology, American Studies, Classics, History, Philosophy and Religion.

CHRISTMAS 1984
8th Epistle of Jim

I must live in a time warp -- I just wrote a Christmas letter last month. My sons finally did it – they've stampeded me into Middle Age??!: just me, not Judy.

To provide a proper place for his new drum set, Jamie relentlessly negotiates for materials to finish his, basement sound room. He has avoided paying his half while pointing out that he gets 50% of the improved property value. His brothers defaulted on the Opel GT, so now he sands, shapes, disassembles, assembles, and repairs while rendering our garage totally useless. Hopefully I won't be accused of giving my children Bondo lung.

Now Jamie and John add theatrical meaning to the song and dance act most teenagers reserve only for their parents. Both were in two plays – "Little Mary Sunshine" and "Don't Drink the Water." With their theatrical exposure, their charisma continues to attract new fans. They are currently not bestowing their charms on particular young ladies, but alternately delight and exasperate their mother.

Apparently neither inherited their father's voice, since they are both singing in the men's choir which doesn't have a monotone section.

John joined the girls' gymnastics team again -- must like female audiences and adulation. He is doing OK in school and only occasionally lets it interfere with his extra-curricular activities; chores are definitely out. We wandered around college campuses trying to figure out where I'm going to dump another $$$. After I vetoed several $$$$$$ private schools, he narrowed his decision to U of M and MSU. The new $39 million performing arts center at MSU and the law quadrangle at U of M (patterned after Oxford) were real highs in our search.

I think Jeff is finally ready to major in academic subjects first and party second. Wonder of Wonders, he wants to go to MSU to increase his academic options. Fortunately, I believe his extra-curricular activities did not sufficiently inhibit his studies to prevent him from transferring from Central Michigan University.

We treated Judy to a new car for graduating a cum laude nurse. If I plead, I'm allowed to borrow it occasionally. Judy was ecstatic to escape from school but is now sufficiently bored to look for work. Since we're bigger than she is, beating on us to do chores is more work than doing them herself. Hence, the next obvious step - Judy hopes to start working part time at a Pontiac hospital in January. Maybe we can be shamed into doing something sometime somehow.

I won the company international business award for endurance and physical stamina -- ten all-expense paid trips to Europe in one year. Twenty-two weeks in Europe to set up three offices resulting in terminal jet lag. This year was so ridiculously eventful, it has left me in a state of sensory paralysis.

Judy and the boys came to visit. While I worked, Judy railroaded the guys on Britrail journeys to Cambridge, Edinburgh, Glasgow, London, Leicester, and Stratford. We all drove to Wales and drank beer in a pub in Aberystwyth on the ocean. In London, Judy and John soaked up culture while the other two soaked up beer in pubs. By the time we got to Frankfurt, we were content to visit old friends.

I prefer to think of myself as cuddly despite all the exercise that's supposed to produce rippling muscles and angular shapes -- at least I'm shaped like a fireplug instead of a pear. Think of me as Teddy Bearish (and Judy as Momma Bearish).

This letter has become more important for me to write than it is to have it read. It helps me to see my life and the people around me with a little more tolerance and humor, the way I perceive God might expect me to. I hope that it helps you see the humor in your lives as well. Take time to reflect. Most of our frantic antics and minor tragedies are part of God's comedy.

Reflection 8: International Business

International Business has been good for the global economy and bad for the planet; it needs to be good for both.

For years, working for a big company was "safe." However, as economies, technological development, travel, population, and corporate greed accelerate, even a delusional person would have a hard time feeling safe.

As long as there is no avoiding risk, we must mitigate the negative consequences. I took significant business risk, but never learned to mitigate the negative consequences. I always had trouble with the idea of making money that I didn't earn. I shudder every time I see one of those commercials where the guy is running after his huge "nest egg".

Western economic theory rests on a few basic notions: that if someone wants something it must have value; that the tension between what people want and its availability is a good gauge of its value; and that free markets do the best job of fixing value because they act knowledgably and in logical ways. Adam Smith, in his "Wealth of Nations," argued that we should leave things alone and let the market sort them out.

In his book "Pulse", Robert Frenay discussed problems of industrial globalization and its associated economics. Just after WW II the industrial powers formed the World Bank to end poverty; the International Monetary Fund (IMF), to sustain the then-prevailing fixed exchange rates; and the General Agreement on Tariffs and Trades (GATT) to provide a framework of international law. In 1994, GATT was subsumed by the newly created World Trade Organization (WTO), with the authority to penalize any member nations – even the richest – whose trade laws impede the free flow of goods, services, and cash across international borders.

Benefits are real. Global infant mortality rate has been cut in half; billions of people live longer, eat better, and have more income. The world's total exports then were $380 billion dollars annually; now it's 17 times that amount.

However, World Bank loans and the IMF's structural adjustment programs make it easy to move polluting industries into the developing world; also, IMF and WTO suppress health, environmental and labor protections by asserting that they hamper open markets. 20% (and rising) of US manufacturing jobs have migrated overseas.

Frenay argues that our environment, built up over 4 billion years, is a form of principal and should be protected by rules that govern financially conservative investment practice. Economic theory must recognize there's only so much energy to go around.

The bureaucratic ineptness and inefficiency of the Federal Government is partly to blame for our current environment and economic state. It is not as easy to fix as it is in business (which is not that easy either, but it is rational). There are 12,000 lobbyists telling Congressmen that what's good for their special interest is good for the country and Congressmen.

Conservatives are concerned about big government but ignore the growing list of multinational corporations that are bigger than most governments. Adam Smith knew that monopolies were a danger to free markets in 1776 and so it is today. Automobiles, computers, media, pharmaceuticals, and oil are monopolies that don't want free markets, they want markets they control.

A real threat comes from the World Bank, WTO, and IMF who support international monopolistic corporations. The diffusion of power through local control, encouraging individual participation, is key for democracy. Republicans and Democrats must come together to fight big business, big government, and big media.

The behavior and rules of the World Bank, WMO and IMF for a global economy are systemically contributing to pollution, sending American manufacturing and jobs overseas and providing tax shelters for companies' foreign subsidiaries. Global Monopolies don't answer to governments but expect governments to cater to them *(it's much worse in the 16 years since this was written)*.

Monopolies, unfortunately, mitigate risk by controlling their markets and eliminating competitors. Many bureaucracies discourage risk taking. The person who fails the least gets promoted. One sure way not to fail is not to do anything and to associate with the final stage of a successful project.

Smaller companies take real risks. Taking risk implies there is some reward and associated happiness, but risk can also involve failure and misery. Small companies' innovations don't reach a controlled (not free) market because monopolies crush them to mitigate their risk.

To solve International Business problems study: Statistics, Anthropology Economics, Political Science, Sociology, Philosophy, Law and Public Policy.

CHRISTMAS 1985

9th Epistle of Jim

MERRY CHRISTMAS. You know the old saying "time flies when you're having..." This year was one decade long. In the sense that adversity builds character, I added a mother lode of character this year. My Mom and Dad died in February and March, Judy's Uncle died this fall, and three other friends also died. Go with God all.

Overpopulation be damned, I don't care to have any more friends or relatives donate for a long while.

On the positive side, with two sons at MSU this year, having extra money to worry about investing isn't a problem. But, if you consider what it costs to feed the two of them, the money I pay MSU is for food and the education is free.

The house feels kind of empty with those two at school and Jamie working, practicing for the school play or visiting his girlfriend. More adjustments - -I wonder if this classifies as growing up or getting old.

Our youngest has turned into a student this year - - so far. I can't decide if he just decided that he needs to do better to go to college, had a major change in chemicals, or his astrological planets are in a favorable position. He also, wonder of wonders, after having it lie dormant for four years got the 1971 Opel (bondo and all) running - - not well, but running. It goes into storage now and won't come out until he pays off his Dad's and brother's share of the car. He delighted his fan club this year with the role of Paul in "Carnival" and Paul again in "Up the Down Staircase."

John is doing well this year in *almost* everything. He is also busy with State Singers and theatre - probably uses up his math reservoir with his music. When John isn't studying or extracurricularring, he's busy thinking up ways to enhance his education, like study Russian in Leningrad or Science in Hawaii this summer. This has the additional benefit of avoiding a summer job. John is going to be expensive.

Jeff now thinks of himself as a person who studies hard and parties hard. Unfortunately, his propensity for partying and possessions seems to generate expenses beyond his earnings - - mother's genes. Speaking of expense, he seems to have discovered latent tendencies toward scholarship. Now that Jeff's a B+ student, he's thinking about going to graduate school.

THREE SONS IN COLLEGE, THREE TUITIONS, THREE ROOM AND BOARDS - - AAAUUUGH.

Judy misses the guys severely. But, her nursing job keeps her busy and tires her out. It's really a tough job - - don't see how she gets through a day. She's good at it though, gentle, but toughened up after over twenty years of survival training with four intense, ego centered males. We now call her Deacon Jones. I was on the church officers nominating committee - guess who was on my list.

Work was a little nonsensical. Sales increased and we lost twice as much as we earned last year. There's an old nautical saying that applies to our management style - it's tough to have a commanding view when one's head is up the aft end of the intestinal tract.

Rudy, our dog, is still cute, cuddly, and hairy as ever, but then so am I - and besides that, I'm smarter than he is, I think.

We all had a tough year, but it brought us a little closer together as a family. Mixed with tears there still has been laughter even at the most difficult times. We reflect on the meaning of life as we continue to write our own chapters in God's comedy.

An important part of reflecting at Christmas is remembering each of you with a Christmas card and this letter.

Reflection 9: God, Mortality, Morality and Law

Reflecting on mortality leads to thoughts of God and religion and to ask: what does it mean to live an ethical, moral life?

Two parents dying in five weeks gave me a heavy dose of my own mortality. Until then, my death was a mere abstraction. Dying happens to other people - not me. I've reserved Isaiah's fiery chariot to go to heaven.

It was a life-altering experience. One associate commented on the significant change in my personality. He said: I transcended from obnoxiously unbearable to marginally tolerable in my business relationships.

Since 1985, I have had an imminent sense of my mortality. I will "not go gentle into that good night." I continue to try to accomplish something of real consequence but have not - with three notable exceptions. We had three sons that are exceptional. But grandma gets most of the credit for that, especially for their civilized behavior that was acquired despite their father's example.

Unless one is very young, the loss of our parents is a signal that we are in the final stage of our life. It's interesting talking to your children about your impending death. They point out that there are many good years left; like they have a clue. Being my kind of crazy is OK but having a brain that doesn't work is not the way to spend my remaining years. A long degenerative process toward death is terrifying to me. *(At 82, 16 years after I wrote this, I published 3 more books. I'm not going gentle into the good night).*

My personal favorite Christian motivator beyond reason is: IMMORTALITY. Only death provides proof. What a great motivator: Live a moral, ethical life as if you are held accountable for all eternity, AND your sins are forgiven.

This brings us to God and religion. There have been several books written by atheists attacking religious belief in God as delusional and a menace. They cite murderous behavior of past Jews, Christians and Muslims and use the Theory of Evolution to explain creation (see Reflection 27).

As a skeptical Christian, one of the reasons that this is so topical is the failure of religion to adopt scientific insights to better understand God's Laws. Too bad, it devalues the message of Christ and requires us to put science and reason outside the realm of religious belief. Reason gives us the best chance for guidance and decisions and accepting God.

Reflection 27 will take the notion of a new (old) Christianity further. A viable Christian religion must be easy for the majority but embrace the minority who are spectacularly expanding our knowledge and understanding of the universe. Spiritual and Scientific insight are not independent realities.

At Christianity's core are the teachings of Jesus Christ. Some feel that only his words represent the true Word of God. In 1820, Thomas Jefferson finished his condensation of the New Testament into what is now called "The Jefferson Bible" by relating only what Jesus taught. Jefferson writes: "We find the writings of (Jesus') biographers a matter of two distinct descriptions. First, a groundwork of vulgar ignorance, of things impossible, of superstitions, fanaticisms and fabrications. Intermixed with these, again, are sublime ideas of the Supreme Being, aphorisms and precepts of the purest morality and benevolence, sanctioned by a life of humility, innocence, and simplicity of manners, neglect of riches, absence of worldly ambition and honors, with eloquence and persuasiveness."

Morality under the law was summed up by Jesus Christ with what some now refer to as the Golden Rule: "All things whatsoever you would that men should do to you, do you even so to them: for this the law and the prophets" (Matthew 7:12).

It is revisited by Immanuel Kant in his Metaphysics of Morals: "Act only on that maxim whereby you can at the same time will that it should become a universal law."

In the 2004 Christmas letter, I discuss the four cardinal virtues of prudence, justice, temperance, and fortitude and the three theological virtues of faith, hope and charity. These virtues and the Golden Rule provide us with guidelines for living an ethical, moral life. However, we need to apply these in terms of rules for ourselves and society. These rules then become the laws of a nation.

Kant tells us in his "Elements of Ethics" that ethics in ancient times was called the doctrine of duties. "The notion of duty is in itself already the notion of constraint of the free elective will by the law. The impulses of nature, then, contain hindrances to the fulfillment of duty in the mind of man."

If you are a citizen of the United States, the constitution and "The Spirit of Laws" is your guide for ethical citizenship. The love of law is fundamental for democracies. Montesquieu says about republics: "In these alone the government is entrusted to private citizens. Now government is like everything else: to preserve it we must love it."

The founding fathers intended that separation of church and state would protect the church from the government not to protect government from the church. In his farewell address, George Washington said: "Of all the dispositions and habits which lead to prosperity, religion and morality are indispensable supports. …reason and experience both forbid us to expect that National morality can prevail in exclusion of religious principle."

If you are Christian, the Ten Commandments and the teachings of Jesus Christ guide the duties of moral and ethical behavior. You must redefine those duties for yourself.

It is important for each person to ask what ethical and moral behavior is, develop a set of duties and constraints and then live by them. Here are a few: obey the law, nurture your family, apply the golden rule, practice the seven virtues, keep your word, don't whine, learn as much you can, forgive other people and yourself for failure, and never quit.

Unfortunately, many Christian communities focus on fabrications and devalue the sublime ideas of religion and science and its application to our national conscience.

> To learn about God, ethics, morality, and law, go to church, meditate and study: *Anthropology, History, Religion, Philosophy and Law.*

10

CHRISTMAS 1986

10th Epistle of Jim

Christmas seems to have come early this year. I haven't really got the Christmas spirit, which may be an improvement because I identify with Scrooge (before the ghosts).

I convinced everyone that Key West was best. Judy takes a circuitous route with the two oldest sons and a big hairy dog: via Detroit - Philadelphia - Southport, N.C. - Key West visiting friends and relatives. Jamison and I fly down, and John and Judy fly back. Jeff gets dropped off at the Cincinnati Airport where he flies to New York for the New Year with his girlfriend. What could be more American than frantic Yuletide behavior? Freedom and mobility really test the nervous system.

In addition to his theatre activities and job, Jamie condescends to squeeze in minimal amounts of scholastic labor. Overall, he's doing well in school but has one major academic aberration. To continue his theatrical activities, he has signed a written contract which requires him to study ALGEBRA two hours a day, six days a week until January 15. Violating the contract would be painful since he will be Henry Higgins in "My Fair Lady" at Adam's High School. He wants to major in Theatre (shudder).

John is doing exceptionally well in college with one persistent exception. What's happened to the Math genes!! - all lost in one generation (almost, see next paragraph). He took several music courses this term, sang in State Singers and the Chamber Choir, and now wants to major in Music. @*!# When do those guys start supporting me!!? They're all going to starve as actors and musicians until I die, and THEN they'll get rich.

Jeff, after sliding through high school and partying for two years in college, suddenly (and for no good reason) became a scholar, and now plans to go to graduate school at NYU for $$$/credit hour. However, he's doing great in CALCULUS - let's hear it for the genes! For someone who was never interested in money, I spend a lot of time watching it flee from my grasp.

One unnamed son had the audacity to ask me why we couldn't own a PORSCHE. I told him if I could ransom him at cost, I could afford a ROLLS ROYCE, but would choose him any day. Maybe we'll celebrate their lives and two graduations with a pig roast in the spring.

Judy has been working as a Registered Nurse for two years and is doing a great job. It's great for her psyche, and exceedingly stressful on her body. On her more 'interesting' days, after work she sleeps, wakes up and eats, and then goes back to sleep until breakfast. You'd think with all that hard work that she wouldn't have time to shop -- but Noooo! She's a natural talent. Even when we go to MSU, her love of sons manifests itself by buying groceries. I thought sending them to college would save $10,000 on food.

As you've probably ascertained from my whimpering, my primary function has been funding family functions. I've developed a strange mentality about money lately. With money flowing out in volume, I figure what's a few $$$$ here or there – I don't want any leftover when I'm gone.

Therefore, John and Judy finally convinced me Hawaii was the place to go. Judy and I went for 10 days, and John was there five weeks in a $pecial MSU Natural $cience class, which gave him a wonderful eight credit academic vacation, and $eparated me from more $$$$s. Hawaii was enchanting, mysterious, primitive, and beautiful. We'll go back to camp and hike in a few years. After all, we only pass through here once.

You'll be pleased to know that I've still got my tubular, cuddly shape despite losing 10 lbs. I'm sure I will never ever see my stomach muscles without vacuum surgery. But to look at my waist is to know there's survival for at least a 30-day famine. I'm definitely getting older, but I'm fighting a terrific losing battle against the aging process.

Christmas is a happy/sad time: to reflect on friends not seen, and parents and grandparents who are gone. It's a time to philosophize on how magnificently we succeed and miserably we fail at being human.

For this Christmas, I wish for you peace with yourself, joy within your families, the warmth of many friendships, and His love on His birthday.

Reflection 10: Communication and Memes

Birth, graduation, marriage, and death are events meriting celebration. The death of loved ones brings sadness but celebrating their life should be mandatory. We celebrated life and Jamie's high school and Jeff's college graduations with a pig roast in the spring of 1987. It involved 15 confrontations with high school participants to not drink the college participants' beer. I would not mix college and high school students and beer at a party again.

Every celebration should involve roasting a pig except maybe a bar mitzvah. College graduates turned the pig on the spit from 7am to 2pm. They drank, philosophized about life, and speculated about the opposite sex. My Jesuit priest friend said that serious philosophical and theological discourse requires alcohol consumption.

I am feeling unbearably mortal. Nine grandchildren will carry my genes into the future. Hopefully, one of my books sends my memes into the future. The Oxford dictionary defines "meme" as: an element of culture that is passed on by non-genetic means, especially imitation (Greek meme: our soul lives on after death).

In his book, "The Selfish Gene," Richard Dawkins defines a Meme Complex as a group of memes that thrive in each other's company such as: political ideologies, religious beliefs, scientific theories and paradigms, and languages. He says that genes are replicators whose competition drives evolution of biological design. Memes are passed on by imitation and stored in brains: tunes, ideas, or catch-phrases. Replicators have traits of longevity, self-copying fidelity, and fecundity. Fecundity is the speed of replication.

Reflections in this book are meme complexes. If I have been insightful and clever enough, they may spread and provide an additional small measure of immortality.

In her paper, "The Power of the Meme Meme," Susan Blackmore suggests that once genetic evolution created creatures that were capable of imitating each other, our brains became the product of two replicators – Genes and Memes. She says memes are governed by simple rules:
1] memes do not have foresight;
2] memes do not care about genes or people - they just reproduce themselves (conversations, TV, newspapers propagate memes);
3] memes, by definition, are passed on ONLY by imitation (learning by trial and error or by feedback is not memetic).

Blackmore speculates in a world full of brains:

1. Why can't we stop thinking? Memes encourage thoughts that compel you to keep thinking them, so we think a lot.

2. Why do we talk so much? Memes that encourage talking fill our brains because they are heard by more people than memes of a shy person like "talking is a waste of time."

3. Why are we so nice to each other? People who are altruistic will, on average, spread more altruism memes because they encourage their host to be friendly and kind as opposed to memes for being unfriendly and mean.

4. Why are our brains so big? Brains are 2% of body weight but use 20% of its energy and are three times the size of ape brains. Early humans learned language and imitation to make pots or knives or catch prey. A quick learner would more easily find a mate; so sexual selection sought big brains.

5. Who am I? Our personalities, abilities and unique qualities derive from the complex interplay of meme-complexes - like religions, political belief systems and cults.

For most of human history memes evolved at much the same rate as genes from parent to child. Telephones, e-mail, fax machines and the Internet have increased the propagation speed of memes. The relative uncoupling of genes and memes may mean that detrimental memes will spread rapidly: dangerous cults, fads, political systems, copy-cat crimes, and false beliefs.

We are constantly bombarded with useless memes from the Internet and television advertising. We hear clever jingles and quips to get us to buy something that we would not ordinarily think to buy; or, infomercials where testimony of satisfied customers urges you to buy their wonderful product.

Science is about discovering the truth about natural law. Consider how easy it is to get ten people to say that something is correct versus proving a scientific theory which may require a scientist 20 years of education, ten years to develop, and another ten years to prove. Most of us "know" very little for sure because it takes a lot of effort to really "know." The danger here is the rate at which we fill our brains with useless (memetic) trivia.

If this topic interests you, study: Applied Math, Genetics and Genomics, Language and Societies, Philosophy and Anthropology.

CHRISTMAS 1987
11th Epistle of Jim

The guys have all been off to school. It will be so nice to have them home for Christmas to visit. College is wonderful - young people get a chance to learn and grow; parents get a chance to rest and recuperate. The only flaw -- parents must send money, send money, send money.

Now they can take care of themselves. Now they're responsible for their own lives. Now I don't have to worry about them - WRONG. It looks like we've got at least five years of parenting before we're a problem to THEM.

Jamie attends Western Michigan University on a theatre scholarship. Now we drive 300 miles to see a play. He is conscientious about acting, but it would be refreshing if he would also study. I remind him that continued funding is contingent upon academic success. Jamie plans to attend UCLA this summer as he did last summer; maybe this could be deductible as a fine arts contribution.

John is working toward a degree in Arts and Letters. He now must go to graduate school. A scholarship would be welcome. Family planning presumed 4 years of college. When he graduates, he will have taken a potty load of courses in Russian, German and Music. Maybe John will get an MBA in International Business and become a Jazz Musician. He has been playing in a jazz band. I wonder if there are more out of work musicians than actors.

Jeff attends NYU and survives on financial aid, a scholarship, and a part-time job. I still send money, but it's hundreds, not thousands. Jeff progresses toward Dad's objective for sons -- self-supporting.

Reading "Zen and the Art of Motorcycle Maintenance" precipitated Jeff's graduation present -- a motorcycle trip through Wales with Dad. Of the many available forms of mobility, a motorcycle may not be in my best self-interest. Let me say: age does not assure good judgment. Sliding around beneath a 400 lb. motorcycle convinced me that perhaps Britain was not the best of places to relearn to ride. Despite knee and ankle damage, we had a great time talking philosophy, riding through the Welsh countryside, and drinking large quantities of beer. We did some upscale trendy stuff too, like go to the theatre in Stratford upon Avon and London.

Judy is reveling, not suffering from empty nest syndrome. When she feels the need to mother, she calls one of her babies long-distance just to make sure he's eating right, getting his proper exercise and bundling up in cold weather - big phone bill. Between being in charge of the church women's group and nursing three days a week, Judy seems to be enjoying life. I'm the only thorn left; and she seems glad to see me even when I get home at eight.

I'm keeping busy at work. Another reorganization resulted in my 6th or 7th new job assignment. Maybe I'll find something I'm good at. Now I'm in charge of Product Development, with people in Detroit and San Francisco - more frequent flyer miles. Someone probably figures I'll do less damage if I'm on a plane.

When my cholesterol level tested at 280, I could feel my heart valves plugging up. Fear drove me to a no fat, no cholesterol diet. In four months, the cholesterol dropped to 190 with a 12# weight loss. I now almost taper from chest to waist -- at least 1^0. Next year perhaps I'll report a visible stomach muscle.

Rudy's been running Judy every night. He's really Judy's pal. She's partial to hairy animals.

Even with the guys living away from home, we're still a family. We all have an opportunity to grow closer now that we do not have the burden of cohabitation. Through our conflicts and frustrations, we continue to generate our own humor. We wish you humor and joy this Holiday Season.

Reflection 11: Mobility and Energy

Mobility enriches the lives of us few while impoverishing the planet.

We Americans think nothing of going from one side of the country to another; we just do it. When we drove from Malaga, Spain to Frankfurt, Germany in a car in one day, our German friends thought us insane. Which in my case is probably true, but who are they to talk anyway? Half of Michigan drives to Florida during winter and spring break.

Europeans joke that Italians race their cars, French hate their cars, Germans love their cars and Americans live in their cars.

Mobility gives us an opportunity to experience other places and cultures directly. It's somewhat artificial because tourist businesses are usually nice if you spend money.

I'm mobility saturated. I haven't seen everything, but enough to find travel to experience other cultures in three weeks or less is not particularly interesting. And travel to experience decadent behavior like a cruise holds no interest for me.

Returning to the USA made me appreciate how much we depend on consuming the planet's resources. A country whose economy booms consumes. And boy, does the USA consume. Grandma actually cried when she walked into a supermarket after coming back from Germany.

Consumption is the basis for our capitalistic system and drives our economy. Unfortunately, we use the planet's resources (especially oil) at a frightening rate.

Our political/economic system determines the way we use, produce, and consume resources, generate wealth, and move our society forward (but lately, maybe backward).

We have to figure out how to power our economy and transport ourselves with less fuel. Using up fossil fuels at our current rate is a very bad idea since we must depend on oil from very unstable Middle East and the South Americas, Mexico, and Canada.

We, as Americans, expect to have many products to choose from. When we buy, we usually buy higher quality, lower cost foreign goods. Is anyone thinking how long this can last. Fortunately, we consume from and owe so much to other countries that they have to support our economy to protect theirs. It's like borrowing so much money from a bank that it can't let you go bankrupt.

Amazingly, we continue to increase our consumption of oil, despite outsourcing production to other countries generating a giant trade imbalance. No one can consume like Americans. Shamefully, we use three times the resources of the average European country. For being the self-proclaimed leader of the free world, there is much that we could and need to learn from other nations.

To assure our polluting reputation, we should give tax breaks on the biggest, heaviest SUVs which consume spectacular amounts of fuel. Oh, wait a minute; we already do that.

One of our biggest problems is that environmentalists are frightening us with flawed arguments on Global Warming. The planet is getting warmer, Carbon Dioxide (CO_2) levels are increasing, but correlation doesn't mean one causes the other. Flawed argument notwithstanding, we can't continue using the planets resources and polluting at the current rate.

Here is what I think is happening. Regulated by government and commerce, driven by corporate practices, and supported by habitat (earth), processes in farming, forestry, mining and industry generate waste, consume and transform habitat to produce products for people; people support processes and create knowledge to provide feedback to change government, commerce, corporate practices, and habitat usage. Read that twice more before proceeding.

Now let's look at the fundamental problem: Flow of consumption and waste is too high for Earth to support. This breaks down into four major problems:

- 500 trillion pounds (no exaggeration) of waste will be generated in the next decade, fueled by population growth and a waste generating lifestyle that fouls and can't be absorbed by habitat (earth).
- Consumption of energy, water, and food to support a waste generating lifestyle and a population increase from 2 billion to 9 billion people in one hundred years.
- Government and commerce organization policies and multinational corporate practices systematically export high waste generating industries to third world countries and eliminate jobs from our economy.
- Politicians and environmentalists are focused on CO_2 reduction which may (probably not) reduce global warming and are not solving the first three problems.

Now remember the wine growing lesson; you can whine about it or mature like a fine wine and become the one person who acts as a catalyst to solve these problems by providing solutions defined in the next reflection.

Remember earlier when we talked about the scientific method. A scientist looks at data and forms a theory which attempts to explain what is going on. However, in order to get funding for your project, you must persuade someone to give it to you. Fear is one of the best motivators to extract money from business or government to fund projects.

Global Warming is an example of fear for funding gone awry. Increasing CO_2 in the atmosphere may cause global warming, but its proponents have not made their case (*16 years later they still haven't but are charging ahead anyway with a net increase in CO_2.*). Many things which can't be controlled may also cause a warming trend - like volcanic activity in the oceans, increased solar heating and cosmic rays. Fear for funding has also showcased the catastrophic events that might occur. Reducing CO_2 is an OK idea, but implementing alternative forms of energy generation is considerably more productive.

Scientists who criticize CO_2 causing global warming are labeled "deniers" and "immoral;" this is political nonsense. The scientific method requires significant amounts of skepticism and continuous attempts to disprove prevailing theories.

NO ONE has PROVEN what is causing Global Warming and NO ONE has or can yet predict what the consequences of Global Warming will be (*still true 16 years later*). The current Global Warming hype is a perfect reason why we all need to take mathematics and statistics in college since we now have lawyers acting as scientists and scientists acting like politicians.

To have an opportunity to solve this problem,
study: Applied Math, Ecology, Earth Science,
and Climate Science.

CHRISTMAS 1988
12th Epistle of Jim

Here we are at Christmas again, Bah Humbug, I need to be visited by three ghosts to get the Christmas Spirit. However, all of our sons will all be here together again; that probably will be just as inspiring and traumatic. They're the blessings that I pray that I'll endure. That and Judy's smokin' Christmas charge card.

Jamie is still majoring in theatre at Western, and wonder of wonders, may even make some money at it. He just signed a contract for an educational television program. Maybe he will become rich and famous in my lifetime and buy his loving father a yacht (yachts are longer than 39 feet). He played the lead role in "Anything Goes". He's very busy acting but did remember to act scholarly two weeks before final exams, He is applying to UCLA next fall as a theatre major. If they want an actor, he's in.

John is still liberalizing his non-major. Besides Russian and German languages and music, he has now added journalism to his non-major. He's becoming a Renaissance man; but maybe not employable in this technological age. He's interested in many things like playing jazz gigs in nightclubs, teaching English to the Chinese or maybe working as a European news reporter. He's an interviewer on cable TV on an MSU campus station. Who knows, maybe he'll be rich and famous TV journalist and buy his loving and supportive father a yacht (yachts are longer than 39 feet).

Jeff is now in his second year at NYU and has become SELF-SUPPORTING. He is working at the New York Hall of Science teaching kids about rainbows with computer animation. Maybe he'll copyright some exotic computer program, get rich and buy his loving, supportive and deserving father a yacht, (yachts are longer than 39 feet). He should graduate in June and hopefully continue to be SELF-SUPPORTING. Jeff has been living in Manhattan and working in Queens. He's turning into a real city slicker. He'll have one giant allergic reaction when he comes home and smells a tree.

Judy continues to enjoy complaining about the nursing profession. Challenges to complain about are important for all of us. The relief of kicking all the chicks out of the nest has passed, but frequent long distance phone calls to give her sons advice help Judy from missing them so much that she wants live-in children again. Our sons come home just often enough to make us thankful for their uniqueness AND independence. The house isn't really empty; besides looking after their four-legged hairy brother, Rudy, we're still acting as a warehouse for all the kids' worldly goods. We should move, leave all the kids' stuff in the house, and not leave a forwarding address.

I won't bore you this year with a long treatise on my battle against fat and aging. Just think of me as a thick waisted exerciser.

Work continues to bring new challenges every day. In the computer business, prices are dropping like boulders, and lots of companies have folded. We continue to show a meager profit which means the company is "successful". It's kind of like successfully surviving a hurricane in a yacht with most of your parts intact (yachts are longer than 39 feet and provide a mobility option that doesn't consume or pollute).

With the kids gone, Judy and I are struggling to get to know each other again. We struggled off to New York, San Francisco, and Hawaii this year. Traveling with two instead of five people is a lot cheaper and almost as much fun.

Sharing thoughts with friends in this letter has always helped me get into the Christmas spirit. Maybe all of us can give gifts to both the people we love and those who really need them. Remember us with kindness and a smile as we remember you in this Christmas Season.

Reflection 12: Environment and Sun

Sun (and wind) provides energy options that don't consume or pollute.

Having all our sons out of the house represented a significant transition for both grandma and me as it probably is for most parents. We miss our children, but for most of us it is compensated for by a new sense of personal freedom. You can be at the center of your life again. Of course, not total freedom, there was still college tuition to pay, returns from college and trips to college where we bought extra food. My friends with daughters tell me it's not food, but clothes. This translates to significant expenditure of MONEY that we foolishly thought might be for our old age. To pay for college, we must die ten years younger (*we didn't*).

Finally, 20 years later, I can reflect on what life is all about. Watching from more of a distance now, I can reflect on the SUN (and wind) for energy and mobility rather than sons.

I thought I invented an approach to solar power generation using solar power to boil water to power steam turbines. Had I thought of this in 1947 instead of 2007, it might have been original. Luz Corporation in 1991 built a solar powered steam energy plant that supplies 100,000 houses in California with electricity.

The fundamental solution to the problem of consumption and pollution in the previous reflection is to preserve habitat by: changing policies and practices in the system; making processes more efficient; changing the content of products to reduce flow of consumption and waste; getting energy directly from the sun; desalinating ocean water; and cutting down fewer trees.

Some partial solutions and jobs include:
- You can become an economist and revise policies of the World Bank, WTO, and IMF and revise corporate practices to prevent systemic increase of consumption and waste by production, products and lifestyle.
- You can become a chemical engineer and research how to make better use of clean solar, nuclear, hydroelectric, hydrogen, fossil fuel, or any other energy generation.
- You can become a biologist and research how to transform habitat for food generation and waste absorption.
- You can become a chemist and research how to desalinate ocean water.
- You can become an architect and use new solar cell technology to manufacture steel roofing imbedded with solar cells.

- You can become a mechanical engineer and research new ways to build more alternative fuel vehicles.
- You can become a chemist and develop materials and chemicals that biodegrade.
- You can become a bioengineer and research new ways to use the heat dissipated by energy plants to drive steam turbines for even more power.
- You can become a physicist and research new ways to use optics to focus the sun to boil water to drive steam turbines.

In his book "Pulse," Robert Frenay points out that "real conservatives never draw on principal to pay for daily needs. ... How many trees can we log without destroying the systems that generate not only new trees, but also wildlife, oxygen and much of our fresh water? And what of the natural capital lost when we squander energy resources and other materials, a cost now missing from market prices?"

If you decide that you want to save the environment, read Robert Frenay's book: "Pulse," Fred Singer's book: "Unstoppable Global Warming," and Michael Crichton's novel: "State of Fear."

Also, get on the Web and search on LUZ. LUZ used 45 acres of solar collectors to provide electricity for 100,000 homes. Extrapolating this to a 100 square mile desert area for solar collectors to power 143 million homes may be impractical, but still you might ask: Why don't we just build a bunch more?

This gets back to being real conservatives. Some folks think that we don't need solar energy because we can slurp oil. Remember, oil is what happens when plants rot for millions of years and plants need sun to grow. I don't want to wait several million years for a fill up when we run out of oil (*this is probably wrong; many energy experts think oil is constantly produced 40,000 feet down*).

> Here are some areas of study to pursue: Biology, Ecology & Evolutionary Biology, Forestry & Forest Science, Plant Sciences, Chemistry, Earth Sciences, Climate Sciences, Physics, Biomedical Engineering & Bioengineering, Chemical Engineering, Engineering Science and Mechanical Engineering, Economics, Sociology.

13

CHRISTMAS 1989
13th epistle of Jim

How very American to celebrate the birth of Jesus at a time and with traditions that have nothing to do with his birth. Christmas for me exemplifies the cornerstones of American Values - Love and Greed.

We had a tragedy this year -- Judy's Dad died. It's been a sad time and not expected. He had heart valve surgery complicated by cancer. Funerals are a celebration of life, so we had a great party. Howard would have enjoyed himself. All of his friends and family were there. I couldn't possibly drink his fair share, but I did hoist a few for him. I'll toast a few for both our Dads Every New Year.

The guys have escaped as far in either direction as they could go without emigrating or getting wet. But Judy keeps close tabs on them by phone. AT&T stock would plummet without her contribution. Judy loves nursing but has gone inactive - the medical bureaucracy got to be a drag. Inactive means they call when they need her; so now she'll work twice as much. Now that she is FREE to plan her time Judy is ready to travel. She only went to California twice and New York once and wasn't pleased to sit home while John and I went to Australia. I promised her Portugal and brought back Opals as penance. She painted the house and lost six pounds. Three more trips like that and everything will be perfect.

Jamie decided that theater at Western Michigan University was like studying in Siberia. Since all the world must be his stage, his future, fame, and fortune obviously are in Los Angeles. So off he went with a little money and a plan to hang out in California until someone discovered him (stat: actors enjoy 98% unemployment). Fortunately, the Jones family must have a hyperactive guardian angel. He is now a full time student at California State University - Fullerton where he has just finished the lead role in a 17th Century play— "The Constant Couple." And to think that last year I was complaining about driving a mere 300 miles to see a play.

Jeff received his Master of Arts Degree from The Tisch School of the Arts at New York University. Good for you. He is writing computer programs that teach kids science at the New York Hall of Science. Manhattan is an intense place, and he seems stressed out lately. To add some diversity to his life, recently graduated brother showed up on his doorstep with bundles of aspirations, little money and no plan. It was heartwarming indeed to hear one son lecture the other on the importance of being EMPLOYED. Just imagine – they can be each other's adult supervision for a while.

John graduated with a Bachelor of Arts Degree from Michigan State University last spring with minors in Music, Journalism, Russian, and German and no MAJOR. He did point out that I had yet to figure out what I was going to be if I grew up. Despite several tense hours of discussion on the above topics and my lack of civilized communication skills and music appreciation, we had a great time on his graduation present trip to Australia in November.

Australia is an incredible space with 12 million people living in five cities and the remaining 8 million living in an area two-thirds the size of the continental United States. Pouches on mammals are the rule rather than the exception with names like Wombat, Wallaby, Echidna, Kangaroo and Koala. We both kept a diary. To make a long story short - we drove 2500 miles in two weeks, saw Adelaide, Melbourne, Canberra, Sydney, hundreds of miles of empty plains, desert, and coastline, ate seafood (lobster included) and drank our fair share of Australian wine. Not to mention, opera house, ferry ride across Sydney Bay, festival in Melbourne, Parliament in Canberra, Casino in Adelaide and a sky containing the Southern Cross. Travelogue available on your next visit

All our sons are gone but not forgotten. We're still writing checks but fewer (Oh happy days). As the requirements associated with being a parent diminish, I really must figure out what I want to be when I grow up; or alternatively, admit that I am now as grown up as I'm going to get (shudder); or just figure out what to do next.

Once again, a parent's death marred our illusions of immortality. We really are short on time here and should enjoy life like there is no tomorrow with enough foresight to enjoy tomorrow if we get there. We've got a brand new decade followed by a new century in front of us. Possibilities abound. Enjoy every day of a Happy New Year.

Reflection 13: Nursing and Medicine

Medical Bureaucracy inhibits hospital care and increases health care costs.

My experience in Nursing has come vicariously by listening to grandma vent and helping her write letters to hospital administrators about the inappropriate ways hospitals save money. Getting rid of administrators instead of Registered Nurses (RNs) was always our first choice, but since administrators are the ones who fire people, guess who gets fired last?

The best choice is to keep nurses and get rid of everyone else. Hospitals try to save money by (sometimes badly) training entry-level people to act as "techs" who do a subset of the nurses' tasks. The job of managing minimally trained and often unmotivated people falls to the RN; so frequently, RNs do the techs work since they are legally accountable; so, delegating work to poorly trained workers is unacceptable. Grandma resigned when the average number of patients in her care doubled; she did not want to put her patients at risk. If you are hospitalized, keep family members near.

Hospitals need to learn what manufacturing engineers have known for 50 years. The fewer job types involved in a complex process, the more adaptable and effective that process can be made. One multi-purpose person is worth two specialists. This is especially true in hospitals.

Here's why. Census, the number of patients, varies day-to-day. This creates serious scheduling problems if a nurse is supported by one to four personnel with different job descriptions (keep in mind, an RN can do all of the jobs). If the hospital has enough RNs to do ALL of the work for a low census including food delivery and janitorial work, the hospital can hire non-medical contract services for a high census saving money and improving patient care.

Despite many advances in technology, drugs, and surgical procedures in the last several decades, patient care suffered from not understanding the principles of process engineering.

Medical costs have reached epidemic proportions. Drugs are expensive because pharmaceutical companies risk billions of dollars in research to bring a product to market and must recover those costs. Doctors must pay off loans for medical school and pay increasing rates for malpractice insurance as lawsuits increase. Inefficient medical and insurance bureaucracies cause healthcare to spiral out of control making it more difficult for individuals and companies to purchase medical insurance. Poor health choices and costs contribute to our inability to compete in a global economy.

We taxpayers pay enough taxes so that 50% of US jobs are Federal, local or state government jobs. Without additional expenditures, we should be able to find efficiencies in government to afford National Healthcare (*much more on this in later Reflections*).

If you want to help people stay well, you might consider Osteopathic Medicine and Dentistry or Pharmacy as well.

To become part of this time-honored Medical Profession, you can become educated in one of the Medical Science areas listed below or you can become a process engineer specializing in hospital processes or an architect specializing in hospital construction.

Medical Science

61] Dentistry
Biologic & Materials Sciences
Cardiology/Restorative
  Sciences/Endodontics
Oral & Maxillofacial Surgery
Hospital Dentistry
Orthodontics & Peds Dentistry
Periodontics & Oral Medicine
62] Human Medicine
Anatomy
Anesthesiology
Biological Chemistry
Biomedical Engineering
Biophysics
Cell & Developmental Biology
Cellular & Molecular Biology
Dermatology
Emergency Medicine
Family Medicine
Human Genetics
Immunology
Internal Medicine
Hearing Research
Microbiology/Immunology
Neurology
Neuroscience
Obstetrics/Gynecology
Ophthalmology
Otolaryngology
Pathology
Pediatrics & Diseases
Pharmacology
Physical Medicine & Rehab
Physiology
Psychiatry
Pulmonary & Critical Care
Radiation Oncology
Radiology
Surgery

63] Nursing
Community Care/Home Health
  Care
Gerontological Specialist
Medical-Surgical Specialist
Occupational Health Nurse
Psychiatric-Mental Health Nurse
Adult Acute Care Nurse
  Practitioner
Infant, Child, Adolescent, Pediatric
  Nurse
Psychiatric-Mental Health Nurse
Women's Health
Certified Nurse-Midwife Program
Nursing Business & Health
  Systems
Nursing Management &
  Administration
Nursing Informatics
Nursing & Health Services
  Administration
64] Osteopathic Medicine
Family Medicine Biochemistry &
  Molecular Biology
Internal Medicine Microbiology &
  Molecular Genetics
Manipulative Medicine Neurology &
  Ophthalmology
Surgical Specialties Pharmacology
  & Toxicology
Pediatrics Physiology
Physical Medicine & Rehab
  Psychiatry
Radiology

65] Pharmacy
Clinical Sciences
Medicinal Chemistry
Pharmaceutical Sciences
Social & Administrative Sciences
66] Public Health
Biostatistics
Environmental Health Sciences
Hazardous Substances
Human Nutrition
Industrial Hygiene
Occupational & Environmental
  Epidemiology
Occupational & Environmental
  Medicine
Toxicology
Epidemiology
Hospital & Molecular Epidemiology
Dental Public Health, International
  Health
Health Behavior & Health Education
Health Management & Policy
Life Sciences & Society
Public Health Genetics
Reproductive & Women's Health
67] Veterinary Medicine
Large Animal Clinical Sciences
Microbiology & Molecular Genetics
Pathobiology & Diagnostic
  Investigation
Pharmacology & Toxicology
Physiology
Small Animal Clinical Sciences
Veterinary Technology Program

14

CHRISTMAS 1990
14th Epistle of Jim

Christmas again. Bah Humbug. Three days before Christmas day and I've finally got my contorted brain in shape to contrive this epistle. It's tough to capture the Christmas spirit with American kids in Saudi Arabia because of a bona fide tragedy named Saddam Hussein. We can't even depend on our enemies anymore. Now the Russians are our buddies. How is our primary export industry going to predict to whom to ship their weapons. This is too much harsh reality too close to home. So, let's talk about the really important stuff - us.

After flubbing my promise of a vacation in Portugal, Judy settled for Australia. She saw Melbourne and Adelaide on her own. I made the mistake of telling our Australian Distributor that "my time was valuable." So, they arranged 15 presentations for me to give in five days. We also spent a weekend in Sydney and walked all over in the rain. Cappuccino was great; opera house was famous, beautiful harbor. We spent the rest of the week in Cairns on the northeast coast - very tropical like Hawaii but less claustrophobic. We took a catamaran to the Great Barrier Reef - great underwater view. Judy got a butt burn from floating and looking at lots of exotic fish, reef, and six-foot-wide clams. I usually think of clams as lunch rather than myself as lunch for clams. All plane rides now seem incidental after our 32-hour 3 transfer return flight.

Judy felt Australia for Portugal wasn't adequate compensation, so she went to San Francisco to see Jamie in a play about Tennessee Williams. Never mind that he got great reviews, he got PAID!! My son the working actor (but only for six weeks). It's an exciting concept -- soon I may be able to retire and manage his vast wealth. And again, how could we not see Judy's "Sweet Prince" play one of Shakespeare's greatest characters. Even his brother flew in from New York to see this great "undiscovered" actor in a momentous portrayal. To think I've complained about driving 300 miles to Western Michigan University to see him in a play. Maybe we have a young Sir Lawrence, but he'd better learn carpentry to pay bills while he is still "undiscovered."

Jeff accepted a position (somehow "new job" seems too common for such a prestigious Institution) with the American Museum of Natural History in New York City. He's in charge of computer exhibits for the museum. Maybe we could even go so far as to imply he's becoming an authority figure at 25 (the mind boggles at the personality transitions that can be made over five years).

John stopped waffling and focused his efforts by doing everything at once - full time master's degree student at NYU in Interactive Media, fellowship to host Russian visitors, Jazz vocalist performing at a local radio station, Chinese lessons, and earns money editing marketing brochures. He commutes to Manhattan from his apartment in an area described by Manhattanites as culturally depressed Brooklyn.

Judy also decided that it was a big hardship to sit at home while I went to Tokyo on business, so she went to New York to visit her first and second born. We enjoyed 100^0 weather on different sides of the planet. Moral: don't visit big cities in summer. Both cities are full of rude aggressive people (the kind I identify with); New York is dirtier, but Tokyo folks are smaller and packed denser. Our two oldest sons double teamed Judy with NYC night life so she picked me up at Detroit Metro moaning about having had enough travel.

Judy's still nursing but only part time. Good thing, she needs two days rest for each day worked especially when she works twelve hours. Tough job but she's good at it. I've got to find her an easier job that pays better so that I can retire.

I've managed to survive another year keeping busy flying here and there while our dog Rudy relaxes at home. I wonder who's accomplishing more. One famous philosopher said that all we're doing is "moving rocks." Maybe if I learn to move big boulders fast enough, I'll move a mountain one day.

Amazing creatures, people. We are smaller in relative size to the universe than atoms are to us, but what grand perceptions and thoughts we have. Watching what we do in the grand scheme of things makes me wonder what we are bringing upon ourselves -- exaltation or destruction. While making your contribution, remember that you are in our thoughts, and we wish you all the (exalted) best in this holiday season.

Reflection 14: Education

We are all here to serve each other. How we serve is a personal thing. Grandma and her sister chose direct and obvious services: nurse and teacher. It never ceases to amaze me that their own bureaucracies hamper these most altruistic service professions (medicine and education).

I wrote about bureaucracy and nursing earlier so we can focus on education. There are no more important jobs than those in elementary education. My solution to current low SAT scores is to replace half of the administrators with teachers, reduce class sizes and constantly TEST students AND teachers for competency.

Many teachers tell me that their jobs are too complex to evaluate and that testing children does not help them. Because teachers don't want to be tested and because educators don't test children well does not mean it can't be done well.

In his book, "How We Think," Thomas Dewey tells us: "Education must cultivate effective habits of discriminating tested beliefs from: assertions, guesses and opinions… (It must) ingrain -methods of inquiry and reasoning - mental discipline… No matter how much an individual knows (hearsay and information) if he has not attitudes and habits of this sort, he is not intellectually educated. He lacks mental discipline. These habits are not a gift of nature. Education must supply the conditions for their cultivation."

Great teachers need to be rewarded, bad teachers need to be fired, and good teachers should be the norm. Teachers need to police and test themselves. At least our kids know more than children in third world countries.

Educators need to understand they are teaching for the child's benefit AND societies benefit. For clear-cut objectives: go back to the Reflection 7 and reread the USMA's learning models.

My concern with "no child left behind" is that all children in the class stay behind. At some point we must acknowledge that children learn at different rates and stop cheating children at all learning levels out of a quality education. Every child who graduates from high school should demonstrate proficiency in critical subjects in order to graduate: math, reading, writing, problem solving and respect for capitalism and democracy.

Testing is the only way that we know with certainty that a child learned something. Most teachers argue that they end up teaching to the test: PERFECT. They need to pass a test that is about being liberally educated as defined by the USMA.

Thomas Dewey identifies what is accomplished when teaching a child how to think scientifically. Dewey proposes that the natural curiosity of a child evolves into deductive and inductive scientific reasoning which is necessary to make informed decisions. Dewey concludes his book with this sentence. "Genuine communication (between teacher and student) involves contagion; its name should not be taken in vain by terming 'communication' that which produces no community of thought and purpose between the child and the race of which he is the heir." Not all of us are leaders but we should have a clear definition of the components of leadership.

Our children must contribute to society in a rapidly changing world. When they ultimately graduate from college, they must have the discipline, knowledge, and skills to begin to contribute in one of the 75 subject areas identified earlier.

If you wish to contribute in elementary, secondary, higher and special education, you must be become proficient in an area below.

Administration	Educational Theory	Jr. High & High School
Supervision	Counseling & Guidance	Teaching
Curriculum & Instruction	Educational Testing,	Art
Institutional & Cafeteria	Evaluation &	Business & Commerce
Management	Measurement	Consumer Economics & Home
Education, General	Family Relations & Child	Management
Pre-elementary	Development History &	English
Education	Philosophy	Foods & Nutrition
(Kindergarten)	Media Specialist	Industrial, Technical &
Elementary Education,	Psychology	Vocational Education
General	Statistics & Research	Language: Spanish, French,
Secondary Education,	Special Education	Latin & Other
General	Deaf & Blind	Health Education
Junior High and High	Gifted & Disadvantaged	Home Economics
School Education	Retarded & Remedial	Mathematics
Technology and Support	Speech Correction	Music
Library Science	Emotionally Disturbed	Physical Ed
Education Technologies	Physical Disturbed	Reading
Food Service & Home		Social Studies
Economics		Science
Technologies		Higher Education, General
Library Technologies		Jr. & Community College
		Education
		Adult & Continuing Education

15

CHRISTMAS 1991
15th Epistle of Jim

As usual Judy caught the spirit of Christmas well ahead of me. Hopefully, I'll get an attack of the Christmas virus so that I can finish this letter before the 25th. A lot has happened with the world and us this year. Where did the USSR go? That was a fast flush for what we thought was a mighty military superpower. Who's got the bombs? Good thing Saddam came along to give us a place to send all those bombs that were intended for the USSR. Our economy is going down the toilet and our kids are poorly educated compared to 25 other "civilized" countries, but we've got smart bombs.

Getting this letter finished is tougher this year than ever. I stressed my little brain at Martin Marietta Aerospace Group in Denver analyzing the state of their information systems for the last 50 days. I spent this last year laboring to build a consulting company. Waiting for my previous employer to realize its potential was getting more like "Waiting for Godot." I must have been unemployed for the first half of the year because I lacked paying customers. Now that three companies have paid me money at least the IRS thinks I'm a business.

Judy nursed full time for the benefits and to make sure that we didn't starve. I discovered that I can easily live on Judy's salary, but Judy has more necessities. So, I guess I'll continue to build Jones Consulting (40 hours to settle on that original name). Judy only works 3 days a week: but, it's a 12 hour day. She then needs to recuperate for 12 hours the following day. So, her work/recovery schedule is a six-day week. Judy loves nursing but her body doesn't.

Jamison is only one MATHEMATICS (Dad's revenge) course away from a BFA in Theater. WORK and RESPONSIBILITIES are looming on the horizon. Can adulthood (sounds like a gangster) be far behind. He had another great year as a Thespian. Who knows, maybe he'll even find work as an actor. Judy and I just had to go to Scotland to see him in two plays in the Edinburgh Theatre Festival. He also did a play in San Francisco and another in LA.

Remember when I used to complain about traveling 300 miles to see him in plays at WMU, then 2000 miles to LA, and now 5000 miles. What next? Off the planet?

John has one semester to go at NYU to get his MA from the Tisch School of the Arts in something still to be determined. John has managed to go to college for six years, get two degrees, and is still exploring alternatives. He works for the Boston Consulting Group doing presentations for pay. He's been translating Russian. He's been writing some musical scores. He has also been working on sending quarter tones from a computer to a synthesizer so that it plays notes between the keys. He is still not sure what he wants to be when he grows up. Maybe he's got his father's adult suppressing gene or maybe it's just the normal male hormonal pattern. He went to Germany for three weeks and Russia for three weeks. He tried to live like a Russian and almost starved. Fortunately, our friends the Zabecks fed him when he got back to Germany. Better try to feed the Russians; they've got smart bombs too.

Jeff actually gets paid for doing fun stuff for kids at the Museum of Natural History. He's making a business out of teaching kids using computers. So maybe he's a certified adult with WORK and RESPONSIBILITIES. He came home last summer only to get poison ivy playing Ninja turtles with the five-year-old twin neighbor boys. He has embarked on a career for which he continues to write his own job description. He has been working on a computer exhibit that teaches kids about global warming (neat stuff). It seems more like playing with the computer than working. But Jeff gets paid for it so it must be WORK.

I need lots of stress just to stay awake during the day. But now I have enough to keep me up at night as well. Not only that, I was 50 YEARS OLD this year. Funny, Judy and I used to be the same age, but she says she couldn't possibly be that old. Jeff says that's only seven in dog years. Rudy is really getting old; he's 84 in dog years. I am enjoying the freedom to succeed on my own terms; I guess that also means that I can fail on my own terms as well.

For this Christmas I wish you the opportunity, courage, and strength to be as free as your physical and emotional well-being will permit.

Reflection 15: War – Strategy and Tactics

The Gulf War was an amazing display of military strategy and tactics. We made short work of Saddam's troops, twice. A new philosophy of warfare (from Col. John Boyd's biography) called maneuver warfare was used in the Gulf. It gave our military and politicians justifiable confidence in our ability to conduct war. Since that war our confidence has risen to the level of hubris (exaggerated pride or self-confidence often resulting in retribution).

Col. John Boyd invented the idea of the OODA (Observe Orient Decide Act) loop and applied it to jet fighters, modern combat, and business. Its basic premise is to react faster than your enemy or competitor can respond. German General Rommel, and American General Patton, demonstrated these tactics in World War II. Boyd's tactics were used in both Gulf Wars and in Afghanistan.

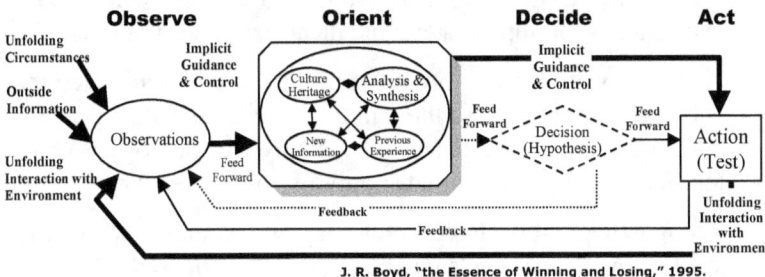

J. R. Boyd, "the Essence of Winning and Losing," 1995.

The OODA loop can operate in seconds, minutes, hours, days, or months. It can be applied to strategy, tactics, and education and to individuals and groups:
- Observe the situation,
- Orient to solution,
- Decide - execute decision criteria (intuitive or explicit),
- Act – perform the action,

"OODA" speed is quite different from the speed of our actions. Doing something dumb, but doing it at high speed, may not provide much of a competitive advantage. Physical speed also has other disadvantages, like momentum (don't turn a corner at 80 mph).

The "Decision/hypothesis" block is the learning part of the loop, where we experiment and, in the process, add new actions to the Implicit Guidance and Control link (reorient for intuitive actions).

Culture (under Orient) is the integrated pattern of human behavior that includes thought, speech, action and artifacts and depends on man's capacity for learning and transmitting knowledge to succeeding generations. *Heritage* is an integrated pattern of behavior acquired from a mentor.

When applying this loop, the better your knowledge, skills, and experience, the quicker and better you can react to your observed situation - whether it is playing basketball, chess, debating, getting a job, building a business, doing scientific research or combat. Remembering the two reflections on education, success depends on how well we learned lessons, past experience and mentors' skill.

If we're so great at modern warfare, what's going on in Iraq and Afghanistan. Sun Tzu in the "Art of War" (6th century B.C.) wrote: "When you do little, even if you are winning, if you continue for a long time, it will dull your forces.... It is never beneficial to a nation to have a military operation last a long time."

General von Clausewitz (1780-1831) wrote: "an enemy's power of resistance is the sum of available means and the strength of will."

Proficiency at warfare notwithstanding, we underestimated the WILL of our enemy and the duration of establishing a peace in the midst of continued violence. The enemy's technology is no match for us but have an unlimited supply of young men who hate us.

Recognizing that we have technology and resources to destroy most enemies, here are some considerations for conflict:
- Understand the region's history and know what is possible.
- Include our allies in our decisions.
- Serve notice to countries that terrorism won't be tolerated.
- Respond quickly and decisively to any terrorist activity.
- Have a realistic timeline and budget to fight a war.
- Have realistic expectations for new governments after war.
- Let local government establish order.
- Set up well protected base camps outside of cities for American soldiers complete with airfields.
- Train local police away from population areas.
- Protect and help rebuild infrastructure and resources.
- Patrol borders to prevent insurgents from creating chaos.
- Lobby the United Nations about militant Islam; like Hitler before World War II, they don't understand the threat *(plus China and Russia)*.

To learn about this study: Political Science, History, Business, Military Officers Training. Search the web for "John Boyd."

16

CHRISTMAS 1992

16th Epistle of Jim

Bah Humbug, Christmas again. It's the first time in 27 years that no one is coming home. Just Judy, her curmudgeon and other hairy friend, Rudy will be home for Christmas.

If you ever gave a thought to keeping up with the Joneses, don't bother; you wouldn't survive the ordeal. This year we added five females!?! to the family, three wives for three brothers and two granddaughters. It sounds like we've got material for half a musical. I had to edit this year's events to keep from writing an epic novel. Usually, I complain about how fast Christmas, Bah Humbug, rolls around every year, but this felt like a decade.

By the way, in case we're moving a little fast for you, we are Grandma and Grandpa Jones. I suppose I should feel much older, but mostly I feel disoriented. Life usually doesn't move fast enough for me, but this year it got a little ahead of me. In one event filled letter I hope to capture the joy and desperation of the year's events AND introduce you to our five new ladies.

Lauren is our first granddaughter (with our genes) and lives in San Francisco with her parents, Lisa and Jamison. Lauren is, of course, practically perfect in every way. I can't wait to give her everything she wants while assuring her that her parents will buy her the really expensive stuff. Lisa says that I can't be left alone with Lauren without adult supervision. Lisa is finishing her BFA in dance. Jamison is working on his MFA in theater. I'm looking forward to them becoming famous and wealthy and supporting us in our old age (a yacht would be nice).

Nicole is our newest granddaughter (with our genes) and lives in Manhattan with her parents, Jackie and Jeff. She is of course practically perfect in every way. I can't wait for her to get a little older so that I can give her everything she wants. Notice an irresponsible pattern here? Grandfathers should help their granddaughters frustrate their parents - it's the law. Jackie said I can't be left alone with her daughter without adult supervision.

Patty and John were married in November and went to Paris on their honeymoon. Additional congratulations are in order since they graduated with Master's Degrees from the Tisch School of the Arts last May. Patty works for NYU counseling students. John continues to do just as he pleases. He is trying to become a published author writing over ten short stories and a Jazz singer singing at Birdland last summer. John supports himself by creating presentations at the Boston Consulting Group.

Judy, who coined the infamous phrase "why don't we ever get to do everything?," got to do everything. At one point, she stared glassy eyed at nothing in particular and said: "I wonder what we'll do next year for excitement." Judy has two full time jobs; one is working as a nurse and the other is building photo albums of the 10,000 pictures she has taken of weddings and granddaughters. Buy stock in Kodak; Judy is supplying at least twenty people with a pictorial history of the year's events. She falls asleep at 10 pm with a 10lb photo album on her tummy. And to think it was just last year Judy said: "we're never going to have grandchildren." Be careful what you wish for, God may decide to really give it to you.

All three weddings were small but singularly unique in their celebration of life and love. Jackie's and Jeff's marriage and reception were outside at Montauk State Park, Long Island. Lisa and Jamison were married in Lisa's childhood Lutheran church in West Los Angeles. Jamison's confirmation Pastor, LeRoy Haynes, assisted in a formal and elegant wedding with readings from the Bible and Shakespeare. John and Patty were married in the United Nations Chapel by her NYU parish priest with a spectacular reception at the top of the Beekman Hotel.

Holy prolificity! We now have a kajillion in-laws. We appreciated their hospitality and availability of daughters who are practically perfect in every way [Judy says I must be nicer to daughters than sons]. We sincerely appreciate the love, nurturing, and trauma to create three young women who can now struggle to nurture Judy's three sons into maturity. Maybe they'll have more luck than Judy has had with me -- NOT!

Now a word about me: I LOST 15 POUNDS! I am one lean mean consulting machine. But alas, one tenacious ball of fat continues to obscure anything resembling a stomach muscle. Jones Consulting was even leaner for the first two-thirds of the year with NO REVENUE, AAAUUUGH. When I consider looking for a job, I lay down for a while and the feeling passed. Fortunately, Xerox hired me for the last third of the year so I can burn and rave a while longer. Also, it appears that business which disappeared MIGHT come back. As I get older, I feel like there is less of my life to screw up so why not take greater risks? Dylan Thomas writes:

Do not go gentle into that good night.
Old age should burn and rave at close of day;
Rage, rage against the dying of the light.

"This has been the best of times and the worst of times." Not making money while someone is spending wildly can create tension, but I'm happy to say bills finally got paid. Aside from that, this has been a year of intense and monumental events. As parents we are proud of our children and look forward to our deserved revenge with our grandchildren. Four grandchildren EACH with a wakeup call to one or two Y chromosomes would be appreciated.

I have come to understand this about being a parent:

Your children are not your children... For their souls' dwell in the house of tomorrow which you cannot visit, not even in your dreams. You may strive to be like them but seek not to make them like you.... You are the bows from which your children are sent forth. The Archer sees the mark upon the path of the infinite, and He bends you with His might so that His arrows may go swift and far. --Kahlil Gibran, The Prophet

Because our arrows were sent forth from tightly strung crossbows, our sons may still feel some stress from the launch. But, as long as we are all on the same planet, our futures continue to be intertwined and Judy and I will monitor their flights and report their trajectories every Christmas. Although I would not have planned this year as it happened, now that we survived it, we cherish all of the memories. We hope your holidays and the coming year are filled with events that generate memories to cherish.

Reflection 16: Generations and Genes

Genes bring a measure of immortality; they contain knowledge to create the next generation.

"Be careful what you wish for, the gods may give it to you." Wishing combined with biological need for immortality through grandchildren resulted in an eventful year. The gods did indeed give grandma what she wished for.

Wishes are curious things; when one wishes one might want to be very explicit and clear about the degree and rate at which the wish is to be delivered. In just seven months, grandma acquired three daughters-in-law and their associated genes to eventually create the next generation of nine wonderfully healthy and intelligent grandchildren (at last: immortality at the cellular level)!

Webster defines: Chromosomes as the part of the DNA that contains genes; and Genes as part of Chromosomes that control inheritance of a trait.

Since your Dad got 23 chromosomes from grandma and 23 chromosomes from me, some of your more annoying characteristics may be attributable to me. As a matter of fact, if you do the math, $1/4^{th}$ of your traits may come from me.

At about the same time Darwin wrote about Evolution, Gregor Mendel synthesized a theory of heredity with discrete units called genes. Genes are amazing little algorithms that immediately start creating grandchildren once an egg is fertilized.

Deoxyribonucleic acids (DNA) are giant molecules that control the building process of Ribonucleic acid (RNA). RNA builds enzymes which control the chemical reactions that determine the cell structure and function and finally our traits.

DNA supervises the production of billions of cells. Within the DNA are 23 chromosome pairs that contain the genes that define our inherited traits (e.g. eye or hair color). As DNA oversees the making of billions of cells guided by RNA and enzymes, genes decide whether an eyeball, brain or butt is created. Fortunately, DNA usually doesn't get confused and mix butt cells with brain cells to produce a butt head.

Darwin's evolution combined with Mendel's genes is called Neo-Darwinism; survival (or my immortality) comes from passing on genes to subsequent generations. This combined theory is used by Geneticists to explain that the present variety of life forms evolved over 4 billion years from simple organisms because:

- The copying process of genes sometimes produces a mutation (new trait) which is not represented by the original genes; a mutation can be random or can result from disease, drugs (Thalidomide) or X-rays.
- Mutation tends to produce increasingly more complex organisms making possible a large variety of life forms.
- Natural selection determines that organisms which survive are ones that reproduce and subsist successfully.

Geneticists study DNA for a variety of reasons:
- To understand our evolution,
- To understand what causes disease like cancer,
- To understand how to produce food faster by growing bigger plants and animals faster.

To understand our evolution, we look at the differences of species at the cellular / chromosome level. At this level most animals look a lot alike. Apparent minor changes in DNA can result in vastly different species. Geneticists created complex adaptive systems computer models of the evolutionary process in an attempt to understand how life evolved.

To understand disease, scientists are looking at correlations between chromosomes and the propensity to contract a disease. Stem cell research has yielded many insights into the causes of disease but has caused a great deal of discomfort for many people because sometimes a human embryo is used.

Scientists are looking at the genetic structure of plants to determine how to get more crop yield per acre. This has led to the genetic modification of much of our food. Although this helps feed many starving people, scientists and others are concerned that these high yield species of plants will be more susceptible to disease and insect infestation.

Cosmologists determined that the universe is chaotic not random; Chaos Theory in Mathematics allows scientists to see order where only random erratic behavior was first perceived. Scientists at the Santa Fe Institute are developing models of the origins of life using an extension of Chaos Theory called complex adaptive systems. Cosmologists acknowledged an intelligently designed cosmos in the last century, perhaps biologists will acknowledge intelligent recursive genetic algorithms and not randomness in this century.

To be a Geneticist, study: Applied Math, Statistics, Genetics and Genomics, and Microbiology.

17

CHRISTMAS 1993

17th Epistle of Jim

Here we are again celebrating the birth of Christ rescheduled for past pagan medieval rituals. Somehow, it seems especially appropriate in this country where Christmas emphasizes our convoluted mixture of puritan ethics and rampant avarice. As you can see my annual attempt to get in touch with my few remaining emotions at this auspicious and celebrated time precipitates my December cynicism.

Judy on the other hand is deliriously happy about having the entire family here for Christmas. Most of you know that to escape this heavily humored environment, the two oldest went east to the Brooklyn Bridge and Jamison went west to the Golden Gate Bridge. Judy is single handedly trying to rebuild the economy in the face of unbridled taxation. She is in double digit presents for her two new granddaughters along with several presents for ten other people. Hardly a day goes by without her arriving at home with something very special for Nicole or Lauren. It's hard for me to conceive of applying the idea of something very special over 20 times; but hey, what do I know, I don't usually catch the Christmas virus until December 24th.

Some of you who have become addicted to my contorted sense of humor expressed concern that I didn't take full advantage of the opportunities for humor that were available in 1992 -- three marriages and two grandchildren in that year. Maybe I was just influenced by a kinder gentler time and maybe I'm getting soft and sentimental in my old age. Or maybe I'm just confused about navigating through our new family infrastructure which got 33 times more complicated. That is a mathematically computable number: $[2^{10}-1] / [2^5-1] = 2^5+1 = 33$ where 2^n-1 is the number of interactions between n people.

Also, the estrogen to testosterone ratio has increased by a factor of 3. That computation is left as an exercise for the reader. Besides, the thought of 6 women pissed off at me at once is 666 times worse than 3 men (evangelically determined). Apocalyptic writings point out that six is not a good number. As you can see, even for those of us who understand advanced arithmetic, my new social interactions, which are not part of my skill set, are making it tough to figure out what's humorous and what's fatal.

Lauren and Nicole are God's gift to us all. Nicole was sent to torment Jackie and Jeff. Lauren was sent to torment Lisa and Jamison. John and Patty are hanging tough and enjoying life. It is a grandfather's divine right to provide advice and counsel to his grandchildren in their aggravation attacks on their parents. Furthermore, I am looking forward to a dozen grandchildren over the next twenty years. My theory is that any of the little power swimmers that evade two forms of birth control will make practically perfect grandchildren. It's amazing how much distress that my little theory generated.

I have some very sad news to report. Judy's mother, Beatrice, died September 2, 1993. Her death was unexpected and came after only two weeks in the hospital. She died in the morning three days after the doctor said she would soon be well enough to go home. She did go home. For her, home was always where Howard was. Howard, her husband died four years ago. Bea missed Howard mightily these last four years. I am sure she is content to be beside him now. Rest in Peace. We love you. We will remember you. Go with God.

Another sad event for us was the death of our dog. Rudy has been part of the family for thirteen years and was everyone's best pal. He greeted us every day and protected us every night. When the guys left, he looked after Judy and walked her most every night. We will miss his cute hairy face and gentle manner. Who knows, maybe he's looking after our parents now. Goodbye old friend.

Judy had a stressful and happy time doing everything in 92, but a stressful and sad time since August. Christmas is helping her survive the ordeal since she keeps busy by bolstering our sagging economy. She has five new family members to buy gifts for. It's tough trying to buy several special things for all these people, but Judy has responded debitably. Judy is still working full time as a nurse which keeps her tired out, but not enough. She's discovered The Jim's Christmas giving solution -- THE CATALOG. Last year, she was falling asleep with photo albums; now it's Lands End, Eddie Bauer, L. L. Bean, or, God forbid, Neiman Marcus. Judy flew all over the country again last year but felt deprived because we didn't go anywhere extra special for our 30th wedding anniversary. She says extra special is Bermuda, Hawaii, Aruba or anywhere that will cost us $1000 per day. Note to family: this is NOT an invitation to help us make San Francisco or New York a $1000 per day experience.

I am cautiously optimistic that I may build a successful business. Success means generating sufficient revenue to pay for Judy's planned trips and other expenses. I have incorporated as "Priority Process Associates, Inc." The 4000 other names that I thought of were already taken. I consulted with Xerox and TCI in Denver [right in the middle of sailing season, damn]. TCI is the largest cable company in the U.S. Potential business looks good, but nothing evaporates like potential. I hooked up with three professors at a local university, two of whom I worked with at Strategic Planning at GM. We're ready, willing, and able to save American Manufacturing and preserve America's position as an economic superpower. It looks like I'm beginning to be successful enough to work twice as hard at being successful.

After last year's kaleidoscope of marriages, births, and travel itineraries, it would appear that this year was less intense. I am happy to say that this year was just as intense, but more focused. Our children are still our children, but they have become adults and are building new families of their own. We have 3 new adult females and 2 wee females to continue to get to know and love; not to mention a 33 times more complex familial infrastructure.

As our perceptions of the universe continue to expand with technology like the Hubble Telescope, it is easy to begin to believe that we humans are insignificant specks of protoplasm on a tiny planet in the far corner of the universe. But my life experiences have convinced me that every living thing is unique and exemplifies our infinite diversity. We humans have been given the most exquisite of gifts, consciousness; the ability to think beyond what we understand through our limited senses; the ability to see, sometimes dimly and sometimes with startling clarity the path of the infinite. Microscopic specks that we are, we are not insignificant, and we are all capable of greatness whether by intention or accident. At this special time, we hope you have the opportunity to see with clarity the path of the infinite.

Reflection 17: Galaxies

The Milky Way is our Galaxy: Let's at least colonize our solar system.

The book, "Cosmos," assembled by Giles Sparrow in a spectacular 14"x17" format is a collection of photographs of our solar system and outlying Galaxies taken by the Hubble telescope and various space craft. This mind-boggling statement is on the inside front cover: "(The Universe) stretches at least 80 billion trillion miles across in every direction around us... We know there are at least as many galaxies as there are stars in the Milky Way (30 billion)." Spanning pages 148 and 149 of the book is a picture of our own Milky Way Galaxy with the statement: "The closer stars get to the center of the galaxy, the faster they orbit. ...there must be something extremely dense and massive .... around which even the central stars orbit. There is only one real candidate for such an object – a giant black hole ...(which) could contain the mass of several million Suns in a space smaller than the orbit of the Earth."

It takes a while for this to sink in. 10,000 years ago, we thought the sky was some kind of painted back-drop. 1,000 years ago, we thought the planets revolved around the earth. 100 years ago we thought our galaxy was the universe. Now we know there are 30 billion galaxies. AND WE CAN'T GET TO THE NEXT NEAREST SUN !@#?*

Our brains really have gotten too big for our own good. We can now "see" the universe 80 billion trillion miles across. Do the math: If we could travel 100,000 mph in space times 24 hours, times 365 days x 100 year life span equals 876,000,000 miles. In a lifetime we travel to about 0.000000000000000000001% of it. AAAAUGH!

Our brainpower seems directed toward making our lives "safe." And what's left is directed toward war and CO_2. We wallow in our fears and kill each other in the name of the same God when we have 80 billion trillion miles of space to explore and colonize.

WE NEED TO GET OUT THERE AND KEEP GOING. Just like aquatic life was meant to get out of the water and onto land, our destiny is off the planet. We have the brains, imagination, and much of the technology, but not the WILL to go. Certainly at least our Galaxy belongs to us complete with a giant black hole.

Mathematics, Newton's Laws of Physics, Einstein's Theory of Relativity, Quantum Mechanics, and The Big Bang Theory of the

Universe have done a nice job of framing our Universe so that cosmologists and physicists have been able to explain a great deal about what is going on out there. Scientists can even measure the mass of the Universe and its rate of contraction. The problem is that the Universe is expanding which suggests that only 4% of the Universe's mass is accounted for by things we are familiar with like suns, planets, gases, and asteroids, etc. The rest of the Universe is composed of Dark Matter and Dark Energy, meaning Cosmologists don't have clue about what it is.

The presence of Dark Matter and Energy has been determined by the fact that spiral galaxies like the Milky Way are spinning at such a rate that they should be shedding stars (Our Sun is traveling at 485,000 mph around the galaxies core). To validate this, George Smoot and John Mather at Berkeley designed the Cosmic Background Explorer to look for extremely subtle differences in space that carry the imprint of the Universe when it was one second old. COBE found them: quantum fluctuations that 13.7 billion years later would coalesce into what is 22% dark matter, 74% dark energy and 4% of the stuff we know about which agrees with the mathematics from general relativity, but not quantum mechanics (ref: New York Times Magazine, March 11, 2007).

Clearly, we need a new theory which explains Dark Matter, Dark Energy and resolves the differences between General Relativity and Quantum Mechanics.

Maybe you'll be the one who discovers that the gravitational constant is not constant but a variable that increases as the density of objects increase as they collapse into black holes.

Grandchildren, there are a bunch of professions like aerospace engineers, physicists, cosmologists, astronauts etc. that will help us explain the Galaxy and GET OUT TO SPACE: your frontier.

To participate in space research, study:
Applied Math, Astrophysics & Astronomy
Aerospace Engineering and
Military Officers Training.

18

CHRISTMAS 1994
18th Epistle of Jim

Cheez, another Christmas. It's now Dec. 17th and I started this letter on Dec. 2nd. I might as well finish this thing because I probably won't be assaulted by the Christmas spirit at all this year; nobody is coming home for Christmas. But I did see our brand-new grandson in New York, Aidan Jeffrey Jones. Cool -- a Y chromosome; way to go Jeff and Jackie: one of each just like you planned. Things were a little tense the last time we were there. Judy walked, sat, and did everything in general with her hand on Aidan's chest.

John and Patty are due in January - their first. Life as they know it is over. Little ?XY? who is due in the next month. Lisa and Jamison are holding at one with Lauren who has joined her theatrical parents and has auditioned for stuff like the poster girl for Mervyn's. Jamison finished his course work for an MFA in theater but needs to act in a major role and/or write a thesis. Lisa finished her BFA in dance and swears she will not go to school again.

That's four grandchildren which is a third of their collective quota. After 20 years of life with children, one develops an intellectual and emotional understanding of responsibility [it almost worked for me]. These impressionable new minds will need guidance to mature into independent thinkers who will bring wit, humor, and wisdom in the same wonderful unique style as their grandfather.

Judy went somewhere on a plane EVERY MONTH. She's piling up more frequent flier miles than I while working full time as a nurse -- pretty amazing. She goes coast to coast - San Francisco, LA, New York, Roanoke, San Diego. She was disappointed that she didn't get to Houston to see her pal Sharon, but she got here. Judy and I just returned from a trip to wine country down US 1 north of San Francisco in the rain. Great expansive vistas viewed while driving on a narrow turtle back road with a 100,000-foot drop to the ocean. We stopped afterward for a late breakfast and Excedrin.

Unfortunately, Judy probably won't be going to San Diego anymore. Judy's Auntie Fern died last summer. She was some significant number of years old and enjoyed every year. She was a pleasure to be with, played mahjong, was an avid sports fan, and loved life and family. When she died the Padres stopped playing baseball. We will miss you, Fern.

Judy is still a major American consumer, but now she is single handedly trying to boost airline industry profits - mostly Northwest Airlines. She's been nursing at the hospital in between transcontinental treks. She's unhappy with the administration's approach to efficiency which seems to mean: give the nurses twice as many patients and work. It does serve the purpose of keeping her tired and away from regularly supporting the economy. She also doesn't seem to notice that I'm at work a lot. The nice part about being self-employed is that I only have to work when I feel like it as long as I feel like it at least 60 hours per week.

I'm beginning to think that I should have declared my business a nonprofit rather than incorporating this year. Next year looks like it will be a lot better. I'm taking the position that success comes to people who are too dumb to know when to quit. I feel like I've been rolling this giant snowball up hill now for four years which will soon start rolling downhill out of control. Part of this whole business is to write THE BOOK on this wonderful new business analysis method that leverages the Internet to increase knowledge flow and may be titled "Elementary Executive Coloring Book."

I had a complete physical including a colon cancer test where they checked my tonsils. I'm fine except I'm too fat and my cholesterol is too high. 20 lb, and 40 cholesterol points stand between me and being "low risk." Low risk is a euphemism for: you PROBABLY won't die predictably soon. I've been having a mortality attack lately and THE BOOK isn't published yet. Most American males believe in the myth that if they make lots of money you won't die. We mature males know that if we exercise, eat right and publish THE BOOK, immortality is certain [mature male is an oxymoron].

To celebrate Christmas AND immortality, we should pay more attention to the real meaning of this season and enjoy mortality as the Desiderata tells us: "You are a child of the universe no less than the trees and stars. You have a right to be here. And whether or not it is clear to you no doubt the universe is unfolding as it should."

Take time to ponder what it means TO BE in God's eyes whatever you conceive Him or Her to be. We wish you peace, serenity, and a quiet time to reflect for yourself on what it means TO BE.

Reflection 18: Internet

Internet techno-logy provides the ability to find pearls of knowledge, but it's in a sea of disinformation.

People who claim to deal with "reality" never deal with reality but respond to specific stimuli. Reality is bigger than we are and beyond our perception, but not beyond our imagination. Thank goodness for imagination so we can perceive reality. Thomas Dewey in "How We Think" tells us: "The proper function of imagination is vision of realities [not] exhibited under existing conditions of sense-perception."

Expanding our perception helps us see more of the reality around us. We can now see germs and viruses with microscopes. We see distant stars with telescopes. We see our planet from space. Seeing more helps us understand more which helps us see more. We need to use our imagination to continue to see and understand.

Awareness of our environment and universe has expanded exponentially in the last 500 years. We are looking at the atom and at the outer boundaries (maybe) of the universe. It amazes me what mankind has accomplished on its seeming path to self-destruction.

If you are a thinker this is an awesome time to be living. You can just sit on the Internet and find stuff to think about (so much for relationships). Ask a question, get 314,159 answers. The internet, however, does not promise the right answer. From those responses, you can take a week to find THE answer. But I have wallowed in computer stuff a long time so I can usually find actionable knowledge amongst the crap to innovate an answer. Rate of innovation is about one's ability to change knowledge into value.

The Internet generates so much useless data that it makes the acquisition of knowledge on the World Wide Web difficult. However, using the proper search techniques can provide huge quantities of useful information, which can eventually be synthesized into actionable knowledge. The problem is that most people accept and use the first piece of information (usually crap) that they find to reinforce their opinion.

In business, getting the information right is critical. The ISO (International Standards Organization) has defined what accuracy of information means in terms of a Record. ISO 15489 defines a record as information created, received and maintained as evidence and information by an organization or person in pursuance of legal obligations or in the transaction of business. A record should correctly reflect what was communicated or decided or what action was taken. An ISO15489 compliant record must have:

- Authenticity: proved to be what it claims to be and created by the person at the time claimed.
- Reliability: trusted as a full and accurate representation of its contents.
- Integrity: complete and unaltered.
- Usability: can be located, retrieved, presented, and interpreted.

The government commission (SEC) that regulates business will put the president of a company in jail if his company's financial information does not conform to this ISO 15489 records standard.

Unfortunately, the information on the Internet is not held to this standard. Using the Internet as a resource for information requires that you the user validate that information as having authenticity, reliability and integrity.

This has been referred to as the information age, but it is mostly about disinformation. Remember earlier we talked about memes, the scientific method and OODA loops. If we are going to Decide and Act, our Orientation process (science) must involve making sure our Observations (memes) have Authenticity, Reliability and Integrity. Only then, do we have information that we can trust.

Note that you can buy your way to the top of the search engine Google list and control information in that way. This will be an important social issue (*google now 'harvests' your personal data*).

Crap notwithstanding, the Internet holds great promise for the exponential expansion of knowledge. By leveraging cheap highly functional and connected computers, trusted knowledge in all fields is accelerating, reinforcing, enabling and building on each other.

At the present rate of innovation, science will continue to raise ethical questions such as human genetic modification both to eliminate disease and to improve performance. You will need to be "USMA liberally educated" to make or influence decisions on the ethics of such research.

To involve yourself in providing trusted electronic information, study: Statistics and Probability, Computer Science, and Law.

CHRISTMAS 1995

19th Epistle of Jim

Aaauuurgh!#@?&# Christmas again. Scrooge didn't come around until he was 70, did he? So there's still time for me to catch the Christmas virus one of these years. Judy of course is having a wonderful time as is evidenced by the fact that one of our bedrooms looks like a retail clothes and toy outlet. She now supplements her store foraging with a significant amount of catalog purchases. One day someone will do a market study on Judy's Power Christmas Shopping.

Everyone came in October for our niece Julie's wedding. Twelve people resided in our house/warehouse; eight adults and four children if you go by chronological age; or, four adults and eight children if you abide by the female expectation of male maturity. Maturity is grossly overrated. The house was plenty big enough until everyone had to go someplace at the same time, like the wedding; then, we were three bathrooms short.

Our grandchildren, Christopher, Lauren, Nicole, and Aidan provided a great deal of the spontaneous entertainment at the wedding. Aidan [Jeff & Jackie's one year old] ran back and forth on the dance floor, bouncing off mirrored pillars for three hours. 9-month-old Christopher [John and Patty's first] stood up, sat down, and was carried around while being awesomely cute. Cute is a standard Jones chromosome. Nicole [Jeff & Jackie's 3-year-old], whose chocolate intake is usually restricted, ate chocolate all night and ran and danced in frantic circles. Princess Lauren [Jamie & Lisa's 3-year-old] presided over her Mad Hatter's Court in her Alice in Wonderland dress. Is grandparenting fun? We get to play with them, give them back and watch them exhaust our children.

Judy has reduced her nurse work to two 12-hour days per week to make time for extracurricular activities. She's her piano teacher's pet student but isn't ready for the Met yet. She also spent a 1000 hours and dollars refinishing my mother's piano; I did my best but wasn't able to avoid contributing. We haven't traveled nearly as much as Judy would like. She only got to New York twice,

California twice, Florida, once, and upper lower Michigan twice this year. She got to do everything, but everything wasn't enough. Next year maybe we'll go to Australia and Bermuda as well as all of her usual trips so that she'll get enough of everything.

Business was pretty good this year. I almost made as much this year as when I had a real job. I do seem to work hard for not much money. I do whatever I want as long as I do it 70 hours a week. Someone asked how I knew if I was working without having a real job; if I'm awake with a pulse, I'm working.

I am always entertained by "practical" people who think I should get in touch with "reality." Most of today's things, structures, and business were just a product of someone's imagination 100 years ago. Imagine talking to someone in 1900 about planes, electrical appliances, television, computers, satellites, moonwalks, social security, Medicare, and organ transplants.

On His day, take time to reflect on the "reality" of your soul's immortality and the "practical" impact of the imagination of a Man 2000 years ago who taught us about love, community, forgiveness, and immortality.

Reflection 19: Fine Arts

Art, music, literature and theater provide insight into life and science.

Consciousness is such an amazing gift. Grandma once said: "Why don't we ever get to do everything?" I don't understand why everyone isn't learning something all the time.

I am told by nonreaders that they learn by doing, which is fine, if you don't want to learn much. I am also told this generation must be entertained to learn. How limiting is that. Here we've developed language and writing over the last 5000 years. It provides a way for us to try to know everything.

My family has provided me with insight into topics that I might not have introduced myself to had they not been interested: music from John, theater from Jamison, media from Jeff and medicine from grandma. In order to understand what they are doing, I have read their books, gone to events, and listened to hours of tapes covering economics, philosophy, music, theater, ecology, physiology, and religion.

The problem is the ratio keeps getting smaller, when I divide the volume of information that I know, by the volume of information that I know I don't know. So, the more I know, the better I understand how dumb I am.

I'd like to speak about something of which I know nothing: Jazz. This business anecdote came out of a conversation with John Jones.

In jazz, there is a well-established and accepted idea of "playing outside." This means that an experienced jazz musician can deviate from the original structure and the rest of the band will follow. The idea is to go "outside" enough to create tension and hence excitement.

The problem in business is similar for out-of-the-box jazz musicians as for organizational innovators. Many innovators suggest radical strategies that are organizationally discordant and don't realize the benefits promised. Playing outside is no excuse for not understanding structure. Going too far outside without a thorough understanding of the musical - or organizational - structure, results in unpleasant and discordant musical - or organizational - performances.

The farther out-of-the-box the idea, the more verification is required. A powerful systems view is mandatory for reinventing any large organization or government.

CHRISTMAS 1995

That view of business and Jazz applies to anyone wishing to have variety and innovation in his/her life. Too little change and you're bored poopless, too much change and you're scared poopless. Physiologically speaking: poopless is a dysfunctional state.

Grandma took up painting in retirement and I took up writing. And, as one friend put it, we are halfway to Russia living on Beaver Island at the top of Lake Michigan. We are out of the box, but not too far. I would like to sell a house and sail to Australia. Grandma says that travel plan scares her poopless. I reassured her with - Sailing in a typhoon couldn't be any worse than being home alone with three sons.

Grandma's painting definitely falls in the category of Art. My writing is more reporting than Art. We could call it: constipated journalism to continue the bowel metaphors. I am hoping that grandchildren read through it and find some topic worth pursuing.

Some writing that falls into the art category has led me to scientific investigation like Michael Crichton's book: "State of Fear" which is fiction about environmental science. Because of his novel, I ended up reading "Pulse", "An Inconvenient Truth" and "Unstoppable Global Warming" and started planning the development of my own personal solar energy system.

Jamison has had major roles in professional presentations of Shakespeare's plays: Hamlet in Hamlet, Banquo in Macbeth, Timon in Timon of Athens, Romeo in Romeo and Juliet. We understand much of English Language usage from Shakespeare. We can also be introduced to many abstract concepts and Mathematics such as Tom Stoppard's play "Arcadia" about the development of Chaos Theory. And we can also learn about science and its possibilities from half of Isaac Asimov's 200 books.

"To be or not to be" an artist, musician, writer, or actor is the question. You can study in many of these areas in Arts and Humanities, but if you do, encourage your parents to work harder at getting rich or marry someone who is rich.

To participate in the arts, study: Classics, Fine Art,
Language and Literature, Music, Theatre and Film.

20

CHRISTMAS 1996

20th Epistle of Jim

Yahhuh, Christmas again. Someone said they were going to the politically correct version of a Christmas party - a Holiday Party; not even Xmas. Now we can focus totally on commercial aspects of HOLIDAY...Augh No wonder it's the only time of year that I become mildly depressed. What would happen to our economy without the holiday season? Maybe I'm thinkin' too much but it would be really scary, if I tried to think and nothin' happened.

We're subsidizing both retail business and travel businesses. With John in New York City, Jamison in LA, and Jeff in Brisbane we're on a plane to somewhere all the time. Jamison, Lisa, and Lauren are coming for Christmas.

Then, we leap on a plane to see Jeff, Jackie, Aidan, and Nicole in Australia. That's right AUSTRALIA!?! Cheez. I used to complain about everyone going as far as they could in either direction without getting wet. If Jeff went any farther, he'd be coming back. He surfed the Internet for job opportunities and surfed all the way to Australia. Thank goodness for modern transportation and navigation. We can get there in a day by plane rather than six months by square rigger.

That of course means we'll have to go to New York no later than March to see John, Patty, and Christopher. I won't complain anymore about traveling or the next thing that will happen is we'll have a Jones family on the moon.

Jeff is setting up a multi-media department for Queensland University of Technology in Brisbane. John is continuing to build his Mac computer business while working at becoming a published fiction writer. Jamison is learning the acting system in LA which has not yet made him a millionaire. The grandchildren are keeping their parents entertained, but I haven't had sufficient opportunity to influence their behavior in positive but parentally exhausting ways.

Judy had her obligatory minimum six trips in the inter-continental United States with an added trip to France. She said that I could come along if I really wanted to. She, sister Janet, and friend Barb whose son got married on the French Riviera went together. They went to Paris - Moulin Rouge, Louvre, Champs Elysees, Notre Dame, Monaco, and the Riviera for the wedding.

This year was really in the toilet business-wise. Year-end business was the only thing that kept it from being a total swirly. I spent the first half of the year trying to work with Xerox where vice presidents proliferate. I was talking to eight at once. I concluded that the probability of getting anything done is 2^{-n} where n is the number of vice presidents. If you do the math, the probability of anything happening was 1/256.

I finally got THE BOOK written in February, written in April, written in June, written in August. The good news is reviewers thought it was a significant technical contribution. The bad news is that most of my readers thought someone else should have written it. Comments like "this looks like a 300-page outline of a 1200-page paper" was one of the kinder remarks made about my writing. I knew I was in trouble when a Ph.D. engineer with 35 years' experience said it was hard to read; he did, however, refuse to stop reading it. I can't imagine why people think it's hard to read, it only has sixty process diagrams and six dead philosophers.

This has been an introspective year. Not finding work for the first half can do that to you. Writing a book and wondering if you're a legend in your own mind can also be ego shrinking. Judy thinks I'd have to expel a lot more hot air to deflate my ego to marginally manageable size. I considered getting a real job for more than two consecutive days. Fortunately, I received no offers that I couldn't refuse. Introspection is cleansing to the spirit: like a barium enema.

To write the book, I spent a great deal of time reading philosophy, management, and technical texts. Truth is a really cool thing to search for. It is everywhere, of course, and no one sees it. So even glimpsing it from time-to-time is breath taking. Writing this book was like that for me. I can't imagine why people devote their lives to greed and power when searching for holy grail is an alternative. Prophets are about religious truth [not religious leaders]. Even for non-Christians, Jesus Christ was a major league prophet. Some religions spell it profit. Christmas is about celebrating the Truth -- both its mysteries and the search [everyone should tip windmills].

For Christmas and the New Year, I wish for you a worthy Quest.

Reflection 20: Charts in 1421

Innovative historical (and scientific) analysis by one person can change everything.

Modern navigation today involves keying in latitude and longitude into your hand-held Global Positioning System. GPS uses satellite signals to determine the direction and distance to get there and your actual direction traveled. It was not so easy for European sailors since no one could accurately determine latitude and longitude until the 1600's or so we thought.

Consider this: Columbus was sailing with charts that were copied from Chinese charts. One reason that Columbus refused to believe that America was not Japan was half the natives he encountered descended from Chinese sailors.

Consider this: when Captain Cook in 1772 claimed to have discovered Australia, the head of the map department of the British Admiralty protested that the Admiralty had maps showing Australia drawn 250 years earlier. Consider this: the Chinese charted North and South America and Australia in 1421. Where did I get such weird ideas?

In his book, "1421 The Year China Discovered America", Galvin Menzies provides an overview of the quest: "Chinese fleets commanded by Admirals Zheng He, Yang Qing, Zhou Man, Hang Bao and Zhou Wen... charted every continent in the world (from 1421 to 1423). Admiral Zheng He's claimed to have visited three thousand countries large and small appeared to be true...

"Magellan saw the Straights of Magellan on a map before he set sail... The (400 foot long) Chinese ships had charted the world, they could determine longitude by means of lunar eclipses, and by comparing charts they were able to resolve any remaining longitudinal differences and complete the first map of the world as we know it today. ...it is now time, at last, for us to redress the balance of history and give credit where credit is due."

According to Menzies, the reason we haven't known about this were twofold: when the admirals returned to China, a new emperor was in power who believed that Chinese colonization went against the wishes of God so the maps and remaining ships were burned. But the Portuguese sailor who traveled with them brought charts to Portugal where they were carefully guarded; they were probably used by Prince Henry the Navigator (1394-1460) to train Captains and Navigators who would colonize the world for Portugal.

This is no unverified theory. Many Native Americans have Chinese DNA and there are Chinese shipwrecks all along the east and west coasts of North and South America. What have historians been thinking for the last 500 years?

An historian is an individual who studies history and who writes about history. Most generally, historians are the writers, compilers and narrators of history. Historians are concerned with the continuous, systematic narrative and research of past events as relating to the human race. Modern historical analysis usually draws upon other social sciences, including economics, sociology, politics, psychology, anthropology, philosophy, and linguistics (ref: Wikipedia encyclopedia).

To the social sciences used by historians, Menzies brought another dimension to historical analysis because he developed his theory by studying old charts. Menzies was a navigator in the British Navy who was fascinated by old charts. The detail in these old charts suggested that whoever drew them could compute longitude which the Chinese did in the early 1400s; over 200 years before the Europeans. The Chinese used astronomy and applied mathematics to develop their navigation methods.

If you have a hard time believing this, read the book or get online at www.1421.tv. You will see where the 24 shipwrecks are along the coast of North and South America. You will also see where the Chinese landed in America and stayed. You will be able to review which Native America tribes have Chinese DNA. You will come to understand that horses were introduced to America at that time.

You will be able to see where the Chinese mined in Australia before 1000 A.D. Furthermore, you will be introduced to Chinese artifacts that have been discovered around the world like porcelain, jade, dies and materials.

Here is an example of where there was a general consensus on several origins of America's discovery until ONE person challenged the consensus view. In history as in science, you don't vote on who's right.

Menzies book was regarded as nonsense among historians until Siu-Leung Lee's (PhD, Chinese-historical professor) published his 2017 research paper that confirmed Menzies "debunked" assertions (see Reflection 31: 1434).

If history fascinates, you, study Anthropology, and History.

21

CHRISTMAS 1997
21st Epistle of Jim

For the entire year I'm so happy almost nobody can stand me. Then, along comes Christmas -- aaaugh. The hypocrisy of Christmas's importance to the retail industry does me in. Fortunately, some of you must be allocating funds expected by merchants to the poor and needy because almost everything was on SALE for us last minute shoppers. Awesome. It's one thing to buy something on sale, it's quite another to find what you had intended to buy TO BE on sale.

Patty's and John's Daniel Patrick arrived in July. He started out at a little over six lbs. but porked up to 18 lbs. in four months. He is very good natured except when milk isn't available. Christopher at three has a head start at being a zoologist; he knows most of the animal species and is fond of imaginary elephants and tigers. He and Daniel brought their parents to visit at Thanksgiving. It's amazing how many bubbles they generated in our jet tub with a little shampoo.

When she isn't flying somewhere special, Judy percolates in HER Jacuzzi tub in HER new bathroom. Judy appreciates it soooo much that she had to point out that the rest of the house looks shabby by comparison. I violated my cardinal rule of work avoidance. Worse, I ignored Jones' Minimal Marital Discordance Law: every home requires a major flaw to make all other flaws look inconsequential. Nothing is ever perfect.

Judy and I started the year by going to Brisbane to see Aidan, Nicole, Jackie, and Jeff. Brisbane is a million-person city with spectacular scenery, ocean waves rolling onto a rocky coastline, rain forests, deserts, and is surrounded by outback with few people. A minor drawback is bugs the size of small mammals and lots of poisonous snakes. Tropical splendor comes with big bad beastly bugs (b4s). When not attached to trees like koalas, albino aboriginals Nicole and Aidan spent a great deal of time being transported on my shoulders.

In May, we gathered in San Francisco for Jamison's graduation with an MFA in theater. Lauren has already developed attractive female syndrome - she's busy making rules for the boys (and grandpa) who keep pestering her. I didn't know boys paid attention to girls until glands kicked in after 12 -- wrongo. Our visit was great since Lisa and Jamie moved to a wee house, 67 steps up a hill, the day before I got there. I still couldn't avoid a significant amount of lifting and unpacking. Nothing is ever perfect.

Judy and I went to Key West in April. I had a consulting assignment and worked six to eight hours per day. I used email to collaborate, get reference material and send progress reports. Judy enjoyed herself immensely without me. I was required to take her to dinner every night and swim in the late afternoon in the marina. I think she would do well wintering in the Keys with me working all day. She suns while I generate invoices; perfect for HER.

There is a saying "You cannot discover new oceans unless you have the courage to lose sight of the shore." I've been wallowing off-shore for over six years now. I am doing better than mediocre. The thought of corporate bureaucracy suppresses any urge to get a real job. Paradoxically, unique skills at perceiving and solving complex business process problems seem to be balanced by a general lack of basic sales and marketing skills.

Because of business uncertainties and age, illusions of being safe keep disrupting my thoughts. Our entire society is occupied with being safe, which, of course, is impossible. Helen Keller said, "Security is mostly superstition. It doesn't exist in nature... Life is either a daring adventure or nothing."

When asked, "Speak to us of houses," Kahlil Gibran answers: "What have you in these houses? And what is it you guard with fastened doors? ... Have you peace, the quiet urge that reveals your power? Have you remembrances, the glimmering arches that span the summits of the mind? Have you beauty, that leads the heart from things fashioned of wood and stone to the holy mountain? Or have you only comfort, and the lust for comfort, that stealthy thing that enters the house a guest, and then becomes a host, and then a master?"

I wish for all of you, the peace for dreams and the quiet urge that reveals your power to reach for them.

Reflection 21: Reflection and Philosophy

Training prepares us for a career. Education expands our world view by exposing us to knowledge that continues to reveal new truths.

Plato wrote about the teachings of the philosopher Socrates 2400 years ago. Aristotle was Socrates' student. They began an argument that lasted 2000 years. Socrates attempted to see the truth by asking questions of the wise men of his day and showed that their thinking was wrong. This is more important today than ever. Much of what you see and read today has not been well thought out or worse it is intended to mislead you. Key questions to ask on any important topic include: How did you arrive at your conclusions; how did you test your theory and what facts support your ideas?

I am only going to deal with one philosophical question: What comes first - ideas or reality?

Socrates believed that all natural things or ideas were merely shadows of what he called forms or ideas. Aristotle thought forms or ideas come only after we experience natural events or things. Socrates would say that the form or idea of a pig existed before you saw pigs. Aristotle would say you must see the pig to imagine pigs.

Philosophers argued about this for the next 2000 years while, no doubt, consuming large quantities of wine. This argument was renewed with Rene Descartes in the 16th century, rebutted by John Locke and others in the 17th century and finally resolved by Immanuel Kant in the 18th century. I like these three guys a lot. Here's how the arguments went.

Descartes was convinced that certain knowledge was attainable only through reason. He wanted to prove philosophical truths in the same way someone would prove a mathematical theorem. Descartes was the first to build a philosophical system based on what was learned since Plato and Aristotle "invented" philosophy 2000 years earlier. Descartes maintained that we can't know something is true unless we can clearly and distinctly perceive it.

Descartes doubted everything, especially our senses, which he thought might deceive us. His doubt was the only thing he was certain of. Descartes said when our reason recognizes something clearly and distinctly - as the properties of a circle in mathematics – it must necessarily be so.

My next guy is John Locke, who was born in 1632. Contradicting Descartes, Locke claimed that all thought comes from our senses and before we perceive anything, the mind is an empty slate.

We return to whether we see the truth by reason or our senses, which brings us to my favorite: Immanuel Kant, (born in 1724). Kant thought Descartes went too far in his arguments for reason and Locke overemphasized learning through the senses. Kant showed that all our knowledge of the world comes from our senses, but our reason determines how we perceive the world around us. Our concept of time and space and the idea that everything that happens as a matter of cause and effect is determined by reason.

So what's the big deal? The argument was resolved by Kant into a system that laid the foundation for modern science (philosophical discourse continues with 20th century philosophers like Russell, Wittgenstein, and Habermas). First, we perceive a bunch of events, like apples falling, balls rolling, etc and we develop a theory for movement. Then we test the theory to make sure that we can predict how balls roll and apples fall. Isaac Newton looked at the planets, saw how they move through the sky, applied previous theories for movement was divinely inspired to develop physics.

Charles Darwin looked at species evolved across the world and wrote "On the Origin of Species by Natural Selection." Gregor Mendel developed the Theory of Genetics which, combined with Darwin's theory, has evolved to Neo-Darwinism which attempts to explain the evolution of life.

So, our senses observe how things happened, our reason helps us formulate a theory, which allows us to predict what will happen. We then are able to observe whether what actually happens is what we predicted. We expand our knowledge of how things work and expand our perception of what is going on around us. 1000 years ago, we perceived the world, now we perceive 30 billion galaxies.

Pursuing an education is not just about learning facts for a career. It's about expanding your world (and Universe) view by being exposed to knowledge, writing, and thinking that came before us and continues to reveal new truths. Some argue that we never really see the truth. But it is awesome to get a little closer to the truth than anyone else *(see Reflection 37)*.

To learn how Western thought, philosophy and science evolved, study: Science, History, Philosophy and Math.

22

CHRISTMAS 1998
22nd Epistle of Jim

Christmas is coming, but I managed to ignore it until I observed a bedroom full of boxes with Santa and Christmas tree paper strewn all over. Judy's credit card is tied to Northwest's frequent flier program. She's accumulating circumnavigation credits by purchasing carpet for three rooms, all new kitchen appliances AND Christmas presents. She's awe struck by a dishwasher that doesn't require washing dishes by hand. We also got a TV for her AND my remote which requires a Y chromosome to operate properly.

After ten years of almosts, should haves, and unfavorable acts of God, we finally won BOTH Mackinac races. For those of you who are unfamiliar with big time yacht racing (yacht's are bigger than 39 feet), there is a Port Huron-to-Mackinac and a Chicago-to-Mackinac Race. I promised to brag at least once a day from last July until next July. We managed to find our way up both Lake Huron and Lake Michigan faster than anyone else. Since I navigate, I am especially pleased not to have to explain why we didn't get there first: "second is the first loser."

After six years, I finally have an almost real job. Since I wrote the job description, it's a little surreal. I got tired of trying to convince people that I was really smarter than I look and that they should really give me a purchase order to postulate and pontificate. Now I have really excellent salespeople to tell people that I'm really a LOT smarter than I look. Judy especially likes this job stuff and has taken charge of the paycheck that shows up every few weeks.

Judy still works very hard for twelve hours two days a week at the hospital. I am so happy that she works those two days because she is ecstatic the other five days not to be working.

AS always, Judy's been on the move with trips to LA, NY, and OZ. Since Jeff (who is running the Multi-media Dept. at QUT in Brisbane), Jackie, Aiden (4), and Nicole (6) moved to Australia, Judy makes exceptional use of her frequent flier credits to get us there. Aidan and Nicole say G'day and air playne like every other

Aussie. We also took a lap around northern New Zealand this time; no marsupials, boiling mud, loooong beaches, green lipped mussels, fast sailboats, and OUR Cup.

One benefit of hurricane George trashing our place in Key West is that BOTH Jamison (who got rave reviews from the LA Times for "A Lion in Winter") and John (who runs his multi-media business in NY) and families are coming home for Christmas. Imagine that, I (?) get to play with Lauren (6), Daniel (1), and Christopher (4). If there are no real adults nearby, we'll eat chocolate, ice cream, and cake. The real adults will probably be more expensive to please: like dinner at Charlie'$ Crab with several bottle$ of wine.

Someone recently told me to face reality with which I agreed completely. Kant in the 18th century explained the reality of observing events as consisting of: phenomenon - what we experience, and neumenon -- what we don't experience. Scientists have been successful because they develop multi-dimensional models to predict events and then map them back into a dimensional space that we can experience. A black hole in space was proposed by Steven Hawking long before one was "observed." One might conclude that a black hole is all neumenon because it can be experienced only by observing the space around it.

How many dimensions is reality? Do you ever wonder what is going on in dimensions five and six? Do you ever wonder where 10% of the electrons go when scientists have observed that "they just disappear." Santa certainly travels in one of those other dimensions because how else could he deliver presents to the whole world in one night. Do you ever wonder how many dimensions God experiences?

I certainly hope that these multi-dimensional ramblings don't qualify me for me committal and that you experience all of the dimensions of Christmas.

Reflection 22: Wind and Navigation

Wind is power, wind is motion, wind fills sails. I love wind.

One of my serious avocations in life is to understand wind. Wind has been God's gift to commerce and travelers since the dawn of history. The earth's rotation provides a natural west-to-east wind. Also, hot air at the equator flows up and toward the poles as cooler, low-level air flows to the equator to replace it; this is called a Hadley Cell. Disparities between water and land temperatures also create wind from all directions. Wind blows hard, it blows soft, it swirls and eddies and it destroys. Wind is power, wind is motion, wind fills sails and wind pushes and pulls sailboats. I love wind.

Sailing for me has less to do with the boat and more to do with wind. Every piece of gear should be carefully placed on the boat to make optimal use of wind from any direction relative to the boat. A sailboat race was never me and competitors, it was about discovering the true path to the finish. If you did not finish first, you did not find the Way. If you did finish first, you still may not have found it, but you were closer to it than anyone else.

What awesome power exists in a hurricane. Tornados have higher winds, but they traverse a much smaller area. Hurricanes can cut a 100-mile swath in the landscape. Too bad we can't harness the power of a hurricane to keep the USA lit up for decades.

Wind, tides, and solar power could be capitalism's answer to benevolent consumption. It is God's energy gift to us humans. Our weather engine is powered by the sun and its complex patterns are divided into four zones (this is about the northern hemisphere; the southern is an exercise for the reader):

- Equator to 20^0 Latitude: This is the tropical zone where the north / south air of a Hadley Cell is the strongest, but it is also influenced by the 900 mph Earth's rotation (0 mph at the poles); Upper air becomes southwesterly and lower air becomes northeasterly. I know nothing about this area since I pass over it at 30,000 ft. on the way to Australia to see Jeff and his family.
- $20^0 - 35^0$ Latitude: This is the subtropical high-pressure zone where the high-level tropical zone air descends to create persistent high-pressure cells with no clouds or rain; this band holds most of the deserts AND tropical paradise islands like the Florida Keys which are in the wind band of the descending tropical Hadley cell. The high pressure makes for a general feeling of well-being especially while sailing or reflecting (while drinking wine) in the Keys.

- $35° - 70°$ Latitude: This is the zone of changeable westerly winds where large weather systems, traveling eastwards bring rain and strong winds interspersed with light winds and little clouds; this climate provides the environment for people, crops, and livestock. I know this zone; Lake Michigan and Lake Huron at $41°$-$46°$ North Latitude is where I live and participate in sailboat races as a helmsman and navigator. Wind and weather in this area is described by one word: variable.
- $70° - 90°$ Latitude: The polar region is a zone where high winter cooling generates the north / south winds of a Hadley Cell; it's really cold with snow and high winds. I think I may like to visit this zone, briefly in the summer.

Temperature decreases as air rises because to rise it uses up its internal heat energy in dry air at a rate of $5.4°$ F / 1000 ft. If the air contains water (in the form of humidity), air holds less water as it rises, and its temperature drops until the humidity reaches 100%; the water then condenses into tiny droplets and clouds form. As air continues to rise, the droplets turn to ice; as they grow bigger and heavier, they fall through the clouds capturing other crystals to form snowflakes. In the middle latitudes these snowflakes turn to water again as they pass through the warmer air to fall to the ground as raindrops (or occasionally hail).

There is a whole bunch of other stuff to know like conduction, convection, radiation, conservation of energy, Coriolis effect (toilet swirlies), geotropic and gradient winds, typhoons, hurricanes, fronts, jet streams, and Rossby waves. You can learn more about them by reading Ralph Hardy's little book called: "Teach Yourself Weather."

Let's discuss sailboat racing strategy which involves chasing your way around isobars. Here's how it works.

A low-pressure cell which causes a weather front is a depression where the upper wind takes away more high-level air than it brings in; wind at low levels flows inward and upward to balance the flow. The earth's rotation causes a counterclockwise rotation at the surface. The opposite occurs with high pressure aloft causing air to flow down and outward in a clockwise direction. The direction and velocity of these spiraling winds can be estimated by looking at isobars which are lines with the same mean sea level (MSL) atmospheric pressure. The wind direction is approximately $20°$ to the isobar as the wind spirals in or out. The speed of the wind will be indicated by how close the isobars are together. If they are close together, it indicates that the atmospheric pressure is changing rapidly which means a high wind speed.

Surface weather charts used by meteorologists and crazed sailing navigators show the weather by indicating the fronts superimposed on top of a chart of the area. Weather models will predict and plot the position of the front and its associated isobars on the map in six-hour increments over 3-5 days.

Your job as a sailboat racing navigator is to OBSERVE the wind speed, direction and barometric pressure and the local wind conditions (hot land and cold water can create their own mini-weather system). You, also, OBSERVE the direction of the boats competing against you. You then ORIENT yourself by determining how much the wind and direction vary from the model predictions and project where the position of the weather system will be over the next six hours. You then DECIDE on an optimal direction for the boat to go to take best advantage of the wind velocity and direction both now and six hours from now. You then ACT by informing the owner about which direction she / he should point the boat.

If the owner disagrees with your well thought out and erudite opinion, you consider whether the owner's opinion has merit. If it does, you need to revisit your OODA loop with input from the experienced members of the crew. If the owner's opinion has no merit, you point that out and reiterate your position LOUDER. If you are confident in your assessment, you continue in this loop until the boat goes in your recommended direction or you are thrown off the boat.

To become a meteorologist study Applied Math, Climate Sciences, and Physics. To race a sailboat, talk to grandpa.

23

CHRISTMAS 1999

23rd Epistle of Jim

I think I managed to get past Christmas without being inflicted with the spirit. It whizzed by a week early. Jeff, Jackie, Nicole and Aidan came from Australia via Singapore, London, and New York to visit us for a week and left on the 23rd. There was enough energy in this house to power Detroit.

Jamison and Lisa went Scuba diving in Key West this summer. Jamison connected through Detroit with a precocious package. We gathered up Lauren at the airport, drove to Charlevoix, MI, took a boat to Beaver Island and stayed for 4th of July weekend. She threw candy off the back of a truck in the parade while I ran alongside hoping that I wouldn't have to catch her or have a cardiovascular event.

We are anticipating TWO NEW GRANDCHILDREN this year. Count em in cosmological order: Jamie and Lisa's BABY6 Jones and Lauren, John and Patty's Christopher and Daniel, and Jeff and Jackie's BABY7 Jones and Nicole and Aidan. We may yet achieve grandfather's politically incorrect vision of 12 grandchildren. Most of us grandparents that had three or more children wish that the same blessing be bestowed upon our children along with a mortgage. Which reminds me, John and Patty purchased a way cool house in Dobbs Ferry, NY with (as I see it) a lower-level grandparent apartment. It takes a REALLY BIG Y chromosome to have three children and a mortgage and NOT mature. I now have family members who are at my level of maturity.

A potentially calmer, wealthier Judy started Yoga and a stock investment club. She took a class on how to search the Web for medical information. Now she surfs the Web for jokes for her grandchildren, sends animated greeting cards, and checks her stock portfolio. She was so appalled with the response of my cast-off computer that I gave her a computer, perfume, and a plane ticket to Key West. Hopefully the improved response of her new computer will limit verbal abuse directed at technology and contribute to a calmer, wealthier Judy.

Since Jamison, Lisa, Lauren, and BABY6 will be in Key West over the New Year, Judy was ready to walk there if I didn't get plane tickets. I look forward to flying during the holiday season with the same level of enthusiasm as having a root canal. Root canals remind Judy of me during the holidays.

Management couldn't figure out how to run the company, so they sold it to another company who is now trying to sell it again. During this buying and selling, I got reorganized out and found another job with Xerox who has been reorganizing itself for six months while its stock drops. Once again, I seem to be a part of the entertainment in a corporate comedy.

THE BOOK IS PUBLISHED. Notice that I didn't say finished. After developing the methodology for 20 years, revising the book 30 times over the last three years and paying $??K to technical writers, I declared it done. Sales have been amazing; at the current rate I will have sold 5000 copies by the year 3000. Buy two books on amazon.com for productive use as doorstops or bookends: "The Document Methodology".

Despite mixed reviews, I liked every part of the book; especially the chapter conclusions where a deceased philosopher speaks to five directors of Monstrotech, inc. on critical unstructured ideas within the chapter. Gibran wrote: "If (a teacher) is indeed wise, he does not bid you enter the house of wisdom, but rather leads you to the threshold of your own mind." Hopefully, the book does that for its limited readership without requiring psychotherapy; in truth, the book is written as well as I knew how to write it.

Of the two ways we achieve some measure of immortality, children or personal accomplishment, my best bet seems to be children. Maybe I should try to be nicer to them, so they remember me well. NOT. I conclude that I did well as a remedial parent because their other parent was exceptional, I love them ferociously, and I would STILL do anything that I thought would benefit them (whether they like it or not;-)

With my newly acquired semi-literary skills I may write another book entitled: "Christmas Letters to My Friends." In the meantime, we wish for you, love of family (conflict notwithstanding), a calmer, wealthier spouse, pride in your children (You may strive to be like them, but seek not to make them like you - Gibran), and personal accomplishment (Life is either a daring adventure or nothing – Helen Keller).

Reflection 23: Flow of Knowledge

The flow of knowledge started with the dawn of human history, but got its foundation and initial structure from the Greeks in 400 B.C. It then moved steadily and slowly forward until 1500 A.D. After Kant's philosophy, Isaac Newton's physics, Freud's psychology and Darwin's Theory of Evolution, and major advances in mathematics and engineering, knowledge started expanding at a torrid pace. We learned more in the last century than in all of history.

In Plato's dialogue with Theaetetus, Socrates defines "to know" as "to possess knowledge," and attempts to answer the general question: "What is knowledge?"

> "...let us now suppose that in the mind of each man there is an aviary of all sorts of birds, ...flying anywhere and everywhere.
>
> ... whenever a man has gotten and detained in the enclosure a kind of knowledge, he may be said to have learned or discovered the thing which is the subject of that knowledge: and this is to know ... he may resume and get hold of the knowledge which he long ago possessed, but has not at hand in his mind ... possession of knowledge is not the having or using it."

The Internet and books, in a Socratic sense, "possess" knowledge in aviaries of computer networks and libraries. But often people don't "have" the knowledge because they can't or don't know how to get that knowledge when they need it. When this happens, people who need knowledge to perform a key task recreate it, or continue their work without knowledge, increasing the risk of failure when it would have been easy to succeed. Until any organization can use its knowledge to apply and inquire about its knowledge through both its formal and informal systems, it and the people in it "possess" knowledge but don't "have" the knowledge.

At this point it may be useful to distinguish between:
- **Noise** as an incomprehensible jumble of images.
- **Data** as the result of monitoring events.
- **Information** as data organized into patterns.
- **Knowledge** as information which has meaning and has been validated through:
    - Quality of Information – authenticity, reliability, integrity
    - Quality of Method – analytical, statistical and logical methods used to build the information base, and
    - Review by peer group to validate structure and content based on its correspondence to something real, coherence with other propositions, and pragmatism (does it work).

Documents are the explicit form of communication and contain noise, data, information, and knowledge formatted for people. Good documents:
- Format a structure for understanding complex synthesis of diverse data aggregates (paper, electronic, audio, video).
- Represent knowledge objects or products of enterprise processes.
- Guide classification for creating an enterprise knowledge library.
- Reside in many media, including computer files, paper, video, audio, microfilm, aperture cards or microfiche.

It is important that we make decisions based on knowledge not on information, data or worse: noise. The reason science and mathematics are so important to the evolution of knowledge is the process by which theories facts, and knowledge are validated.

Testimonials in infomercials are either noise or information but they are not knowledge. Testimonials may also be lies.

In order for a reporter to accurately report events, she must corroborate data by finding two independent sources. If the reporter fancies herself a journalist, she theorizes to add her bias to the data without peer review by experts.

A lawyer through rhetoric and reference to precedent "proves" his point to a jury most of whom have no idea what correspondence, coherence or pragmatism means in terms of validating his assertions. A lawyer told me that the general rule for courtroom success is: "pound on the evidence if it supports your client, otherwise pound on the table."

Lawyers and journalists methods don't ensure truth. Science may not either. But compare this to the Scientific Method where a theory is presented to the entire scientific community associated with the discipline and everyone tries to disprove the theory. This approach has accelerated the progress of science because scientists can rightly trust their community's knowledge.

To be a scientist, study Math, Biological, Physical and Social Sciences. To understand the scientific community and "Truth," study, Anthropology and Philosophy.

24

CHRISTMAS 2000
24th Epistle of Jim

I had to wait until after Christmas to catch the spirit. Jamison's and John's families were here for Christmas. That is a lot of energy. Judy and I alternated between exhilarated and exhausted. Patty, John, Daniel and Christopher met nine-months-old Ian. Daniel was concerned "THAT baby" would drool on and chew on his toys and books (and to his dismay Ian did). Lauren took charge and kept Christopher and Daniel properly supervised.

Judy and I spent the first week of December in Australia visiting Jackie, Jeff, Nicole, Aidan and another new person, six-month-old, Anna. Anna, my pal, preferred me to Judy, which generated concern about Anna's judgment. But some of us would have no friends if everyone had "good" judgment. Aidan trash-talked me: "I'm going to kick your butt at Chess" were his exact words. Fortunately, I won MOST of the time against a SIX-YEAR-OLD. At his current rate, I won't be able to beat him by next month.

We stopped again in New Zealand on the way to Australia and continue to be enchanted by black sand beaches, dark green foliage and recent volcanic activity. We were reminded that New Zealand has fewer people than sheep when we met several hundred of them on the main highway between Wellington and Auckland.

Judy travel involved three trips to LA and NY, one to Key West and one to Australia. Now we have SEVEN practically perfect grandchildren to follow around until we drop. Judy needed to take a thousand pictures to adequately chronicle the year's events.

My book is doing as well as Thoreau's book, "Walden" and better than Van Gogh did with selling his art. For the record, Thoreau lost money on his two books and Van Gogh sold one of 2881 paintings. If fame comes posthumously, I can wait.

Work at Xerox is a study in corporate comedy as its stock reflects. What I do is at the discontinuity of Xerox' strategy and operations; so I continue in my own business comedic role.

Modern manufacturers would be out of business with 0.1% defects or variation in their process. Our election process may have disqualified 2% of or 2 million votes. We don't and won't really know who WE elected. We do know a total lack of understanding of "viable" processes and statistical analysis got G. Dubyah elected. Al G. needed more divined Democrat dimples to win.

Unlike business and elections, variations in the processes of life are where a lot of blessings lie (e.g. children). In the coming year, stop just coping with your blessings for a moment and count them. We wish you Happy Christmas, many blessings in the New Year and the strength to endure them.

Reflection 24: Counting

Most people's knowledge of mathematics requires an emergency upgrade.

I am confounded by the fact that my Democrat friends think Republicans stole the presidency from Al Gore in 2000. If the Democrats had one statistician amongst all of those lawyers, Al Gore would have gotten his recount.

I sat in wonder as I heard one prominent Democrat after another explain to me how to count dimples and chads and ask who would I trust to count: a human or a machine? My conclusion from that whole charade is that Democrats can't count and that Republicans and the Supreme Court were smart enough to know it (but they probably couldn't count either).

The exercises below came from a paper by Mike Sterling called: "So You Think You Can Count, Philsak?"

Counting Exercise One: If there are 60 people in a room, what is the probability that two people have the same birthday, if any? Would it be about 60/365 or around a 17% chance that somebody in the room has the same birthday as somebody else? NO. It is almost 100%. It can't be? We just can't count because we don't know how. It's not our fault. It's in our genes. It's called the Birthday Problem and the graph below shows a graph of the probability. Parents and teachers think it's OK for Johnnie not to be good at Math until he tries to get elected president. Without statistics, we have to stick to political BS'ing and PowerPoint.

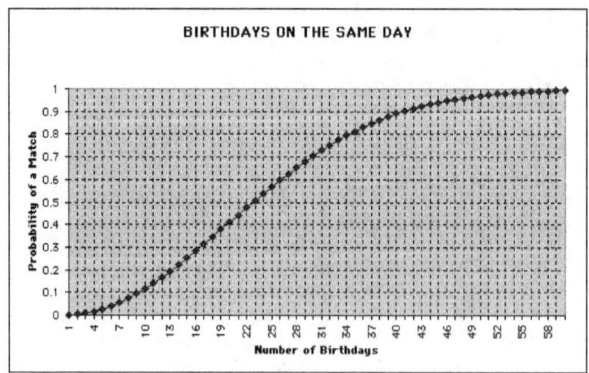

How did we go wrong? We can't be expected to duplicate what it took thousands of years to learn and finally wrote in obscure books that few educated people study. Our ancestors saw one, two or many wolves in a pack and did not care about common birthdays or exact counts.

It's not just 60 individuals divided by 365, it's whether Lauren shares a birthday with Nicole or Aidan or Chris, or Anna or Ian, Oliver or Kate, or Dan. But we're not done. We have to start again with Nicole sharing a birthday with Aidan or Chris, or Anna or Ian, Oliver or Kate, or.....Dan; and then follow that up with Aidan and go through all the labor of counting combinations. This is called combinatorics and you've never encountered it. To create that graph, we must know something from probability theory.

Counting Exercise Two: If you ask your science teacher if you tossed a coin 10 times, would the probability of getting exactly 5 heads be 50%? He might agree and explain that of course to get a feel for this obvious fact, you'd have to make maybe 40 trial tosses of 10 coins each and that would prove it empirically. Do we have a bad feeling about this? Consider 4 tosses and 2 heads. With 4 tosses we can figure that we could get combinations like these listed symbolically.

HHHH	No good		THTT	No good
HHHT	No good		HTTT	No good
HHTH	No good		HHTT	Good
HTHH	No good		TTHH	Good
THHH	No good		THHT	Good
TTTT	No good		HTTH	Good
TTTH	No good		HTHT	Good
TTHT	No good		THTH	Good

So there are 6 possibilities where you get exactly two heads and there are a total of 16 ways we can achieve results. So the probability of getting exactly two heads (or tails) is 6/16 = 3/8 = 37.5% and not 50%. But the teacher asked about tossing 10 coins not 4. There are 1024 ways to toss 10 coins and get different combinations like HTTHHTTTTH. And, there are 252 ways that we can get exactly 5 heads. So the probability of getting exactly 5 heads is 252/1024 = 63/256 or 24.6%.

For adults who didn't understand this, your knowledge of mathematics requires an emergency upgrade.

You really, really need to study applied mathematics and statistics; otherwise, like most politicians, lawyers and journalists, you won't be able to tell whether statistical arguments are rhetoric or reason.

Study math and statistics

CHRISTMAS 2001

25th Epistle of Jim

Bah Humbug. Now we need Christmas to coerce consumers to consume and get the economy jump-started. I would like to inform you that we are "doing our patriotic duty" and consuming even more than normal. We built a way cool house in Key West.

Jeff, Jackie, Nicole, Aidan and Anna are doing great with the poisonous snakes and bugs in Queensland which are preferable to recent visitors to Manhattan. Both Jeff and Jackie have quite a few friends in Manhattan where they had lived for ten years. They still would like to come back to the U.S., but the luster is off the idea.

John, Patty, Christopher, and Daniel are doing well, but being within 30 miles of ground zero has been traumatic. They lived within a hundred yards of the World Trade Center until two years ago. Their old apartment building was condemned as a result of damage from the attacks. We thank those of you who called and expressed concern and relief that our family was OK.

Jamison, Lisa, Lauren and Ian are living the good life in LA while Jamison continues to pursue his career as an actor; no easy task. Judy spent two weeks there in September and bonded with grandson Ian while thoroughly enjoying and exhausting herself. Ian not only moves a lot, but also requires that you move with him. She got to spend five extra days in California, since her return flight was on September 13th.

While Judy was in LA, I consulted at Siemens and returned on the first flight from Frankfurt to Detroit after September 11. Since most of us in Frankfurt airport's six-hour line were Americans, we entertained ourselves with the new and not working version of security which featured 25-year-olds with machine guns designed to prevent anyone from getting on a plane. While we Americans genuinely appreciated their concern for our safety, the Germans did not appreciate our humor. I was never happier to be back in the good old USA. Judy's sister Janet and husband Rick eased the trauma of my return by retrieving me at the airport and Lufthansa eased my US Customs' declarations by losing my luggage.

This was a difficult year for many of us. I think we hallucinated that two big oceans would be enough to protect us from any evil that existed in the world. Abraham Lincoln's Thanksgiving Proclamation and prayer in 1863 is relevant to me 138 years later:

"…..We know that by His divine law, nations, like individuals, are subjected to punishments and chastisements in this world… We have grown in numbers, wealth and power as no other nation has ever grown. But we have forgotten God… We have vainly imagined in the deceitfulness of our hearts, that all these blessings were produced by some superior wisdom and virtue of our own….. It has seemed to me fit and proper that God should be solemnly, reverently, and gratefully acknowledged, as with one heart and one voice, by the whole American people……"

I would like this letter to be more entertaining, but humor seems inappropriate when Americans are killing and being killed. Peace on earth continues to elude us. Making "One Nation under God with liberty and justice for all," work for American has proved elusive; making it work for the "World" will be even tougher. The answer to the question - Why us? – appears to be: Americans are the only ones with the grace and resolve (and military) to even try.

I wish for all of you as well as the leaders of every country and religion, the wisdom to bring about Peace on Earth in this decade. I wish for each of you tranquility of spirit and joy in your experiences with family and friends.

Reflection 25: Islamic Terrorism and Peace

Not facing the problem of Militant Islam now may make it impossible to fix in the future.

What a tragedy for humankind is terrorism. I cannot believe that we can continue to pervert religion to justify unprovoked attacks on any society. 9-11 was an atrocity of global proportions. I cannot believe the restraint we have used in both Afghanistan and Iraq. I was in Munich, Germany at the time of the attack. I could not tell whether the Germans were more appalled at the attack or the potential American response.

Our politicians "Imperial Hubris" (*hubris* is exaggerated pride or self-confidence resulting in retribution) assumed that winning a battlefield war would bring peace to a region that has warred with itself for over 3000 years. Our diplomatic skills seem to be limited: one party bumbles while the other panders and postures. Political hubris can be comical, but not when Americans are in harm's way.

The U.S. has attempted to establish democracy "friendly to us" in Iraq, but innocent people who should be experiencing new freedoms are dying in our effort to make peace in the midst of an Iraqi civil war. War must destroy the enemy's will to fight with us and each other. We haven't done that. Why?

In his handbook, "The Prince," Machiavelli advises that there are three ways of holding defeated nations: "The first is to despoil them; the second is to go and live there in person; the third is to allow them to live under their own laws, taking tribute of them and creating within the country a government composed of a few who will keep it friendly to you." Democracy requires more than a few.

We are supporting Iraqi militia to establish order while terrorists and militia kill each other, innocent Iraqis and American soldiers. Sunni and Shiite Muslims, sects of Islam, have been killing each other over religious differences for over a thousand years. Saudi Arabia is sending Sunni insurgents to Iraq to help the 15% minority Iraqi Sunnis kill Shiite Iraqis and Iran is sending Shiite insurgents to help Shiite Iraqis kill Sunni Iraqis. Our military is trying to help stabilize the new democratic Iraqi government, all of which is new because we dismantled the entire infrastructure of the old regime.

Our Constitution guarantees separation of church and state while Islam requires Islamic law. Once Muslims are a majority, a nation is governed by Islamic law. In the despotic governments of the Middle East, people look to Muslim clerics for guidance. Even a democratic Iraq will end up being governed by Islamic law.

Islamic law in the Middle East is not kind, benevolent or rational. Countries under Islamic law stone raped women for adultery, kill people, who denounce Islamic faith, chop off hands of thieves, imprison people for free speech and don't allow women to vote.

The UN has no desire to police rogue and despotic regimes or to deter terrorist attacks. Letting people suffer intolerable oppression is the world's greatest evil. Although it may be the most humane thing we could do, the U.S. experience in Iraq demonstrates that we don't have the resources to be the world's peacekeepers. We must work with our allies to make the UN (and police) effective in enforcing international law with despotic regimes.

Machiavelli advises: "one ought never to allow disorder to take place in order to avoid war, for it is not thereby avoided, but only deferred to your disadvantage." However, after trying to build democracies in Bosnia, Afghanistan, and Iraq, we should revisit how to proceed after a military action.

We must get American military out of harm's way without abandoning Iraq to terrorists by getting troops out of the major population centers and letting Iraqis police their own people. We must establish well-fortified bases within Iraq to protect Iraqi assets so they can support their own restructuring and so that we can prevent further infiltration of insurgents (*we failed and are paying*).

Many Middle Eastern countries harbor, pander to and support terrorists. Militant Muslim terrorists have been terrorizing leaders of these countries for many years. Negotiating with governments is a waste of time both for the UN and the U.S. since these governments are more afraid of terrorists than they are of the U.S. or world opinion. At the moment these Middle East leaders are happy to have their local terrorists killing U.S. military rather than themselves. Negotiating and waiting only makes this worse.

Islamic terrorists are nurtured, trained, and harbored in countries which may include Iran, Syria, Iraq, Saudi Arabia, Afghanistan, Pakistan, and who knows where else. They all should be put on notice that acts of terrorism against any country will precipitate a military response. To make this threat more viable we need to begin to eliminate our dependency on Middle Eastern oil now.

Militant Muslims are like cancer, not facing the problem now may make it impossible to fix in the future *(it's worse 16 years later)*.

To try to fix this problem, study: Arabic, History, Religion, Government or Military Science.

26

CHRISTMAS 2002

26th Epistle of Jim

Surprise, I almost have a Christmas spirit and am only semi-scrooged. Part of the reason is that I waited until four days before Christmas to write this letter. I just went shopping for Judy and got something that I really like. Check with Judy later to see how I did. I always buy presents I like, thereby, assuring someone benefits.

Jeff's family think they might stay in Queensland. We met them in Byron Bay on the beach between Sydney and Brisbane. Jeff strongly recommended that we drive the 400 miles from Sydney rather than fly. His motives became clear in an email with addresses of four vineyards in the Hunter Valley (100 miles north of Sydney). We bought three cases, processed two, left a half and extracted a half case. Judy got to visit her very favorite ENORMOUS Botany Bay fig tree in the botanical gardens in Sydney before flying back to the U.S.

When we got back to the U.S. we stopped for a short visit with Jamie's family. Judy spent three weeks there earlier chasing Ian around while Jamison worked on a movie and Lisa choreographed an AIDS benefit in San Francisco. Jamison was in four movies this year, but all of them are in the can (not released). Jamison and Lisa are working on their own production scheduled for release in May.

One week BEFORE we went to Australia, we went to New York to visit John's family. Since Judy retired as a nurse, she is becoming quite militant about seeing all her grandchildren REGULARLY. They moved to a hundred-year-old house in Hastings which is five miles closer to Manhattan than their old house. We are going to visit them on Christmas day and John says to bring my tools. Ya think that there may be a few things to do.

While Judy was in California, I consulted at the American Bureau of Shipping where they approve vessels as seaworthy. I visited a General Dynamics shipyard. As I was issued my hard hat and safety goggles, I was informed that they might not allow me on their 839-foot cargo vessel without steel toed safety shoes.

They weren't fond of yachting people or their boat shoes. This boat was HUGE and cruised at 30 mph; it held 600 truck tractor-trailers and 300 cars. Imagine my dismay when I discovered its 12" toy steering wheel. Big guys should have big parts.

We spent January and February at our new home in Key West. I can now tell you from personal experience that the weather is definitely better in those months than in Michigan. In January, Judy kept referring to next month as July. We came back in March because Judy missed her friends. After two below-freezing days she decided maybe her friends could come and visit her.

9-11 and Afghanistan have made us appreciate more than ever what we have and have us feeling more patriotic. However, my commitment seems shallow compared to the signers of the Declaration of Independence who committed treason under English Law punishable by hanging. That's patriotic commitment. Despite our desire for peace, our nation was created and is sustained with the blood of patriots. Thank you, veterans and future veterans. We are in your debt. With all the talk about war, remember what Thomas Jefferson told us to protect:

"We hold these truths to be self-evident, that all men are created equal, that they are endowed by their Creator with certain inalienable rights that among these are life, liberty, and the pursuit of happiness. That to secure these rights, governments are instituted among men deriving their just powers from the consent of the governed."

Our government and military make war with our consent. It is my heartfelt hope that the new year finds us at peace. But, if it's war, let it be only about protecting these self-evident truths.

We wish for you life, liberty, and the pursuit of happiness in this season and throughout the coming year.

Reflection 26: Ships and Seas

Accurate knowledge of past designs and maritime accidents are critical to establishing rules and tests that insure a new ship is seaworthy.

America has lost most of its ship building industry. 85% of the larger vessels are built in Asia (Korea, Japan and China) while less than 1% are built in the U.S (ref: Korean Maritime Institute). The U.S. delivered 45 deep-draft ocean-going naval and merchant vessels in 1953. There were 23 built in 1980 at the end of the Carter administration (ref: coltoncompany.com). None were built in 1988 at the end of the Reagan administration. We can thank management and union bureaucracies for building more expensive ships and the U.S. government for letting another major U.S. industry slip away.

My limited knowledge of ship building comes from a consulting engagement at the American Bureau of Shipping. ABS is a Ship Classification Society. If you are a ship builder and want to float your boat, it must be approved by one of several major ship classification societies: Lloyd's London was first in 1760, France, Italy, ABS, Norway and Japan were added (1828-1899), and six others came later (1936-1975).

How is a ship classified? Over the last several hundred years, governments and classification societies have defined an ever-increasing number of criteria that must be met for hull structure, propulsion size and reliability, and mechanical and electrical sub-system requirements. Every time there is some kind of maritime accident, it is analyzed in detail and more rules are generated. To be certified as safe in hurricane force winds and seas, all aspects of ship design and construction must pass volumes of reviews and tests. Accurate knowledge of past designs and maritime accidents are critical to establishing the rules for shipbuilding.

ABS must review the designs of the ships that it classifies. Builders are not too happy with the time taken for this review process because every day it takes to finish it costs them $50,000. However, if ABS screws this up and the boat sinks, the owner may not be too happy; not to mention the ship's crew.

An ABS competitive advantage over other classification societies is its Hull Analysis program which calculates the required frame structure and hull thickness. Of all the things to get right, hull construction would be at the top of my list.

Once the boat is built, it must be surveyed to ensure that it is built to the design that was reviewed. Needless to say, the surveyor is under some pressure to get the boat surveyed, so the builder can sell the boat and the new owner can put the boat into service.

I asked a ship builder in San Diego - How does a boat captain determine if his ship should leave port? The response was: when the boat is fully fueled and the cargo is on board, he leaves no matter what the weather report says. Sailing into a hurricane doesn't appeal to me much.

Since time, money and oil are at the foundation of first world country economies, ships are getting longer so they go faster. Why longer to go faster? The speed of displacement hull boats is limited by the square root of two times the water line length; that's because as the boat goes faster the bow wave gets bigger. If a boat is 450 feet long; its top speed 30mph. If a boat is 800 feet long, its top speed is 40mph. I leave calculation as an exercise for the reader.

The 839' boat that I boarded in the San Diego shipyard had two separate propulsion systems with 37,500 horsepower each: that's PROPULSION. The boat also looked like a warehouse inside with steel I-Beam pillars and cement floors. Actually, imagine a warehouse going through the water at 30mph and you've got the picture.

Now, imagine this ship in a hurricane with winds in excess of 120 mph and 80-foot waves. The boat I toured was 80 feet from bottom to top; so that would put the waves crashing over the top decks. If I were driving this thing, I would hope ABS did their job, however long it took.

A hurricane on the ocean is terrifying but consider a storm on the Great Lakes. Some of these ships that easily survived hurricanes on the ocean break apart in the Great Lakes because of the wave period. On the ocean an 80-foot wave will be 400 feet long. On the Great Lakes a 40-foot wave is 80 feet long making it much steeper and placing more stress on the hull. To learn about the Great Lakes read Jerry Dennis's book: "The Living Great Lakes."

In his Letters of Travel, Rudyard Kipling wrote: "There is a quiet horror about the Great Lakes which grows as one visits them. Fresh water has no right or call to dip over the horizon, pulling down and pushing up hulls of big steamers… Lake Superior is all the same stuff towns pay taxes for (fresh water), but it engulfs and wrecks and drives ashore like a fully accredited ocean – a hideous (and awesome) thing to find in the heart of a continent."

To become a Marine Architect or Oceanographer study: Applied Math, Earth Sciences, Climate Sciences, Mechanical Engineering.

CHRISTMAS 2003

27th Epistle of Jim

Here we are at Christmas again, but this time Judy and I are in the Keys. Without snow it doesn't feel like Christmas, thank goodness. Jones Law: The ability to endure cold goes up 1° F for each year of life after 60.

Oliver Jack and Katherine Grace arrived this year. Both started out small, but have tripled their body weight on mother's milk. There might be a lesson there for us porky old guys: no dairy. We now have nine grandchildren; can you believe it. God granted my wish: all parents are outnumbered by their children. A little chaos might help them mature, although, it didn't seem to work on me.

Jamison, Lisa, Lauren, Ian and Oliver continue to be our fine arts family in LA. Jamie has been in several plays, movies and TV shows, but we are still waiting for him to hit the BIG time so he can buy a sailing yacht for his father to "maintain." He and John wrote a screen play that they are trying to get funding for. Jamison has a new high-tech process that will allow them to make this movie for less than $100K instead of $5 million. Want to invest in a movie?

John, Patty, Chris, Dan and Kate are doing just fine in NY. They bought a 100-year-old house in Hastings and have discovered that it is an ongoing "investment." At least they'll recover their investment, as opposed to the three boats that I have and don't sail in the Keys. The family visited us at Thanksgiving "up north".

Jeff, Jackie, Nicole, Aidan and Anna are becoming Aussie's. They have now been down under for almost six years. Jeff just got put in charge of a Research center in Brisbane that he created by schmoozing up $8 million in investment capital from industry and $12 million from the government. Maybe he can schmooze up work for me and $100K for a movie.

Judy has retired from nursing after 17 years. She is happy and sad to be done. If she could find a more relaxed situation, she might get back into it. That would be great because now she is alone with a credit card seven days a week. She's been flying to both coasts to visit grandchildren. At Easter she flies to Australia and I get to tag along. My investment skills and Judy's travel and credit card keep me working.

If that's not enough, we bought a lot on Lake Michigan on: where the hell is Beaver Island? To be exact: 45°34.5' N 85°32.9' W or 50 miles north of Traverse City. Judy's expenditures pale in comparison to our builder, Ernest Martin, husband of my niece Julie and father of Madelynn and Katelynn. We put in the foundation this fall with lots more money to follow next year.

I'm still at Xerox, but I am not sure why. Xerox has done well as a company but the services group is struggling. I sent an email to the CEO at the beginning of the year outlining the problem: a strategy disjoint from competencies and managers that didn't know it. I copied the email to the senior managers as well. Imagine my surprise at continuing to be employed. After four years, I decided its time to rewrite my Document Methodology book. After it's done, I'll send another note off to the CEO and plan on doing some independent consulting.

Last year we worried about the war. This year we worry about peace. That's progress only if we successfully negotiate it, not just in Iraq but Afghanistan and Bosnia as well; from Romans 8:28 we know that "God causes all things to work together for good for those who love God." Would that be for Muslims who are called to kill for God's purpose or Christians?

At church this year Judy and I endured a six-week program called 40 days of purpose. Unfortunately, it wasn't God's purpose for me or for Judy. It was how to evangelize for the church instead of dare to do great things, God will guide you.

One of the few things I've done regularly in the last thirty years has been to write this letter. My intent is to use them as a foundation for humorously and seriously discussing God, philosophy, family and friends. When I get it done, I'll send you all a copy. Maybe that's my life's purpose.

We wish you peace and joy in this season. We all need to take the time to ponder and wonder. Whatever your religion or theology, we hope that all of you remember this is a time to reevaluate and reaffirm your purpose in life.

Reflection 27: Christianity and Reason

Religion requires faith in the unfathomable while continuing to search for God's many undiscovered laws.

Material about Christian rationalization and belief presented here was derived from four books by:

- Richard Dawkins: "The God Delusion"
- John Polkinghorne: "Faith of a Physicist"
- William James: "Varieties of Religious Experience"
- Elaine Pagels: "Beyond Belief"

You either believe in God (believer) or you don't (atheist as is Richard Dawkins) or you haven't decided (agnostic as is William James). If you believe in God, you may believe He started up the Universe and doesn't interfere (deist) or is a continuous part of our daily lives (theist). To be an Orthodox Christian you must believe in a triune God: Father, Son and Holy Ghost and that Jesus rose from the dead (as Polkinghorne). If you are a Gnostic Christian, you believe in Jesus Christ as a human with divine insight.

Dawkins argues that the universe is explained by genetic theory and Darwin's theory of evolution and no God. Dawkins believes that the workings at the cellular level are adequate to explain the entire formation of the Universe. Genes replicate USUALLY with a high degree of fidelity to create life, but occasionally mutate resulting in a new characteristic. Dawkins believes that billions of years of genetic and memetic (remember memes) actions will produce a human being with consciousness.

That is a big metaphysical leap that takes a lot of belief. Anyone who is part of some monotheistic (big word for one God) religion should have a problem with this. Neo-Darwinism evolved from an elegant, but not predictive scientific theory to a theology for atheists. No one (including Dawkins) can tell how many iterations and in what order this genetic process took to produce us.

The tendency for organisms to self-replicate and produce increasingly more complex living organisms that evolve through natural selection requires very sophisticated laws of replication. This process is amazing and elegant. Mutations and subsequent selection for both genes and memes may or may not be thought of as intelligently guided.

Polkinghorne, who is a Physicist and an ordained Episcopal Minister, points out that biologists like Dawkins are at the same place as physicists in the 18th century. They thought that Newtonian Physics explained the entire Universe without invoking intelligent design. In the 21st century they have "discovered" that dark matter and energy compose 96% of the Universe and they don't know what it is.

If you believe in a Designer of Natural Laws, you are deist. If you also believe in Intelligent Mutation, you are also a theist.

William James, Professor of Psychology at Harvard in 1902, said that because religion is about faith and not logic, we must look scientifically at the benefits of faith to see if religion has value. He sums up religious life to include these beliefs:
- "That the visible world is part of a more spiritual universe that is our true end.
- That union or harmonious relation with that higher universe is our true end.
- That prayer or inner communion with the spirit thereof – be that spirit "God" or "law" – is a process wherein work is really done, and spiritual energy flows in and produces effects, psychological or material..."

Religion also includes the following characteristics:
- "A new zest which adds itself like a gift to life and takes the form either of lyrical enchantment or of appeal to earnestness and heroism.
- An assurance of safety and temper of peace and, in relation to others, a preponderance of loving affections."

Irenaeus architected Orthodox Christianity in 175 A.D. This view was adopted by Constantine in 350 A.D. for the Roman Empire and all known Gnostic writings were burned. The Orthodox view said we are all miserable sinners saved only by faith in Jesus as God.

Elaine Pagels, Professor of Religion at Princeton provides insights into Gnostic Christianity. Gnostic writings were discovered in Nag Hammadi, Egypt in 1945. Pagels points out that Orthodox Christianity was not the only view of Jesus for the three centuries after his death. Gnostic Christianity was a community of believers who accepted Christ's teaching, but not his divinity, and believed that one comes to God through knowledge of self, knowledge of the world and, through meditation, knowledge of God.

Gnostic Christianity allows for adaptation as our knowledge of the world and ourselves expand but is still balanced by defending existing dogma. Since the Orthodoxy divorced itself from science, many of its communities require belief despite contrary evidence.

Christianity descending from Judaism has a great theological history. At its best, it is a religion of grace, comfort, forgiveness, and a powerful force for good. At its worst, it has provided us the incomprehensible murderous behavior of the crusades.

My conclusion is that Christianity has lost its way. When it set itself against science in the 15th century, it denied much of God's new revelation to us. Consequently, religion is regarded by many as inadequate to provide a moral compass for ethical questions like abortion, capital punishment, war and genetic research.

Scientists have faith, but do not suspend reason. Many Christian sects require their members to extol faith and denigrate reason. The gift of consciousness and the desire to expand it gives us the ability to continue to discover, use and live by God's laws.

On the issue of belief, I conclude that I am a Theist Gnostic Christian who believes that God works through laws which are beginning to be discovered by science that explain the Universe, the Earth and us. I experience and look forward to more of the benefits of religion that were identified by James.

Religion requires faith in the unfathomable while continuing to search for God's many undiscovered laws *(much more on this later)*.

To learn about Christianity: join a church.
To learn about religion, study:
Anthropology, Philosophy, and Religion.

CHRISTMAS 2004

28th Epistle of Jim

Christmas is a great pagan holiday, but does it have much to do with Christianity as we celebrate it? In his book, "Mere Christianity", C. S. Lewis discusses the three theological virtues of faith, hope and charity and the four cardinal virtues of prudence, temperance, justice and fortitude. I'll bet five out of seven is the best any of us do, while others ignore all seven. Capitalism and consumption go hand-in-hand with intemperance and imprudence.

Judy and I are in transition. And speaking of consumption, Judy and I own three houses at the moment. It takes fortitude to own three houses and the justice for imprudence and intemperance is property taxes, AAAUGH. Getting the house ready to sell that we have lived and warehoused stuff in for 28 years has been one inconsequential task after another. We are building our third house on Beaver Island. Beaver Island is above your little finger and across from your middle finger on the back of your left hand near the top of Lake Michigan. We hope to live there prudently and temperately.

We enter the Christmas season with Judy and me still in Michigan looking at snow. Prudence should put us south BEFORE snow comes to the north. The only snow that I need to see is in pictures from our friends. A consulting engagement keeps me here. Judy is seriously considering which virtue is better: fortitude in the snow with me or charity for herself in Key West where she will be visited by friends. No person over 55 should have to live above 35^0N in winter.

Jeff's family in Brisbane is taking an around the world trip and will be in LA and NYC at the end of January. We visited them last April in Australia. Jeff started a research center for multi-media stuff in Brisbane and also began a major house expansion; some of it was done by me. After a week of doing what I had just been doing at home, I told Jeff that Judy and I were going to the beach and would his family like to come along? Jeff's imprudence and my intemperate remarks prevailed. We all had a great time.

We plan to visit John's family in New York in February when Jeff and family are there. It will be fun to see them together. John's and Patty's old house in Hastings is like old people who are characters: both require prudent maintenance as they age. The last time I was there, John and I repaired bathrooms (notice a pattern). After applying my plumbing skills, John prudently brought in a plumber who was happy to redo what was done. Plumbing in a 100-year-old house requires fortitude (and competencies).

After a particularly extended period where Jamison had few acting jobs, we prayed for auditions. Jamison got what we intemperately prayed for; wrong prayer. He had several hundred auditions and no jobs. We prudently revised the prayer to PAYED acting work. God must be a linguist. Jamison can be seen on General Hospital for the next several weeks; we hope it goes several months. He also plays a Russian spy on Alias, which is a nonrecurring part at the moment, but he is NOT killed in the episode. Judy and I will visit at Christmas. We look forward to seeing them.

On our tiny little sphere in God's universe, Americans who exhibit no prudence or temperance in their behavior and consumption are warring with Arabs who exhibit no charity or justice in their faith. What does God think about our lack of virtue? Most physicists cannot explain God's universe in less than seven mathematical dimensions.

Understanding God's purpose and living even a marginally virtuous life isn't simple nor is it two-dimensional. If I attempt to prudently and temperately simplify within the three or four (time) dimensions in which I exist (less than three houses, two cars and three boats), maybe I will have the time to reflect on what purpose God has for me. Understanding my purpose in seven theological and seven mathematical dimensions is requiring faith, hope, fortitude and Judy's charity.

During this most religious of seasons, we wish charity in your relationships, faith that you will find your purpose and hope that we will find peace in our not so common seven virtues.

Reflection 28: Australia

Australia is a showcase of evolutionary plant and animal diversity.

Australia's first colonists were part of the most successful felon rehabilitation in English history.

Although I have visited Australia many times, I have not seen enough; the trips have been short and my son has had house projects for me to do. I really like Australia and New Zealand. If anyone in those two countries ever reads this book, please be advised I would be happy to work at a university or business or just hang out at a yacht club.

Australia is a wonderful country that we steadfastly ignore. "In a Sunburned Country," Bill Bryson put it this way: "Australians can't bear that we pay so little attention to them and I don't blame them. ...Australia is the world's sixth largest country and its largest island. It is the only country that is a continent and the only continent that is a country."

Let's discuss some fun facts that Australians don't talk about much. It has more non-human things (especially Queensland) that can kill you than anywhere else on Earth. The stonefish, box jellyfish, blue-ringed octopus, funnel web spider and paralysis tick are the most venomous of their respective species. If you don't get a lethal dose of venom, you could get snacked on by crocodiles and sharks. Bryson relates the Australian's penchant for understatement about poisonous creatures when someone described a Portuguese-man-of-war sting as "a bit uncomfortable." I love this country.

Originally, this reflection was going to be about Australia's B4s: Big Bad Beastly Bugs. A detailed description would be inadequate; you need to experience them. I am convinced that motorcycle insurance is so expensive in Australia because one bug splat on a visor would completely block the cyclist's vision.

Australia is a showcase of evolutionary diversity: its plants and animals are nowhere else. We know about kangaroos, koalas and emus, but how about wombats, wallabies, kangaroo rats, echidnas and my personal favorite, the platypus. This little guy is toothless, duck-billed, beaver tailed and furred, clawed and web-footed, lays eggs and has one orifice for poop and reproduction. After thinking this was a joke, scientists finally decided that it was not a reptile and called it a mammal.

The seasons are all backwards and the sky is full of constellations that most Americans never see. We have, however, heard about the Southern Cross. *Following the Equator* by Mark Twain provides an excellent description of it: "It is ingeniously named, for it looks just like a cross would look if it looked like something else. ...It consists of four large stars and one little one. The little one is out of line and further damages the shape. ... If you leave it out, then you can make out of the four stars a sort of a cross - out of true; or sort of kite - out of true."

No discussion of Australia would be complete without a brief mention of its colonization. Unlike Americans, Australians do not brag about their parents being among the first colonists. "The Fatal Shore" by Robert Hughes chronicles the epic of Australia's founding as a penal colony.

Until Manning Clark's "History of Australia" in 1962, Australia's convict history was ignored by schools and universities. Hughes wrote: "You could not take pride in them or reproach England for treating them as it did. The cure for this excruciating colonial double bind was amnesia – a national pact of silence."

England shipped more than 160,000 men, women, and children as convicts to Australia. No other nation was founded so painfully; it started with 11 ships in Sydney Harbor carrying over a 1000 people on January 26, 1788, and ended in Fremantle on January 1868 with the last convict ship carrying 279 prisoners. Hughes concludes: "the assignment system in Australia was by far the most successful rehabilitation that has been tried in English, American or European history... Assignment dispersed them throughout the bush and kept them in working contact with the free. It fostered self-reliance, taught them jobs, and rewarded them for doing them right."

This reminds me of a joke which Australian's don't think is funny. A New Zealander emigrated to Australia to work. An immigration officer began asking personal background questions including: "Have you ever been convicted of a felony?" The New Zealander responded: "I didn't know that you still needed a felony conviction to get in here." His reward: a return trip to New Zealand.

Until 1901, Australia was governed as six separate colonies with a governor appointed in England. To get an idea of how this worked, let's look at how Mark Twain reported in *Following the Equator*: "The Governor will be in England. He always is. The continent has four or five governors, and I don't know how many it takes to govern the outlying Archipelago. The country governs itself and prefers to do it. ...Thus, the Governor's functions are much more limited than a Governor's functions with us. And therefore, more fatiguing. …He is usually a lord, and this is well; for his position compels him to lead an expensive life."

As an American, it is hard to adjust to how empty Australia is. Most of the country has not yet been surveyed. When you look at a road map, you see a few roads crossing the country. You assume they are main roads. WRONG. They are the only roads.

The Botanical Gardens next to the Sydney Opera House cover 38 acres and contains grandma's favorite plant: a 20-foot diameter Botany Bay fig tree. Sydney is a beautiful city with steep hills on both sides of its harbor. Melbourne and Sydney both have over 3.5 million people. Melbourne is a great city as well lacking only a spectacular harbor. Adelaide, Brisbane, and Perth collectively contain about 5 million people. The remaining 8 million people are spread throughout a land mass that is two-thirds the size of the continental United States.

> *If bug and snake size and venom don't put you off, Australia is one giant science project awaiting further investigation. You can study: Applied Mathematics, Ecology and Evolutionary Biology, Genetics and Genomics, Animal Sciences, ENTOMOLOGY, Plant Sciences, Earth Sciences, Civil and Environmental Engineering, Anthropology, and Geology.*

CHRISTMAS 2005

29th Epistle of Jim

Merry Christmas (at Thanksgiving).

I am writing this letter too early to be annoyed about Christmas commercialization. I am also relieved to survive this year's events. So, no bah humbug. In the sense that "what doesn't kill you makes you stronger," we should be able to lift a house. We are, however, mostly disoriented.

Judy and I are getting this letter out early because we are not where you think we are. We know where we are because "wherever you go there you are." After 28 years in Rochester, we moved to Beaver Island, which is in Lake Michigan north of your little finger and west of your middle finger.

We miss our friends, but apparently not for long. Some of you are already scheduling visits.

At the beginning of 2005, we had a partially finished Beaver Island house, a Rochester house in disrepair, a Cudjoe Key house in a hurricane corridor and no income, but a lot of outgo. With a lot of hard work, hysteria, and luck, we seem to have extricated ourselves from our self-imposed economic black hole. The bad news is that Judy now knows that I have home repair skills. Good news: Judy is so saturated with home repairs she tells me not to do things.

Selling the Rochester house was an exciting experience. We listed with a Real Estate agent with no house sale in four months. This is a two-fold problem, you do not sell the house and since this could not possibly be the fault of the agent, it must be the house. The agent then requires you to complete repair and decorating projects each week. This process leaves you both tired and pissed off. We then put the house up for sale ourselves and Judy sold it in three days. Luck and the web are making real estate agencies obsolete.

Keep in mind that while all this was going on, we were running up to Beaver Island to perform little tasks like installing hardwood floors, sanding and varnishing the loft and hundreds of other details that would bore the crap out of you if this whine goes on longer.

On to another whine. Then there was THE MOVE. I am sure most of you have had a moving experience, but we've lived in Rochester for 28 years. Without divulging her identity, one of us is a pack rat who throws NOTHING away: for example, our sons' third grade English papers. After looking at each of 100,000 items carefully, the item was retained or discarded. We threw out a house load of stuff. We filled a 24x8x8 truck, drove it up to Charlevoix, put it on the Ferry and unloaded it on Beaver Island. Judy then went to LA leaving me to finish the move. I cleaned up the house, filled up a 6x12 trailer and repeated the same process as with the truck.

I did not get to see Jamison's family much this year, but Judy has been there for five weeks while Jamison and Lisa worked. I am not sure which is easier moving a houseful of furniture or watching a two and four year old, but Judy had more fun.

After being involuntarily separated from Xerox, they had to hire me back to consult at Ford. I then failed to get two teaching jobs and decided that I was retired. After interviewing me for a job in June, a company called me back in October for a six-person interview process. I tried my best to convey not only my capabilities, but also, the corners on my personality. I failed to communicate my true nature; they hired me. The job requires 50% travel, but I can work out of the Cudjoe Key residence. My unique job qualification is being smart enough to do it and dumb enough to take it.

The good and bad news is that the main office is in New York City with major consulting groups in Chicago and Los Angeles. The good news is I will get to see Patty, John, Christopher, Daniel, and Katherine more as well as Jamison's family. John's family also came to visit during the move to Beaver Island. The bad news is getting into NYC and LA. However, I have already been to see the New York guys twice in NYC and will soon be traveling to LA.

Jeff's family came early this year to New York on their around the world trip. Since I "retired," we were planning a visit. My new work schedule, however, suggested a 168-hour work week.

LeRoy Haynes, my past Presbyterian minister, and I are working on a book on either God, truth, theology, religion, knowledge, or some as yet to be determined divine inspiration supported by reason. Keep in mind that my theological education came at a tavern with my Jesuit priest friend and mentor, Joe Hopkins.

We wish for you the time to reflect and a divinely inspired year.

Reflection 29: Beaver Island to Manhattan

For one frantic six months before I retired, I lived on Beaver Island and "worked" in Manhattan. Commuting from one to the other was the quintessential definition of Culture Shock - maybe even bigger than German and American cultural differences. Manhattan definitely vibrates at a much higher frequency than Beaver Island. I went from curb-to-curb cars and cabs on asphalt and cement to passing fifteen turkeys and a deer in a ten mile stretch of dirt road between my house and town on the island. I took a two-hour ferry ride, drove four hours to Detroit and flew to New York.

I could deal with Manhattan crowds and pace and easily write reports and manage my team from Beaver Island, but the transition from one environment to the other was a killer. Old human nervous and circulatory systems are not built to deal with transitions like that frequently. My blood pressure is still a little out of whack and I still have nightmares about catching planes. I think that my old age is here, but I'm in denial.

You probably know about Manhattan – Wall Street, Empire State Building, seven million people, subways, cabs, trains, department stores, buses, skyscrapers, theaters, opera, nightclubs, felonies, etc.

Beaver Island is tucked just under the Upper Peninsula in Lake Michigan and is the lake's largest island. It is about the same size as Manhattan, but none of that stuff in Manhattan is on Beaver Island. The town has three real estate agencies, a hardware store, a grocery store, a bank, three restaurants, three bars, three churches, five hotels/motels, medical center, school, tennis courts, library, nine-hole golf course, two boutiques, two art galleries, toy museum, a furniture store, two light houses, at least ten builders, 550 year around residents and about 2000 additional summer residents. There is no mall, drug store, or theater.

We have beaver, coyotes, rabbits, deer, raccoons, turkeys, swans, geese, ducks, eagles, and loons. Rabbits, deer, mice, chipmunks and turkeys eat up our garden. Raccoons eat our garbage. Coyotes and eagles eat rabbits, squirrels and chipmunks. Beaver chew down trees and build dams that flood roads.

Because of its pristine environment, Central Michigan University maintains a biological station here with cafeteria, classrooms, labs, and dorms. Students come to study biology, botany, and habitat.

Believe it or not, the island was declared the only independent kingdom. When Joseph Smith was killed, James Jesse Strang declared himself ruler of the Mormon Church. When its elders disputed this and excommunicated him, he and several hundred followers migrated to Beaver Island driving off its few Irish settlers. Declaring himself King of all the Earth, his coronation took place in July of 1850. He got himself elected to the Michigan House of Representatives. By 1856, his kingly delusions enraged enough of his own followers to get himself fatally shot.

The Irish came back to the island and drove the Mormons off. In one wave 40 families from the island of Arranmore arrived; their descendants still live here.

On Beaver Island, our lone policeman prevents its major crime - DUI - by picking up drunks and driving them home. You can leave your car unlocked with the keys in the ignition, but since beer is viewed as community property, don't leave it on your back seat. People park in the middle of the street while they talk to each other. There are no traffic lights. There are 100 miles of road, but only ten miles are paved. The island is run by families that have been here for five generations who disdain suggestions from newcomers.

Which reality would you prefer – Beaver Island or Manhattan? My sons would choose Manhattan because that's where the action is. I have obviously chosen Beaver Island, because I am where my action is and would prefer to avoid the intrusions and invasions that densely populated areas bring. Television and the Internet allow me to maintain the illusion that a man and his pal Judy can be an island. I occasionally go through cultural withdrawal without theaters, museums, and concerts, but remember we live in Key West in the winter. Besides I'm only semi-cultured.

There are other benefits to compensate for cultural deprivation. We look south over Lake Michigan which stretches 200 miles down to Chicago. At night, a full moon sends a highway of light back to the mainland on black water and provides almost enough light to read a book. You can see so many stars on a cloudless night that one of our friends asked what the haze in the night sky was. It was the Milky Way!

We have freedoms and alternatives that defy imagination. I can sit here on a remote island, look out at the vast expanse of Lake Michigan, and communicate via Internet and telephone with people all over the world. Thank you, America.

30

CHRISTMAS 2006

30th Epistle of Jim

Merry Christmas,

Adopting retail Christmas behavior by writing this letter before Thanksgiving minimizes the curmudgeoning effects of prolonged relentless commercialism. Speaking of retail, Judy is suffering from Mall deprivation, having lived on Beaver Island continuously for six months and will now seek retail therapy as we head for the Keys. Despite its isolation, it took Judy three months to stop saying "I love this house" every five minutes. But, after a winter-like October, we wimps are ready for the Keys.

We spent one wonderful week in July in the Keys with Jamison's family. It rained a lot so we spent significant quality time in close proximity to each other; the house is 880 sq. ft., which is 100 sq. ft. smaller than our Beaver Island house loft. I was amazed at how many consecutive times Ian and Oliver could play their game boy, punctuated by Oliver saying " I winned, I winned." Since I had not seen my children and grandchildren for quite a while, proximity was a good thing, but some found it necessary to play in the rain.

We also spent two wonderful weeks at the Beaver Island house in August with John's family. Proximity was expanded because the weather was great and the domicile is three times larger than the Keys house. Also, Janet (Judy's sister) and husband Rick next door acted as social directors with ATV, tube and Jet Boat rides. We also went kayaking, sailing, swimming and dune climbing.

Dimensionally speaking, 350 sq. ft. is better than 150 sq. ft. per person. Getting both families to Beaver Island next year would bring it down to 210 sq. ft. per person where I will further be able to observe how the inter-familial space-time continuum is impacted by dimensionality, weather and availability of activities.

For the second year, we spent no weeks with Jeff's family. We hope to get to Australia early in 2007. Judy and I will travel rather than repair and renovate their house. We'll see the kids twice for one wonderful week at a time. This will give me the opportunity to observe the Corioles Effect (toilet swirlies go counterclockwise there; clockwise here) on the inter-familial space-time continuum.

After spending the three months adapting to her beloved Beaver Island house, Judy started into a painting frenzy. She can't do one painting at a time because she won't waste left over paint. She also suffers from "it's-not-quite-done" syndrome. Most of her excellent art remains 85% complete. Each painting awaits the last dab of left-over-just-right color from a future palette. Convincing her to sell paintings for $$$$ could compensate for my investment skills.

I retired again in October just in time to install two propane heaters (without asphyxiating myself), a pantry and linen closet, varnished 1000 ft^2 of ceiling and 15 ft^2 of me (Judy supervised and helped) and converted a gas generator to propane (without an explosion). Retirement is strenuous; no wonder so many people retire and die. I need to sit on my butt and write. I can start soon after sanding and painting rusted Keys house support beams. We need fewer houses or more wealth to pay handy men. Maybe we can negotiate a WRITTEN CONTRACT with our sons where they own but we live in the houses until we die while they pay taxes, maintenance, and utilities. After all, they already pay our Social Security and Medicare; three sons should be like a third world insurance policy.

Many of you know, I am writing three books. It's all about EGO. My vision of immortality is posthumous fame. The second edition of my first book will appeal to an audience of five people; but, it represents a lifetime of work in my corporate comedy. The second book should be of more interest since it is a compilation of past Christmas letters with reflections. It will have an audience of at least 100 since I will print and send you one. If you like it, buy two copies on amazon.com give it to friends and instruct them to do the same. If you don't like it, give your copy to an enemy; this is my multi-level marketing scheme. The last book on God, theology and religion will be incomplete and marginally comprehensible, but when published could insure immediate fame posthumously.

Members of both political parties have described themselves as the party of hope not fear. I hope our new electees calm my fears by preventing Iranian Armageddon. Here are a few other suggestions: give tax breaks to American companies; educate all of our children; and my favorite, preserve Medicare and Social Security. Thanks to citizens and not politicians, America continues to be a country where hopes are realized and some fears are calmed.
We wish for you a time to rejoice in the hope that is Christmas.

Reflection 30: Architecture

Building a house on an island with house plans on 8.5"x11" sheets of paper is not something I would recommend for anyone who can not afford to flush fistfuls of money down the toilet. I have done dumber things, but not many.

An important lesson that I learned was that however proud you are of your personally designed house plans, have them redone by an architect. Finding mistakes on paper is far better than correcting them in the middle of the construction process.

I designed the house because, as you can see, it was too simple in concept for an architect. One triangular roof would be way too easy for an architect. The house is spectacular inside. A 24' high living room ceiling 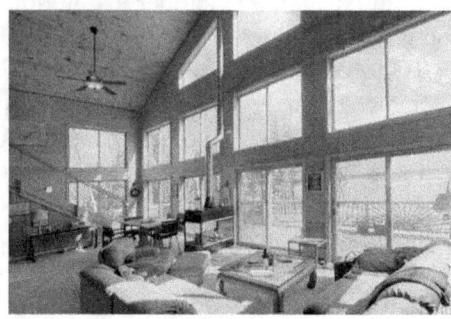 gives the house an open feeling that I have not experienced in a house of this size. With all of the windows, it feels like you are outside. It would be even more special if someone washed those high windows occasionally.

Architecture is an interesting blend of form, function, art and engineering. Judy directed the form and art while I bumbled around with function and engineering.

We did well for amateurs only because of the experience and adaptability of our builder: K & M Contractors. Having at least one person who knows how to build a house was helpful.

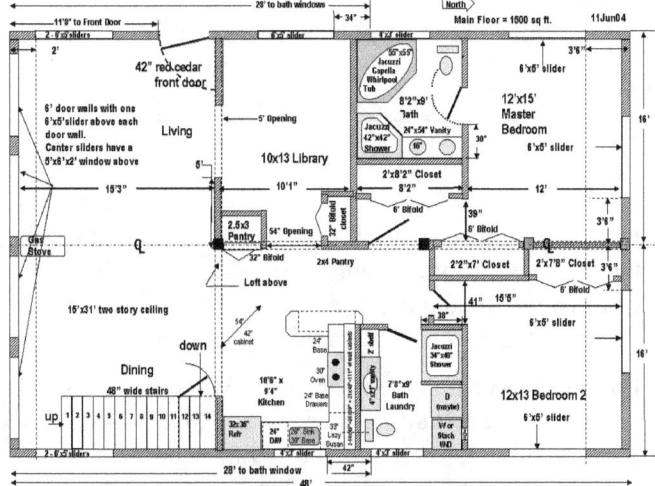

We built the house using the above drawing of the first floor. It is amazing that it came out looking like we intended.

If you build a custom home, here are some simple suggestions:
- Even if you are really proud of your design ability, have an architect redraw it or buy plans.
- Find a quality builder that you can trust; look at three of his houses and talk to the owners.
- Negotiate mercilessly up front and then be nice.
- Require a project plan which clearly shows major construction milestones and completion dates.
- Make sure rough inspection, final inspection and certificate of occupancy are milestones.
- Require every change and its cost to be documented in writing and signed by you and the builder; don't nit-pick.
- Tie your payment schedule to each milestone.
- Make sure your last two payments are big enough to encourage the builder to want to finish.
- Pay on the day that you get your builder's invoice.

Building a custom home has been described as digging a hole into which you throw fistfuls of money. Have a complete physical before you embark on this adventure.

CHRISTMAS 2007
31st Epistle of Jim

Merry Christmas,

I am writing this Christmas letter in early fall, in order to get the book printed; so the usually curmudgeonliness hasn't beset me. I can't complain about money that Judy has spent on Christmas presents either, but quake thinking about it.

I retired last year in October. I still work ten hours a day, but I don't get paid and don't have to travel, but still have nightmares about running to catch a plane. I finished the second edition of "The Document Methodology" in February and anticipate selling at least 50 books because I bought them. I also wrote and published this Reflections book. I know that this book will sell at least 100 books, because I bought them and sent them to you. Remember, if you like this book, buy two copies and give them to friends. If you don't like it, give it to someone that you want to annoy (not me).

Judy keeps really, really busy. In Key West, she is busy with her Art, knitting, piano lessons, tap dancing and hanging out with her friends. She occasionally asks me to look at a painting and tell her how to correct its perspective. On Beaver Island Judy is busy reworking the natural environment around us. Judy needed help to:
- dig up soil in the woods and dump it in her garden,
- plant a garden that feeds chipmunks, squirrels and deer,
- build a retaining wall for her flowers,
- cut back the brush around the house in the woods,
- rebuild too steep stairs (she now glides up her steps),
- clear dead trees around the house,
- build a dining room table from a hemlock door and fallen maple tree (she can now seat ten people),

Needless to say on Beaver Island, I am needed or I could employ half the island to do Judy's "need' projects.

Judy got an ATV. That's an All-Terrain-Vehicle. Judy likes to ride in the woods. She also learned in July that it requires gasoline to propel it after pushing it home and telling me that it wouldn't run. I like riding in the woods except for the 10^{10} mosquitoes, but, more important, it provides horsepower for dragging stuff around for "need" projects. It works great for dragging sailboats down to the shore. I can't say beach, because, although there may be sand on the shore, it is obscured by 10^{10} stones, rocks, and boulders. Judy needs to move half of them elsewhere for a rock garden.

We convinced John and family - Patty, Chris, Dan, Kate - and Jamison and family - Lisa, Lauren, Ian, and Oliver to visit in August. They were each here more than a week, but the time we all were together was four days. That's six adults and six children in one house. Fortunately, we have two full bathrooms, but the logistics were still interesting.

Our nieces Rebecca and Julie, and family – Ernest, Madelynn and Katelynn - Judy's sister Janet and husband Rick were all part of it. Judy tried to participate in everything while I watched and occasionally facilitated. Nineteen people exceed my limit for social interaction. We all had a great time. We had ATVs, jet skis, jet boat, pontoon boat, sailboat, water skis and most important Lake Michigan at our disposal.

Jeff and family are going to visit us in Key West at Christmas. I love Australia, but not the 30-hour trip to get there. Judy is ecstatic.

This has been an interesting year for reflection. Writing a book to my grandchildren and friends forced me to crystallize many old half thought-out ideas. Now they are at least half-baked. I have had to revisit my concept of self, my relationship with God and my interaction with other people. I also looked back on the circuitous path that I took to get here and the paths not taken. I seem to have worked very hard to come to some mundane conclusions, but then again, maybe not. I write under the room full of monkeys' theory, if I write enough maybe a few phrases will be profound.

We miss you this Christmas and would hope upon reflection that you are happy with your answers to the questions: why am I here, who am I, how did I contribute, what is my relationship to God, myself, other people, the world, and the Universe, and what am I going to do next?

Reflection 31: 1434

Menzies 1421 (Reflection 20) claimed Chinese discovered America causing apoplexy among historians. Felipe Fernandez-Armesto, professor of history at the University of London, dismissed his book, 1421 as "the historical equivalent of stories about Elvis Presley in Tesco and close encounters with alien hamsters". But Menzies's book sold a million copies worldwide in 135 countries.

Siu-Leung Lee's (PhD, Chinese-historical professor) 2017 research paper *Maps that turn world history upside down* confirmed Menzies "debunked" assertions that China mapped America before 1430 CE, 60 years before Christopher Columbus set sail.

Menzies could have retired on the profit from 1421, but he put his money into more research and produced a contentious sequel, 1434, claiming that the Chinese precipitated the Renaissance.

In 2005, records were discovered that show the Chinese reached Italy between 1406 and 1435. In the Moorish palace in Toledo Spain, Menzies found an exhibit with a note: "Leonardo embarked upon a thorough analysis of waterways. The encounter with Francesco di Giorgio was… a turning point in Leonardo's training. Leonardo planned to write a treatise on water."

Research revealed that Leonardo had a copy of di Giorgio's civil and military treatise which included canals, locks, pumps, parachutes, submersible tanks, machine guns and hundreds of other machines. This book came from Toccola, a clerk of public works in Siena, Italy. Further research established all of these illustrations came from a Chinese contingent that visited Italy. Leonardo apparently was more into redesign than invention.

Menzies asserts that China precipitated the Renaissance. He argues that a Chinese fleet with ambassadors of the emperor, arrived in Tuscany in 1434 and met with Pope Eugenius IV in Florence. The delegation presented the pope with knowledge from a diverse range of fields: geography, printing, astronomy, art, math, architecture, steel manufacturing, civil engineering, military weaponry, surveying, cartography, genetics, and more. This sparked the Renaissance, including da Vinci's mechanical creations, the Copernican revolution, Galileo's discoveries, and more.

From 1434 onward, Europeans embraced Chinese ideas and inventions, brilliantly reasoned, formed the basis of European civilization as much as Greek philosophy and Roman law.

"The idea that Europeans dreamed up everything in the Renaissance is just to make history more romantic," says Menzies. "There's going to have to be an agonizing reappraisal of the Eurocentric view of history."

But the Chinese went home, they didn't colonize the world. History wasn't affected. That was the end of it. So what?' Academics mishandled Menzies books badly by trying to undermine him. A million people including me wanted to understand his assertions.

Some reviewers suggest that Menzies's strength is that he links known facts that no one had the wit to put together before and comes up with something worth debating. Others have called his books a tower of hypotheses. But his brand of history like a detective novel with clues provide a fascinating read.

Menizies wrote *1421* in 2003 and *1434* in 2008 and *The Lost Empire of Atlantis* in 2011. He argues that Atlantis was not myth; a volcanic eruption and subsequent tsunami devastated the heart of the Minoan empire on Crete and Santorini (Thera). In Crete he found Minoan artifacts, viewed ruins, interviewed scholars, and visited sites; from Crete he went to England (where Minoans mined copper and built Stonehenge??) and on to Lake Superior (where they mined copper). He asserts they stopped on Beaver Island (??) on the way down Lake Michigan and the Mississippi to Louisiana into the Caribbean! They were master shipbuilders, sailors, navigators, mathematicians, astronomers, and made bronze tools from tin and copper. Menzies claims that in 2,000 BCE, Minoans ruled a vast Bronze Age empire with many outposts. If he is right, the Biblical flood (1500 BCE) may have drowned their culture.

Menzies research leads to novel assertions. Most academics argue that Menzies is a poor scholar, historian, and archeologist. However, his "debunked" 1421 book's assertions were confirmed by an academic after 14 years of vilification by academics. A later reflection speaks to extracting novelty from noise. Academics must get beyond rules of "proper" scholarship to examine the truth or falsehood of details and novel assertions.

I can speak from personal experience that academics don't like novel ideas especially if they come from outside their "club."

32

CHRISTMAS 2008
32nd Epistle of Jim

I am writing my Bah Humbug letter in November, since we will celebrate Christmas at the far end of the planet. We drove to NYC to visit John's family, then drove to Key West, will fly to LA to see Jamison's family and will fly to Australia at Thanksgiving to visit Jeff's family. We hope to see quite a bit of Australia in the six weeks that we are there. If we live through this self-imposed stress test, we're good for five more years.

My granddaughters are sufficiently attractive for their fathers to consider locking them in a closet until they are 21. High schools should be segregated on the basis of gender. Since boys will be boys that wouldn't do any good either. Grandparenting is great: you can enjoy parent-child conflict and not be responsible for fixing it. However, occasionally, I find myself included in the conflict for enjoying it too much.

My multi-level book marketing scheme failed. Those of you who liked the book SHARED (my least favorite word). You were supposed to BUY several books and GIVE them to friends and family. Those who disliked the book were supposed to GIVE it to an unsuspecting person. I have been told by several males that it is a perfect potty book as it is divided into three-page segments. Thinking positively, I may sell more than five books this year (available on amazon.com). I am now attempting to write an even less popular book entitled: Faith and Reason. My theologically astute friends tell me not to worry about crucifixion; punishment for heresy is being burned at the stake. What a relief that is.

Judy is knitting gifts thereby significantly reducing expenditures at Christmas. But we will spend even more on our Australia trip, transferring our little remaining wealth to Australia not China. Judy is doing great and continues to paint. It is fascinating to watch her paint because she doesn't draw. She just blobs on paint to create amazing still-lifes, landscapes and seascapes. With my investment skills, I keep encouraging her art efforts as she may represent our only source of income in the future.

Judy and I renewed our interest in Sailing. I spent more time repairing boats than sailing. We now have two 16' Hobie Cats, two Sunfish and three others. Why would anyone have 7 boats? Non-sailors think sailing is romantic until they buy a boat and discover that it requires alarming amounts of work and money. So, people almost GAVE these boats to me while reserving the right to stop by and sail. Now I can spend alarming amounts of work and money on 7 boats. I will try to teach sailing next year so that I can get others to supply work. Judy and I purchased wetsuits to extend our sailing season. My extra weight contributes to a tubular shape, so donning my wetsuit was far less entertaining than watching Judy attempt to get the suit past those parts that make women attractive.

Right after government ineptness finishes driving down stock and dollar value, it will need to raise the Social Security age to 110. On the bright side, anxiety over investments will be reduced, because WE WON'T HAVE ANY, AAUUGGHH !#@$$&@#! Several villains of the current situation have been identified: brokers, bankers, CEOs, Republicans, Democrats, and we who elect them. With the obfuscating rhetoric (bull shit) it is hard to identify the least worst villain. Can we put the entire Federal Government in Jail? Bankers lent money irresponsibly encouraged by Democrats. Brokers gambled irresponsibly aided considerably by lack of oversight encouraged by Republicans. Our dollar was devalued by politicians' irresponsible spending. Clearly our Federal Government may be our biggest villain, or is it.

After WW II the industrial powers formed the World Bank to end poverty, and the International Monetary Fund (IMF) to sustain prevailing exchange rates. In 1994, the World Trade Organization (WTO) was created, with the authority to penalize even the richest member nations whose trade laws impede the free flow of goods, services, and cash across international borders. Benefits are real. Global infant mortality rate was cut in half; billions of people live longer, eat better, have more income; and exports have increased 17-fold. However, World Bank loans and IMF programs make it easy to move polluting industries into the developing world; also, IMF and WTO suppress health, environmental and labor protections by asserting that they hamper open markets. They also support international monopolistic corporations and provide tax shelters for companies' foreign subsidiaries. Global monopolies expect governments to cater to them while migrating 20% (and rising) of US manufacturing jobs overseas (ref: Pulse, Frenay).

[The Jones' variation of] Western economic theory rests on a few basic notions: that if someone wants something it is because [advertising tells them] it has value; that the tension between what people [are told to] want and its availability is a good gauge of how much they will [borrow to] pay for it; and that free markets do the best job of fixing value because they act in [predictably irrational or marginally] logical ways. Politicians argue: leave the market completely alone and let the market sort them out, so that monopolies can contribute large sums to their election campaigns. Meanwhile small companies' innovations don't get to market and create more jobs because monopolies crush them to mitigate their risk while sending existing jobs overseas.

The Jones FIX IT Eight Step Program:

Step 1: Jail brokers, bankers, CEOs, politicians, and people whose greed caused this mess (and how about term limits?).

Step 2: Eject the 12,000 lobbyists that pay our congressmen to insure that OUR government serves THEIR special interests.

Step 3: Fire inept and inefficient government bureaucrats who waste our tax dollars.

Step 4: Restructure the WTO and its policies to serve nations and people not monopolies.

Step 5: Loan money only to people who can afford to pay it back.

Step 6: Oversee brokers, bankers, CEOs and politicians to stop them from stealing from stockholders and taxpayers.

Step 7: Stop funding unilateral military attempts to build secular democracies in all (but especially in Muslim) countries.

Step 8: Throw the bums (politicians) out who don't fight big spending, big business, big government, big media and the WTO.

We encourage our politicians and leaders to replace their most evident seven behaviors: sloth, pride, envy, lust, gluttony, greed, and wrath; with chastity, temperance, diligence, humility, patience, abstinence, and kindness. Perhaps our significant reduction in assets will help us remember that this season is about charity to our most rapidly increasing demographic: the poor.

We wish for you the love, grace and hope for a better seven behaviors in the future.

Reflection 32: Black Holes

With government spending what it is, you might feel your assets are going down a black hole. So, what are they.

Black Holes' extreme gravity draw in stars or anything else if their orbit brings them into it (not even light can escape).

Every galaxy (Reflection 17) has a Black Hole at its center. Black holes could be a portal to another universe and our cosmos could have been born from one. While the accepted theory is our universe began as the big bang, yet another theory is that our universe was born from a black hole opening in another parallel universe and that each black hole in our cosmos could be a gateway to another universe. At our beginning of time, 13.8 billion years ago, there was a dense and super-hot energetic point where the laws of physics did not apply – known as a singularity which is at the event horizon of a black hole.

There are a few ways in which a black hole can form. Scientists believe the most common instance is when a star, thousands of times the size of our sun, collapses in on itself known as a supernova. Another way is when a large amount of matter, which can be in the form of a gas cloud collapses in on itself through its own gravitational pull. Finally, the collision of two stars can cause a black hole. A black hole rips a hole in the fabric of space-time.

This has led some to believe that the Big Bang was actually a black hole opening in another universe, allowing the matter which has spewed through from that portal to create our own portal. The matter that has been spewing through for 13.8 billion years may explain why the universe is ever-expanding.

Some of this Reflection comes from NASA's curriculum course on Black Holes for high school seniors in an advanced math course (see http://spacemath.gsfc.nasa.gov). A black hole is simply an object whose gravity is so strong that light cannot escape from it.

Before Princeton Physicist John Wheeler coined the term black hole in the mid-1960s, no one outside of the theoretical physics community paid this idea much attention. Because no material particle can travel faster than light, once a body is so massive and small that its escape velocity equals light-speed, it becomes dark. This is what Laplace had in mind when he thought about "black stars." This idea was ignored for over 100 years.

Once Albert Einstein developed his Theory of General Relativity in 1915, the behavior of matter and light in the presence of intense gravitational fields was revisited. This time, Newton's basic ideas had to be extended to include situations in which time and space could be greatly distorted. There was an intense effort by physicists and mathematicians to investigate all logical consequences of Einstein's theory of gravity and space. Within a year, one simple body was investigated with complex mathematics.

The German mathematician Karl Schwarzschild investigated what would happen if all the matter in a body were concentrated at a mathematical point. In Newtonian physics, this is called the body's center of mass. Schwarzschild chose a particularly simple body: one that was a perfect sphere and not rotating at all. Although this may sound vague, the mathematics is not. There are four basic kinds of black hole solutions to Einstein's equations:

- Schwarzschild: These are spherical and do not rotate. They are defined only by their total mass.
- Reissner-Nordstrom: possess mass and charge but do not rotate.
- Kerr: rotate and are flattened at the poles, and only described by their mass and amount of spin (angular momentum).
- Kerr-Nordstrom: possess mass and charge, and they rotate.

Black holes can come in any size, from microscopic to supermassive. In today's universe, massive stars detonate as supernovae, and can create stellar-mass black holes (1 solar mass = 2×10^{27} tons). When enough of these are present in a small volume of space, black holes can absorb each other and can grow to several hundred times the mass of our sun. If there is enough matter (i.e., gas, dust, and stars) for a black hole to "eat," it can grow even larger. The black hole at the core of our Milky Way has a mass equal to nearly 5 million suns. The cores of massive galaxies have supermassive black holes containing the equivalent of 100 million to 10 billion suns.

In its 15Nov2022 issue, Science Alert reported that "Using a chain of atoms in single-file to simulate the event horizon of a black hole, a team of physicists has observed the equivalent of what we call Hawking radiation – particles born from disturbances in quantum fluctuations caused by the black hole's break in spacetime."
Is creating black hole phenomenon a sane idea??!!??

33

CHRISTMAS 2009
33rd Epistle of Jim

I am once again muddling through this Christmas letter, but it's later and I'm grumpier. Unlike Scrooge, I don't need Ghosts to get right, I live with Grandmother Christmas. Judy continues to knit gifts thereby significantly reducing expenditures at Christmas by spreading supply costs over the entire year. Judy also continues to paint (quite well I think), but I am still looking forward to "sharing" in the wealth and fame that will come from her excellence in the arts.

Last year we flew to Australia for Christmas with our Brisbane family. This year we fly to California to spend Christmas with our LA family. Last year we drove up and down the southwest coast and northeast coast of Australia. This year we plan to loop from LA to Vegas to Santa Fe to Tucson to Phoenix to LA and stop at a few sights along the way, like the Grand Canyon and Hoover Dam. I didn't think retirement was going to be this strenuous.

Our trip to Australia last year was way cool. We saw Ayers Rock, Perth, Australia II, the Tree Top Walk, stromatolites (3-billion-year-old oxygen emitting rocks), the Whitsunday Archipelago at the Great Barrier Reef as well as 3000 miles of nothing. We saw a golf course near Shark Bay with sand fairways and asphalt "greens". We waited until it was 106 degrees in the shade for our strenuous walk of 5 miles around Ayers Rock between 10 am and 2 pm. It should have taken two hours, but we had to stop regularly to see if an ever-reddening Judy could cool down; nope. A stranger suggested that one would have to be daft to walk around it in the heat of the day; strenuously daft would be me.

Perth is a very English looking two-million-person city with no northern suburbs, just scrub and sand. NO people or buildings exist 15 minutes north of the city center; pretty weird, especially when you drive for two hours in the dark and only encounter a truck train every 15 minutes. Picture a 1.5 times size semi pulling two additional 1.5 semi size trailers where the last trailer seems to have a mind of its own. We drove a boxy, left-hand-manual-shift

Mitsubishi camper (named whiz-bang for the door closing sound after a 2am pee) that went sideways when passing these behemoths. Australians fear none of their multitude of poisonous snakes and bugs and crocs and sharks, but truck trains and daft tourist drivers (keep LEFT) are another story.

Australia II sits in a cradle with all its sails hoisted at its very own maritime museum in Fremantle just south of Perth. For those disadvantaged few who are unfamiliar with sailboat racing history, Australians, in the sailing yacht Australia II, took the America's Cup from us after we had retained it for 125 years. The Australians declared that date 26 years ago a national holiday. Sailboat racing is more than important down under; it's religious.

South of Perth are very large almost redwood size tingle top trees with very sensitive root systems. So, Ecology minded Australians (greenies would love it there) built a tree top walk. It looked like an inverted suspension bridge and allowed us to walk 100 feet ABOVE the ground in the treetops. Judy took tree pictures while I took bridge pictures. Note: being on the Beaver Island Eco-Tourism Committee, I might be classified as a skeptical fringe greenie.

In Australia, we took a 3-week trip west and a one-week trip north. That made for a strenuous 4000-mile drive. We stayed at campsites on the west coast and experienced eco-tourist lodging on the east coast. Australian eco-tourism finds a remote area like the Whitsundays and puts up a 3-star hotel (with no TVs), a four-star restaurant and WiFi everywhere. After discovering campsites with private bath houses, there was no going back; especially after Judy came face-to-face with a six-foot kangaroo on her way to the loo.

Last year we saw all of our children and grandchildren in a happy strenuous-ridden month period. We saw our NYC kids at Halloween, our LA kids just before Thanksgiving and Brisbane kids at Thanksgiving. Our seventeen-year-old granddaughters and niece think I'm daft to offer to buy them burkas. Daftness is a consequence of raising children. They should all come to see us in our dotage like our NYC family did in April. Unlike his Uncle Jamison who plans to inherit it, John's son Dan offered to buy the Keys house, probably with hyper-inflated dollars.

Judy's interest in sailing waned this year after watching Jamison and I turn turtle (e.g. sail is pointing straight down under water) in our Hobie 16 in 300 feet of water in Lake Michigan. It took a very strenuous 45 minutes to get it righted while we progressed rapidly toward Chicago 200 miles south. As we were sailing back, our neighbor Terry and our brother-in-law Rick motored out to meet us which prompted Jamison to quip: "now they save us after we saved ourselves." We did appreciate their effort, because going to Chicago upside down would have been really strenuous. I added a righting system, but just the daft idea of a "righting system" for 55^0F Lake Michigan water has kept Judy off the Hobie.

I saw a great bumper sticker: "Re-elect no one." Daft politicians think that they can spend their way out of debt. While they bankrupt our country, I struggle to find clever ways to avoid financial ruin. A Dan/Jamison Keys time-share payment won't help since US dollars will be worthless. An innovative solution may be provided by our son Jeff if he continues to consult in Australia and employ me; he can pay me in Australian dollars! Hopefully, income tax won't go to 75%.

I am strenuously struggling with the 14th rewrite of my book on God, Faith, and Reason. A revelation or two might help, especially since I have adopted Alfred North Whiteheads theology which is based on Quantum Physics. I always felt blessed to have a skeptical nature which confounded my Lutheran school teachers. Trying to think what to believe while the church says, "just believe" and science says "just reason" has been the source of my lifelong comedy. Science requires belief; religious belief without reason has terrifying consequences. Fortunately, we Americans don't stone people for heresy yet. I, like most scientists, seek to know the mind of God (daftly arrogant) and how climate will really change.

We wish for you, peace, joy and the energy to endure the strenuous blessings of this season and a warmer (?) planet.

Reflection 33: Quantum Physics

$$i\hbar \frac{\partial \psi}{\partial t} = \frac{\hbar c}{i}\left(\alpha_1 \frac{\partial \psi}{\partial x^1} + \alpha_2 \frac{\partial \psi}{\partial x^2} + \alpha_3 \frac{\partial \psi}{\partial x^3}\right) + \alpha_4 m c^2 \psi$$

Since Whitehead's theology is based on Quantum Physics, I spent several months trying to understand its mathematics; but not to worry, I don't understand the equation either. Paul Dirac was awarded the Nobel Prize in physics in 1933 for the implications of that one equation which resolved more than a few contradictions in theoretical physics.

So, what's it to you. Since quantum physics is now at the heart of computer chip design, it is not an exaggeration to say that our lives now revolve around the consequence of that equation. There are more than a few computer chips in your cell phone and computer and distressingly over 100 micro-processor chips in your car.

From Wikipedia the Dirac equation is the first theory to account fully for special relativity in the context of quantum mechanics. It was validated by rigorously accounting for the fine details of the hydrogen spectrum. The equation implied the existence of a new form of matter, antimatter, previously unsuspected and unobserved and which was experimentally confirmed several years later.

Even Dirac did not fully appreciate the importance of his results, the explanation of spin as a consequence of the union of quantum mechanics and relativity and the eventual discovery of the positron represents one of the great triumphs of physics.

Insightful as that equation was in the 1920s by the mid-1940s, it was generally accepted among leading scientists that Dirac's theory of quantum electrodynamics suffered some mathematical flaws.

Enter Richard P. Feynman. Feynman first met his hero Dirac during Princeton's Bicentennial Celebration in 1946. When they met first time, the entire conversation was: "I am Feynman." "I am Dirac" (silence). Later Feynman claimed Dirac spoke only this: "I have an equation. Do you have one too?"

Feynman was to introduce Dirac who had been invited to speak on elementary particles during a session on the future of nuclear science following the war. Feynman disliked the work Dirac was presenting, which was a re-statement of his work that led to difficulties in quantum electrodynamics. Feynman addressed the crowd with "so many jokes that Nobelist Niels Bohr... criticized him for his lack of seriousness." He closed on remarks somewhat in conflict with the message of Dirac's coming lecture, addressing the unsettled state of the theory of quantum electrodynamics.

The two men met again in 1948, when they both attended the Pocono Conference. Feynman recalled that "There have been many conferences since, but I've never felt any to be as important as this." 28 of the world's leading physicists attended the conference, including Oppenheimer, Bohr, von Neumann, Fermi, and Dirac. When Feynman gave a lecture on an "Alternative Formulation of Quantum Electro-dynamics", reformulating the theory which had earned Dirac his Nobel Prize, it was not well received, as Bohr, Teller and Dirac all raised objections. The audience's negative reaction motivated Feynman to publish four papers:

- *Space–Time Approach to Quantum Electrodynamics (1949).*
- *The Theory of Positrons (1949).*
- *Mathematical Formulation of the Quantum Theory of Electromagnetic Radiation (1950).*
- *An Operator Calculus Having Applications in Quantum Electrodynamics (1951).*

These papers won Feynman the Nobel Prize in Physics in 1965 for "fundamental work in quantum electrodynamics with deep-ploughing consequences for the physics of elementary particles". Dirac, Feynman's hero-turned-opponent motivated a life's work which altered physics' trajectory and established Feynman as one of history's eminent physicists.

The main principles of quantum mechanics (QM) include:
- Wave–particle duality describes every quantum entity as either a particle or a wave; also, "particle" or "wave" does not fully describe the behavior of quantum-scale objects.
- Heisenberg's uncertainty principle: position and momentum of a subatomic particle cannot be predicted from its initial conditions.
- Superposition: particles exist in multiple states simultaneously: e.g., an electron can exist in multiple locations at once.
- Quantization of particles: energy and angular momentum, are quantized, meaning they only take on certain discrete values.
- Entanglement: particles become entangled; they are linked in such a way that the state of one particle depends on the state of the other, regardless of a large distance between them.

These QM (goofy) principles have important implications:
- Materials Science: QM is used to study properties of materials at a quantum level, leading to development of new materials with unique properties, such as superconductors and super-fluids.
- Technology: QM is applied to design of electronic devices, such as transistors and microprocessors. QM has also been used in cryptology, sensors, imaging, and superconductors with zero electrical resistance.
- Chemistry: QM explains behavior of atoms and molecules. It is used to calculate the electronic structure of molecules, which determines their chemical properties and reactivity and the periodic table. This has led to a better understanding of chemical reactions and development of new drugs and materials.
- Information: QM principles are applied in the field of quantum computing. Quantum computers use quantum bits, or qubits, to perform must faster than classical computers.
- Biology: QM is used to study behavior of biological systems at a molecular level leading to a better understanding of biological processes, such as photosynthesis and enzyme catalysis.
- Astrophysics: QM is used to study particle behavior in extreme environments, such as black holes and neutron stars. This has led to a better understanding of the universe and its origins.

Dirac's equation and Feynman's corrections laid the ground for quantum physics as it is practiced today and the expansion of quantum physics into the sciences as well as technology.

So again, what's Quantum Physics to you. **EVERYTHING.**

34

CHRISTMAS 2010
34th Epistle of Jim

Here is yet another yuletide missive from your Christmas Curmudgeon. I wrote this in the Keys, so at least it's mostly warm. Having experienced over 60 of them, I can say that a white Christmas is over-rated. Did it snow in Bethlehem on the first one? – not likely; Christ was probably born in early autumn, while our Christmas day was originally a pagan holiday. Those of you who reside above 35^0 latitude or 4000' altitude deserve white Christmas.

Judy discovered quilting this summer, considered by many to be an art form. It consisted of scouring Michigan for material and then meticulously and tirelessly sewing little squares of it together. Judy spent several weeks each to make some way cool quilts for Oliver, Ian, and Kate. They were transformed into Thanksgiving presents when she showed them off at Thanksgiving requiring additional presents for Christmas.

Last year we visited Jamison and family in LA for Christmas and took a lap around Arizona and New Mexico. We walked the entire Las Vegas strip and stayed two days at the Grand Canyon because a snowstorm obliterated visibility on the first day. Santa Fe was 10^0F! Not a retirement temperature. AZ and NM are cold in the north, with no water and Mexican gangsters in the south; great scenery, but not a residence option. Global warming would make Beaver Island perfect.

Jeff came from Australia for business in San Francisco, New York, and Chicago. He took a 50-minute flight from Chicago and met us in Traverse City. Getting off Beaver Island can be problematic which, in fact, turned out to be an understatement. The ferry did not run because the 40mph winds with 50mph gusts were making 12'-20' waves in Lake Michigan, so we flew; proving age doesn't guarantee wisdom. The six-passenger plane was tethered on the ground with a rope securing each wing to a truck. Gusting winds create significant up lift followed by a down draft, which resulted in an exciting take off and an even more exciting landing.

Lauren at Syracuse University and Nicole at Brown in Providence are now acquiring knowledge for $$$$$; both are close to New York City precipitating a Thanksgiving dinner and housing plan for 13 Joneses at John and Patty's house. 13 self-actualized Joneses in one spot and a first-floor remodeling in progress with no kitchen on the Friday before Thanksgiving with no sink or running water on Tuesday is the definition of chaos. Patty baked pies while the sink and dishwasher were installed on late Wednesday. By Thanksgiving, she had cooked six pies and a 21 lb. turkey with all of the trimmings in her belated, beautiful Just-In-Time kitchen.

To protect us from 'passionate' island environmentalists, I again violated my 'don't frustrate yourself by participation rule' and volunteered to be on the Beaver Island Natural Resources and Ecotourism Commission. We didn't want to be ushered off the island to protect some endangered species like dwarf irises or monkey flowers. I proposed that Beaver Island be a socio/eco-model and laboratory since it is one of the most bio-diverse and endangered of 32,000 Great Lakes islands. The controversies and hostilities around the modeling idea would make a great reality TV comedy. Earth can obviously take care of itself, but some restoration may be necessary for it to continue to sustain us.

I completed the 18th draft of the book entitled: Faith and Reason. For a pre-publication copy, send an email to: jimijones@aol.com and promise to return a critique within a month of receiving the book. This little 90-page book grew out of pub discussions with Father Joe Hopkins, S.J. in the late 1960s. The book describes the faith and reason necessary to illustrate God's immanence in the universe and is partially explained by Philosopher / Mathematician Alfred North Whitehead's theory of organism that embraces the sciences in support of the authority of religion:

"The order of the world, the depth of reality of the world, the value of the world in its whole and in its parts, the beauty of the world, the zest of life, the peace of life, and the mastery of evil, are all bound together - not accidentally, but by reason of this truth: that the universe exhibits a creativity with infinite freedom, and a realm of forms with infinite possibilities; but that this creativity and these forms are together impotent to achieve actuality apart from the completed ideal harmony, which is God."

We wish for you a life that harmonizes creativity with infinite freedom, and a realm of forms with infinite possibilities.

Reflection 34: Permaculture

Participation on the BI Eco-tourism Commission resulted in me being conscripted into an Island Permaculture project. Sep Holzer in Austria and Bill Mollison and David Holmgren in Tasmania "invented" Permaculture which has three ethics: care of earth, care of people and fair share, and 12 Principles:

1. *observe and interact* with nature to design solutions that suit the environment.
2. *catch and store energy* in systems that collect resources at peak abundance as needed.
3. *obtain a yield* to get truly useful rewards as part of the work.
4. *apply self-regulation and accept feedback* to ensure that systems function well.
5. *use and value renewable resources and services* to reduce dependence on non-renewable resources.
6. *produce no waste* by valuing and making use of all available resources.
7. *design from patterns to details* in nature and society to form the backbone of designs.
8. *integrate rather than segregate* by putting right things in the right place to support each other.
9. *use small and slow solutions* that use local resources and produce more sustainable outcomes.
10. *use and value diversity* to reduce vulnerability to threats and take advantage of the local environment.
11. *use edges and value the marginal* to leverage the diverse, and productive elements in the system.
12. *creatively use and respond to change* by carefully observing, and then intervening at the right time.

Full disclosure: my unsubstantiated opinion of how permaculture is proceeding in the USA, Australia, and Austria appears to be an unscientific whole earth religion which may be the best way to promote it but not the best way to feed billions of starving people. The island permaculture group rejected my proposal that follows.

Permaculture Project Description.

Objectives: Design, plant, harvest crops in a permaculture garden.

Method/Approach: Define a portfolio of programs and science projects where the primary labor force will be K-12 students, teachers, parents, and a permaculture project coordinator.

The portfolio of projects will be integrated with school curriculum: plant biology, statistics, geometry/trigonometry, ecology cycles, conservation, and agriculture. Beyond the K-12 curriculum, researchers, parents, teachers, and the community would be introduced to complexity theory, agricultural engineering, aesthetic / functional Permaculture design, Adaptive Management and Portfolio, Program and Project Management. A portfolio of projects for food production are defined in the context of a sustainable community guided by the Green Globe[1] Standard. A Design of Experiments varies critical parameters in the permaculture plots to accelerate evolution of Best Practices.

Outputs and outcomes:
- Food from the permaculture garden.
- Validated list of Key Performance Indicators (KPIs) for projects.
- Performance statistics from monitoring KPIs.
- Agricultural Engineering K-12 subjects to complete the project.
- Problems and solutions that were relevant to the projects.
- Two journal papers to outline Best Practices: one for education and one for permaculture design.
- Assessment of community's transformation to permaculture rather than shrubs, flowers, and grass.

Portfolio of Permaculture Laboratory Programs

Program 1: Permaculture Garden

KPIs: Soil Quality Measures, Food and Nutrient Volume yield.
- Project 1.1: Design Garden and Prepare Soil.
- Project 1.2: Plant and Manage Garden and report progress.
- Project 1.3: Harvest Food

Program 2: Community Outreach

KPIs: # Students, Teachers, Parents, other and # private gardens

---

[1] The Green Globe program began at the UN Rio de Janeiro Earth Summit in 1992, where 182 heads of state endorsed principles of sustainable development. By 1998 Green Globe's program was extended to corporations and communities and its membership rose to 500 in 100 countries. A strategic alliance was formed with the Sustainable Tourism Cooperative Research Center in Australia to act as a global research facility on sustainable tourism and promote Green Globe's program. Its standard includes principles for A] Sustainable Management (9), B] Social-Economic Systems (9), C] Cultural Heritage (4) and D] Environment (3).

- Project 2.1: Set up a Program Infrastructure (Program Office, PM Info System, Volunteers)
- Project 2.2: Charter a Permaculture Community of Practice.
- Project 2.3: Meet regularly; communicate progress; assign work.

Program 3: STEM Education

KPIs: Science and Math Test Scores
- Project 3.1: Define a science K-12 permaculture curriculum.
- Project 3.2: Develop a permaculture laboratory guidebook.
- Project 3.3: Establish Design of Experiments for permaculture.

Proposal Notes: Permaculture and STEM

Goal: Support STEM education through the design and implementation of a Permaculture Garden

Strategy: Guide Permaculture Garden development with science and mathematics.

Approach: The students (and parents) will learn elements of scientific, mathematical, and engineering disciplines:
- Permaculture design: identify mathematical curves for seed disbursement and other plants for aesthetic appeal.
- Agricultural Engineering – introduce agricultural engineering concepts for farm management.
- Geometry and Trigonometry – define curve types and geometry to model seed disbursement.
- Design of Experiments – Identify and measure key soil, seed type/disbursement, & nutrient parameters.
- Statistical Quality Control – define and measure processes, times and variation and product variation.
- Plant Biology – Identify plants best suited for fertilization and ongoing food production.
- Ecology cycles – Develop a model of the cycles involved in food production to facilitate measurement.
- Concepts in conservation – Postulate how to get the best food production over time.
- Complexity Theory – Use the ecology cycles to introduce complexity models necessary for analysis.
- Adaptive Management Methods - optimize the proposed approach to permaculture.

Design Aesthetics: may (or may not) be a key factor in the disbursement of permaculture in a community. Many people spend significant effort, time and money gardening for aesthetic reasons only. Design permaculture gardens that people consider beautiful to tend rather than their current lawn and garden. This may include flowers and green ground cover that can act as fertilizer.

Scientific Method: Permaculture is full of unsubstantiated assumptions and evolved by trial and error with little mathematical or statistical analysis. Also, various concepts taken as fact are not; e.g. pesticides and chemical fertilizers are bad, organic is better, genetically modified plants are bad. This and other permaculture dogma meet no standard of scientific truth. Part of a SCIENTIFIC permaculture study must consider if the judicious measured use of chemical fertilizer, pesticides and genetically modified seeds are in fact bad or would significantly improve the yield and quality of food generated by a permaculture garden.

Portfolio: programs and projects are defined to guide teachers and researchers in the design, implementation, and operation of the Permaculture Garden (ref: PMI Body of Knowledge).

STEM Community of Practice will be established to inform and educate the community.

Process models of permaculture are developed and revised based on informed research.

KPIs are developed and measurements will be taken to assess, adapt and direct progress.

Curriculum is outlined for student subjects with problems that can be formulated and solved by applying the curriculum in subjects for Permaculture research, design, and adaptive management.

Models: Students will be introduced to concepts from environmental literature, complex systems and models as well as applying concepts from their STEM curriculum.

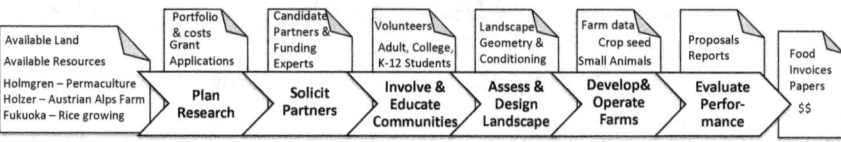

35

CHRISTMAS 2011
35th Epistle of Jim

Yahhuh, Judy and I are celebrating our 70th Christmas. Judy is reveling in the joys and retail ambience of the season, while I contemplate its absurdities (e.g. pepper spray shoppers to get to a toy). Did you catch that I am 70% of the way to a century. Aaauuuugh. Stress of the aging process as the downhill ride gets steeper and faster is commonly known as Geezer Anxiety Syndrome. GAS precipitated my intense emotional need for dark red, heavy, thick, silky, integrated wine. I went right out and bought a case of too expensive Australian Shiraz. As you will see, this was not enough to alleviate my emotional crisis emanating from my GAS. Also notice that my GAS was not so debilitating as to overcome my inherent cheapness since I purchased $Australian Shiraz$ as opposed to $$$$French Bordeaux$$$$$.

After becoming a geezer in April, Judy and I celebrated our 48th wedding anniversary in June with dinner and a too expensive wine at the Rowe Inn in Ellsworth, Michigan, where they have a relaxed atmosphere, gourmet food, and one of the best wine cellars in Michigan. As luck would have it, in the course of an extended discussion, the proprietress lamented that her clientele would not buy wine over five years old. She then uttered the magic words: 30% discount on wine older than five years; this resulted in a significant expenditure for a case of too expensive wine. This relieved my GAS and ended my abnormal need for retail therapy.

Judy has enjoyed a very busy time this year painting; this of course turns our entire house, except for my one little corner office, into an art gallery. She 'discovered' the joy of painting birds. Her birds have personality: Mafia cardinal, killer hawk, professor pelican, baby and stern mother eagle, pedantic parrot, and rowdy roosters. Her sheep all have a happy vacant Alfred E. Newman stare.

As if painting were not enough, Judy was also on the Baroque on Beaver Board of Directors (BoB-BOD). This involves significant amounts of work, requiring me to be marginally supportive. The BoB-BOD brings 40 professional musicians from all over

Michigan to Beaver Island. While on the island, they performed seven concerts. Since I'm only semi-cultured, I attended only four, but I provided moral, schlepping, and bartending support.

Grandson Aidan in Australia graduated from high school in December and will start university in January in Australia. Granddaughters Lauren at Syracuse and Nicole at Brown are in their sophomore years. I would conjecture that Jeff and Jamison had something equivalent to a GAS attack as they wrote multiple five figure checks each year to educate our grandchildren. Thank you.

Since Judy and I spend summers on the shore in northern Michigan and winters surrounded by the Atlantic Ocean in the Florida Keys, we don't get much sympathy about the weather, but I try. In the winter, I called friends in the north and lamented the hardships of having to keep out of the sun while trying to keep cool in the middle of the day. Responses were spectacularly unsympathetic.

Another GAS exacerbator is the maintenance required to take up residence after a house sits empty for six months. This year was especially exacerbating; in our absence, our Beaver Island house rafters became a condo for 95 bats. Everyone who does not have resident bats informed us about how eco-friendly they are and that they eat 3000 insects per night. They also crap toxic guano. Evicting them was way expensive and really pissed off the bats who spent several days literally hanging around outside the house.

I printed (not published) the 20th draft of yet another book: Faith and Reason. I argue that both faith and reason are required to understand God's purpose for us: unreasoned faith produced infamous atrocities, but without faith there is no place to start reasoning. I sent it to 25 people. Response was spectacularly underwhelming. Some people just want to believe and didn't like the idea that faith required reason. Other people could not acknowledge that reason required faith. The book's last page had a quote by Douglas Hofstadter on consciousness and reality:

"Poised midway between unvisualizable cosmic vastness of curved space-time and the dubious, shadowy flickering of charged quanta, we human beings, more like rainbows and mirages than like raindrops or boulders, are unpredictable self-writing poems: vague, metaphorical, ambiguous, and sometimes exceedingly beautiful."

We begin to comprehend 'Reality' only with mathematical abstractions, imagination, personal transcendence, and faith. We wish you the transcendent Christmas joy beyond imagination.

Reflection 35: Knowledge from Noise

As I struggled with the idea of "Faith and Reason," I was led to the idea that God nudges humanity toward divine wisdom in the noise and nonsense of life. Remember from Reflection 23, a document may contain noise, data, information, or knowledge and every useful act can be viewed as: Knowledge flow to value.

Wisdom
Understanding
Knowledge
Information & Observations
Facts & Data
Noise & Nonsense & Novelty

Noise > Data > Information > knowledge (tacit, skills, prescriptive)

Value = Artifact (for an Engineer)

Flow represents an organization's processes.

Knowledge validates information.

The figure represents an extension to Reflection 23 and are standard knowledge definitions from Knowledge management which over-simplistically derive one from another.

- Noise (or novelty/) is any undifferentiated thing assaulting the senses; it is pervasive, ubiquitous, auditory, visual, textural.
- Data is derived noise when it transcends the purely sensual and has cognitive pattern; when it can be discerned and differentiated by the mind (this transition of noise to data is not that easy).
- Information is derived from data when it is assembled into a coherent whole which can be related to other information in a way that adds meaning . . . a difference that makes a difference.
- Knowledge is derived from verified, validated information when it has interacted with other information in a useful form (knowledge is validated, trusted information: ISO 15489).
- Understanding is derived from knowledge when related to other knowledge in a manner useful in conceiving, anticipating, evaluating, and judging.
- Wisdom comes from understanding when informed by purpose, ethics, principle, past memory and future projections.

Novelty can be revealed as a mathematical extrapolation or scientific theory but, most new knowledge is revealed by intuition – seeing things in ways never observed before. Art, literature, Newton's Laws, Darwin's Theory, Confucius' analects, Christ's parables, engineering, mathematics, architecture, science, and technology are evidence of a continuous stream of revelation.

Extracting data, information, and knowledge from Internet noise and real life can be an extensive time-consuming process. There may be novelty in the noise that could precipitate a new reality. Knowledge Management implies data is simply (???) derived from noise (and novelty) which is not that easy as is shown in the table.

• data recorded with uncalibrated instruments	• conclusions from cherry picked facts
• false statements and theories	• conclusion derived from out-of-context knowledge
• unsubstantiated claims to be scientific	• knowledge imbedded in a cloud of nonsense
• irrelevant statements about a person's activities	• assertions falsely claiming scientific derivation
• observations derived from bad data	
• information that incorrectly summarizes data	• claims of causation from correlation in data
• information derived from an inadequate subset of data	• hypothesis posing as (untested) theories
• large volumes of irrelevant data (AI, Big Data)	• corrupt data, information, knowledge anomalies

Knowledge includes tacit, skills, empirical, prescriptive, and scientific knowledge constrained by maintainability and sustainability. These categories are centered on learning various processes to acquire knowledge in engineering and technology.

Tacit Knowledge cannot be explained or justified; it has an important role in many forms of craftsmanship. E.g., drywallers can seldom explain the hand movements by which they even out a surface faster, and with three times less spackling, than me.

Engineering may attempt to systemize tacit knowledge by:
- Mechanizing a work process performed by craftspeople.
- Teaching to make learning a skill possible without a long apprenticeship.
- Controlling other people's work by codifying the extensive (tacit and explicit) knowledge of experienced workers into subtasks that are easier to teach, learn, and perform.

Practical Rule Knowledge: Developed by trial and error as "rule-of-thumb" such as making load-bearing parts strong enough to carry twice the intended load but with no theory to choose '2' as a safety factor. With rule-of-thumb knowledge, it can often be routinized making it possible to perform a task without attention.

Systematic Engineering Knowledge is obtained through studies by engineering scientists in universities and industry.

Technological development has been driven by craftsmen systematically trying out different constructions and methods.

Applied Natural Science: Engineers were educated in math and physics to employ natural science to develop new technology. Knowledge comes from many areas: physics, chemistry, biology, and earth sciences. Technology is now based on natural science, tacit and rule knowledge, and knowledge based on systematic investigations of technological constructs.

Idealization in Engineering restricts one's attention to certain important properties to study an object and not get lost in detail. Idealization distorts the original design or it can leave aside components in a complex object to better focus on those remaining.

Engineering science has important metaphysical and epistemological differences from natural science:
- It provides value to humans rather than search for physical truth.
- It serves the needs of a practical profession, namely engineers.
- Its ultimate objects of study are human made, not natural objects.
- Its objects must be understood in terms of complex combinations of physical and functional characteristics.
- It incorporates forms of systematized action-guiding knowledge not based on natural science.
- It operates on a less abstract level than the natural sciences and refrains from many of their idealizations.

Novelty is something incomprehensively new, not predetermined by knowledge requiring theory, validation, and subsequent generalization into one or more forms of engineering knowledge.

36

CHRISTMAS 2012
36th Epistle of Jim

Judy and I will celebrate our 50th Wedding Anniversary next June; congratulations to me and condolences to Judy. I married up. Surprisingly, Christmas is fast approaching, and I haven't gotten myself too grumped up yet.

We celebrated our 49th Wedding Anniversary with dinner and a way too expensive wine at the Rowe Inn in Ellsworth, MI again. After extensive negotiations with hostess/sommelier/owner Laurel, I bought a case of wine. She insinuated that I was cheap. I call it value engineering. We drank most of the wine at John's house in NYC at Thanksgiving. The LA Jones family was also there, so we were with John, Patty, Jamison, Lisa and six of our grandchildren. Twelve people in a house with 1.5 baths required a shower schedule. Judy and I had the premium library suite on our blowup bed with the esteemed benefit of its adjacency to the 0.5 bath.

Judy has evolved to becoming a doggy portrait painter along with sheep, birds, and landscapes. Our houses are studios with multiple art projects. While dabbing on 2-4 canvases simultaneously, Judy extends her creative talents with knitting and quilting projects along with gardening (but that's mostly outside). Judy also flew to LA for two weeks this year while Jamison swashbuckled through The Three Musketeers in Denver. Niece Rebecca and her parents attended the opening; Lisa went later. Alas, we did not.

John and Jeff are putting their media skills to good use. John assembled and presented a 39 media display event in Times Square to introduce Microsoft's Windows 8. Jeff just finished a 54 media display center called the cube for Queensland University of Technology. Forty years ago, I labored mightily for twelve months to put line graphics on one digital display, now the guys display color animation on multiple displays in a few months.

Grandson Aidan has started university at QUT in Brisbane as a Math major; it's in the genes:-). Granddaughters Lauren at Parsons in NYC and Nicole at Brown in Rhode Island are in their junior year. Anna will start high school in January in Brisbane. Christopher has his own band and hopes to attend Skidmore in upstate New York next year. Daniel had singing leads surrounded by girls in two school plays. Chris and Dan have discovered the one immutable law of sociology: music attracts females. Kate loves softball; playing ball with your granddaughter is way cool except for the pulled calf muscle. Old age comes at a bad time.

We actually had a summer with eight weeks of 70^0-90^0 weather on Beaver Island this year; where summer can come and go on August 15th. Spending summers on the Beaver Island shore and winters surrounded by ocean in the Keys is great, but getting back and forth seems more formidable as I sink into the quagmire of geezerhood.

Just when Judy and I congratulated ourselves on an uneventful, rain free trip from Michigan to NYC to Florida, pieces of a bearing and piston rod began rattling around in the engine. After six hours with various mechanics and service people, Vero Beach Chrysler agreed to absorb most of the cost of a new engine under warranty. We arrived in the Keys in a rental car at a grumpy 11pm instead of a jolly 3pm, with an unhappy 12 hour round trip a week later.

Because we left late, we saw snow and even worse an Oct-Nov heat bill; breathtaking. It may be cheaper to have a house at 25° latitude to avoid heating a house at 45° latitude. Here is a counterintuitive case where less latitude is better.

In working for Jeff, I sat alone in a loft office at 45° north latitude (half way to the North Pole) pontificating on work group processes and behaviors for companies at 27° south latitude. The Internet helps me maintain the delusion that I am an island and an expert; an expert resides over 9,000 miles away (from 45.3° N 85.3° W to 27.5° S 153.0° E is 9040 miles). For you navigators, I retain expert status in Key West (24.5° N 81.8° W) as well.

I finished the 24th draft of the book, Faith and Reason, and will publish it sometime in the spring. Based on comments that previous versions were arcane and turgid, five people may read this version; so the good news is that for lack of interest, I probably won't be stoned for heresy. The book evolved over the last 40 years starting in tavern discussions with Jesuit Priest Joe Hopkins; he may be pleased or will just roll over in his grave. I will send a copy if you ask and critique. 'Duh' or 'ugh' are unacceptable comments.

We wish for faith in the light of Christmas and search for truth and God precipitated by reason in the New Year

Reflection 36: Value from Knowledge Flow

I went through various stages to establish a foundation for how value for humanity is precipitated. The argument for a system engineering methodology assumes that for an organization (or religion) to be viable, it must deliver 'value' of some sort. This section will postulate the types of value that may make an artifact (product, service or religion) appeal to people. Value of an object or service has many different aspects outlined in the table.

Quality	NASA Systems Engineering Guide, Standards: ISO 9001 / ISO15489, 6 Sigma
Ethics Morality	IEEE Code of Conduct, Hippocratic Oath, etc... Seven Virtues, Seven Sins, Mores, Duty, Rules Theology: Panentheism, Christianity; Islam; Judaism; Hinduism; Daoism
Economy Industry	NPV, ROI, CBA in 19 Sectors: Manufacturing, Healthcare, Energy, Aerospace, Agriculture, Computer, Telecommunication, Education, Construction, Electronics, Mining, Transport, Pharmaceutical, Entertainment, World Wide Web, News Media, Music, Food, Hospitality
Health	Medicare with co-pays based on age: 50% young to 20% old to 0% Vet Michael Porter's IPU for Healthcare Delivery, APQC for organizations
Social Science	Utopia: Plato, Jesus, Thomas More, John Rawls=anti-dystopian Law (prevention dystopia): Hobbes (Leviathan), Montesquieu (Democracy), Locke, Smith, Rousseau (Social Contract), Habermas (legitimation), WEF GCI
Ecological Science	2018 WEF GCI with IoT and sustainability criteria, world model Energy – Hybrid vehicles, EVs, NG pipelines, Constrained Fracking Local Solar, Wind/Hydroelectric/Upgraded Nuclear power Habitat – GMO fertilizer/pesticides/crops (increase yield/soil restoration) Sensible lumbering – strip cut NOT clear-cut forests
Human Needs (Maslow)	1. Biological/physiological: air, food, drink, shelter, warmth, sex, sleep 2. Safety: protection from elements, security, order, law, stability, etc. 3. Love/belonging: friends, intimacy, trust, acceptance: family, work. 4. Esteem: dignity, achievement, mastery, respect (status, prestige). 5. Cognitive: knowledge, curiosity, exploration, meaning, predictability. 6. Aesthetic: appreciation, search for beauty, balance, form, etc. 7. Self-actualization: realize personal potential, seek personal growth. 8. Transcendence: beyond self (mysticism, nature, service, science, religion)

Value is usually guided less by ethics and intellectual pursuits than it is by utility, recreation, comfort, and security. An extensive view of value and novelty contends that engineering transforms humankind by leveraging natural laws (e.g. Biology, Physics, Chemistry, Sociology) to create new and novel artifacts. Engineering must evolve to provide a system and discipline that is morally guided and sustainable. Value must:

1] Benefit Individual well-being,

2] Precipitate and validate novelty,

3] Charge societies with value,

4] Provide a foundation for creation of desirable artifacts.

Maslow's account of human behavior focused on what goes right not on what goes wrong. He stated that human motivation is based on people seeking fulfillment and change through personal growth doing all they are capable of. A person finds meaning in life that is important to each him/her self. Motivation for self-actualization leads people differently: creating works of art, literature, sport, classroom, or corporate success. Maslow's categories are useful for guiding an engineer in developing an artifact, but his idea that one must ascend from level 1 to 8 is problematic.

Consider Victor Frankl's premise that humans are motivated by a "will to meaning," an inner pull to find a meaning in life. His six assumptions of 'Logotherapy' include:
1. The human being is an entity consisting of the body and mind.
2. Life has meaning under all circumstances, even if miserable.
3. People have a will to meaning; it prepares them for suffering.
4. People always have freedom to activate the will to find meaning.
5. Life presents demands; good decisions must follow conscience.
6. Individuals are unique; in situations, one looks to find meaning.

Value = Artifact (for an Engineer) which
- Is derived in engineering design between developer, his organization and customer (or marketing).
- Satisfies Cost Benefit Analysis for an organization constrained by value for a sustainable society.
- Improves socioeconomic criteria measured by Net Present Value, Balanced Score Card, and GDP.
- Has Many different aspects as identified in the table and Frankl's will to meaning.

Engineers gain significant insights by modeling knowledge flow to value. Organizational and government bureaucrats have had no model of knowledge flow to value to set sustainable policies. Solutions are proposed based on value to them and frequently inflict more problems than they solve. Bureaucrats must know how its organization's knowledge flows to value to set policy to outline a portfolio that better leverages existing skills, processes, and technology that improves the delivery and quality of its artifacts.

37

CHRISTMAS 2013

37th Epistle of Jim

I continue my annual search for that illusive Christmas Spirit: Bah Humbug. We've been in the Keys since October where it feels more like July than December. A newsworthy cold front here is 65^0F. After living in Michigan for 65 years, having the A/C on at Christmas feels surreal, but very nice.

We celebrated our wedding anniversary in June: half a century! Congratulations to us. We stayed at the Odawa Casino in Petoskey for two nights and had our anniversary dinner at the Rowe Inn in Elsworth. We also celebrated in NYC with John's family and drank Dom Perignon - a present from Jeff.

I am restoring my 24'/30 year old sailboat. What's a few thousand dollars when the price of a new one is $40,000 and rising as our dollars devaluate. I am also Judy's dofer with house-painting and new-floor projects. Judy keeps painting; the artistic version; Judy has 30 paintings hanging in the living room and another 20 in other rooms; ten are for the birds (e.g., pelican, parrot, eagle, heron, etc.).

After receiving several critiques of my book, "Faith and Reason," I will rewrite it ONE more time. Maybe it's not too late for a little "divine inspiration." Speaking of the divinely inspired, I sent a copy of the book to the new Pope six weeks ago, but he hasn't gotten back with me yet. He must still be reading it or he trashed it.

Jeff, John, and Jamison all have college age children. Have you taken a look at tuition? Holy deficiticy. Unfortunately, only the Feds can print money without risking incarceration.

I have been irrationally rationalizing sailing from California to New Zealand and beyond; not to worry, not in my 24 footer, but maybe in a 38 footer. Some old people get delusional. Judy and I may take a transatlantic cruise (big boat, good food, etc.) to get a better idea of the delusion of a transpacific adventure. I have less life to screw up, so I better move while I have moving parts. We wish you a happy and an adventurous New Year.

Reflection 37: Engineering Philosophy

Alfred North Whitehead's *Theory of Organism*, contributed significantly to my *Faith and Reason* book as well as to a philosophy of engineering. He proposes that the only reality is process, and that objects change moment to moment. One may perceive a rock as the ultimate fundamental unchanging object, but at the quantum level it changes every nanosecond (it keeps its shape by obeying physical laws). One sees projections of reality, considerably altered by one's fields of consciousness.

New knowledge can be revealed from mathematics, or science but Eastern sages argue new knowledge is revealed only through "divine inspiration" in transcendent meditation with the Absolute. When a novel insight is revealed to an engineer with respect to a problem, it will be used to create value in an artifact. The question to be answered for an engineer is: how do I transcend my limited perception of reality to acquire novel insights? Whitehead proposes all reality is a dynamic stream of consciousness. He segments perception into three stages[2] providing a detailed view of how one's mind processes external stimuli as constituted in the past (causal efficacy), as taken up into the present (presentational immediacy) and as reference to immediate future (symbolic reference). Since the two primitive modes of perception are incapable of error, symbolic reference (human consciousness) can introduce it.

Whitehead's ultimate principle of reality is a process event called an *occasion*.[3] Creativity does not exist in any other form than occasions. Whitehead says that creativity is *novelty of instance*. Novelty of instance is a new result derived from previously actualized old data; *novelty of kind* introduces new data into the stream of process. God influences novelty of instance in all things identified by 'descriptive words' such as 'yellow' and 'car.' There are an infinite number of these eternal objects.

---

[2] **Causal Efficacy** is represented by fields of consciousness, where humans are unconsciously influenced by objects in their past before perceiving something with their senses.
Presentational Immediacy is when one's senses perceive the external environment and projects it into symbols of mind interpreted by past objects.
Symbolic Reference is the conscious process whereby symbols transition into meaning when causal efficacy and presentational immediacy elicit consciousness, beliefs, emotions, and usages. No one directly perceives external reality.
[3] **Occasions** apply not just to human apperception, but to animals, plants, rocks, etc. and all reality from atom to cosmos.

Eternal objects[4] 'exist' as potential but are activated only when an occasion realizes a particular combination of objects. An observer prehends in a mode of causal efficacy to anticipate the appearance of "a yellow car" in his stream of consciousness. Upon perceiving a vehicle in the mode of presentational immediacy, he limits occasion with his subjective aim[5]: model and color.

Value is tied to Occasion through the harmonizing of prehensions (god's consequent nature) with eternal objects (god's primordial nature). Aspects of value are the building blocks for individual and societal ethics. Whitehead defines God as immanent and primordial in the universe and the purveyor of all knowledge in the form of eternal objects (much like Plato's Forms), which exist prior to all perception of reality. We as humans approximate these eternal objects into disciplines: e.g., engineering physics, genetics, literature, music, etc. Whitehead contends novel ideas result from intuiting reality and the harmonizing influence of God (abduction).

Whitehead and Peirce assert that aesthetics and imagination are essential for novelty, apart from which knowledge cannot increase. Reason is not described as opposite to (aesthetic) sentiment and imagination, while reason is not reduced to sentiment. Novelty undermines all forms of determinism and materialism at all levels of logical discourse. Once novelty is admitted, this kind of approach must be abandoned, and requires a new understanding of experience, knowledge, and the universe as advocated by Sanders Firstness and Whitehead's god's primordial and consequent nature.

Maslow's hierarchy of human needs that identify what humans value and along with cost/benefits, ethics, sustainability, etc are used to define what is valued in the engineering of artifacts.

Kuhn's paradigms describe how engineers communicate effectively and also provide the foundation for explaining how engineering precipitates radical change when novel ideas are validated.

---

[4] **Plato's Theory of Forms** asserts that non-material abstract forms (or ideas), and not the material world of change known to us from sensation, possess the highest and most fundamental reality. To Plato, Forms are the only true objects of study that can provide genuine knowledge. Whitehead's eternal objects are the application to process reality of Plato's Forms.

[5] **Subjective Aim**: a projected concrete form in which to resolve diversity of feelings of the primary phases of the process. From prehending data and admittance of new possibilities comes a unified ideal for the end result.

These philosophers' ideas provide the foundation for how engineers ideate and think, communicate, and work in groups to design, develop, validate, prototype, redesign for manufacture, manage themselves, and manufacture artifacts. They must consider consumers, management, quality, cost, development, material availability, manufacturability, maintainability, standards, codes of ethics, and societal constraints.

Society has been transformed to its detriment and benefit by artifacts developed by engineers. Most engineers eschew society; so, we have engineers transforming society who are unconcerned with its consequences. Lawyers and others who govern society know little about how anything works. To engineer novel artifacts, a Theology of Engineering (Reflection 40) has been identified as the source of revelation to create novel artifacts by engineers. Also, since over two thirds of the world's population believe in God, God must be considered as an element of value for people and society.

System engineering methodology based on *knowledge flow to value* must be employed to coordinate all disciplines to resolve legitimation crises emerging in societies and the environment that were precipitated by engineers' artifacts. Improving prosperity and sustainability within a community is a wonderfully complex problem. A system engineering methodology must be built upon the explicit and implicit flow of knowledge through functions to deliver value. It must use static and dynamic models to provide the facts to measure, manage and transform environments. Process models must support every aspect of engineering.

Rather than simply generating profit, engineering must improve quality-of-life, while minimizing impact on environment, and supporting the economy as a Complex Adaptive System (CAS). From a system engineering perspective, societies, organizations, and the environment are a CAS that is only partially understood by governments, management, scientists, and engineers. Multiple problems will require a portfolio of projects within programs to manage, schedule, and use environmental resources and engineered artifacts which can denigrate or sustain the environment.

System Engineering is critical because it represents the ways in which engineering projects are managed within and between its mechanical, electrical and information disciplines. This System Engineering view absent mathematics and statistics, can inform and educate people about the sophisticated, comprehensive and successful ways engineers engineer.

38

CHRISTMAS 2014
38th Epistle of Jim

My usual trepidation about Christmas was exacerbated by the lunacy of an IRS claim that I owed them enough money to significantly contribute to reducing the national debt. I missed a 1099. Recalculating my tax liability indicated an underpayment of 35 times less than the IRS estimate. I breathlessly await their reply. Moral: triple check your tax submission.

I was looking forward to global warming on Beaver Island, but it has been renamed climate change by Ecology Evangelists to my everlasting dismay. I was hoping for four seasons on the island instead of the customary winter-spring-fall. Since Islanders enjoyed 12 feet of snow last winter, previously dry wetlands for the last six years were again wet. This created a six-week mosquito season. While I huddled in the house, Judy worked in the garden fully covered with a head net to avoid the need for a transfusion.

After 73 years of ignoring cautions about sun damage, my skin failed me in the form of various distractingly ugly rashes, which were treated by the doctor with drugs in the anthrax prevention category; with three pages of side effects including extreme sun sensitivity. I now have something to talk about at cocktail parties when the conversation turns to body part replacement and skin cancers. Judy and I both had a couple of skin cancers, but they were too mild to be adequate for geezer cocktail conversations.

Judy continues to paint, knit, and quilt. Frequently, she has four to six projects active, which cover every available surface and much of the floor space. She loves to paint plants, but her real genius is painting birds, dogs and cats with personality. She continues to put her art in shows and is dismayed when it sells. She enjoys her own creations. We have over sixty paintings hanging in each house. In a stroke of genius, I encouraged her to hang up paintings instead of leaving them in piles, thereby making more surface area available while distracting her from the idea that the Keys house needs paint.

I would very much like to reduce our travel between winter and summer residences from 5000 miles to 0. However, Judy has a legitimate concern that all her stuff might end up in the ocean during a visit from a wind named George or Wilma. We checked out a couple of places with four seasons. Beaufort, SC was more than 50% wetland (swamp) and looked like it might have a three-month mosquito season called summer. Smith Mountain Lake, VA looked good to me, but not so good to Judy despite having the largest Kroger store in Virginia. We both liked Fernandina, FL where one historic house was occupied by my father in his youth.

I have devolved from sailor to marine repairer as I spent more time refurbishing sailboats than sailing. Standing rigging is what holds up the mast. Being corroded and frayed, I began to imagine it failing while under sail resulting in breaking the mast and having the mast tear out a large portion of the deck. Judy might not be too happy about that. She has just recently convinced herself to sail again after watching me cruise by the Beaver Island house upside down in our Hobie headed for Chicago.

I just finished the 31st draft of "Faith and Reason" and sent it to the printer for yet another prepublication printing. I continue to amaze myself with the breadth and depth of my ignorance. This version has been significantly impacted by Eastern theology. On a positive note, I received a reply on a 28th prepublication copy that I sent to the Vatican. It also included an autographed picture of Pope Francesco. Our Catholic friends were far more impressed by the two-line Pontifical reply and picture than they were with my book.

It was surprising to me that Jesus was held in such high regard by Eastern sages as reflected in the books: "The Sermon on the Mount according to Vedanta" and "Living Buddha, Living Christ." Eastern sages claim each of the major religions is a path to realization of the Ultimate Reality, which is the true goal and purpose of human life. Each person should remain steadfast in his own religion as a path to his ultimate manifestation in God. Isn't that just amazing!!??: Eastern religions don't think that you go to hell if you don't believe their way.

We wish for you during this holiday season a spiritual harmony with self, family, community, and God. Namaste.

Reflection 38: Legislative Lunacy

My IRS problem could have been avoided with simple straight forward bank reporting rules. But no, the more regulations requiring oversight assures employment in federal agencies.

If anyone wants to know why I think lawyers shouldn't be writing laws, buy the book: "The Affordable Care Act" (ACA – Obama Care). It's 624 pages, single space, 10-point font with maybe 100 pages of law and 500 pages of gibberish. Yes, I have read most of it as well as multiple summaries including California's summary and implementation of the law. Parts of it are used in Reflection 44 on fixing USA healthcare.

So originally, I thought our major government problem is that we are governed by a confederacy of clowns. I could list some, but just read today's news to see what nonsense government has inflicted on the American people as with Obama Care. However, this is only the tip of the legislative lunacy iceberg. In the 4th revision of their book, *Rulemaking*, Kerwin and Furlong introduce the Administrative Procedure Act (APA) that was enacted into law in 1946. APA has been the spawn of the massive legislative lunacy that is now inflicted on all American. The APA defines a Rule to mean: "the whole or part of an agency statement of general or particular applicability and future effect design to implement, interpret, or prescribe law of policy."

Unfortunately, the rules issued by agencies are law; they carry the same weight as legislative, presidential or judicial orders. A few agencies that carry out law and policy include: IRS, DOT, FTC, FAA, EPA, FDA, etc....

Now consider what a monster this has created. The table below represents the pages of "Rules" issued by Federal Agencies:

Year	Pages	Year	Pages	Year	Pages	Year	Pages
2002	145,099	2007	156,001	2012	174,557	2017	186,468
2003	144,187	2008	157,972	2013	175,494	2018	185,434
2004	147,639	2009	163,327	2014	175,273	2019	185,984
2005	152,271	2010	165,491	2015	178,352	2020	186,069
2006	154,100	2011	169,252	2016	185,131	2021	188,321

Note that under President Obama the rules increased by 27,159 pages from 2008 to 2016 demonstrating his assertion that he did not need Congress to enact legislation (under Trump rules increased 938 pages).

Of the 164.5 million employed people in the USA, 14% are government employees, including 4.0 million federal, 5.5 million state employees; and 14.2 million local government employees.

My idea was to require lawyers to get an undergraduate degree in Engineering first. But as frequently happens, my ever so clever original idea wasn't original. Texas A&M College of Engineering and School of Law "offer a combination degree program leading to the BS in Interdisciplinary Engineering (ITDE) and Juris Doctor (JD) degrees. This program is structured to allow students to complete it in six academic years, reducing the typical time to completion for sequential degrees by one year." Interdisciplinary Engineering curriculum can be translated as "systems engineering."

So why a Systems Engineering Degree? When solving organizational effectiveness, efficiency and adaptability issues, system engineers frequently turn to established standards. Some of the standards used by government agencies include:

ISO 9001: At national and municipal levels, transparency in government is increasingly politically expedient. ISO 9001 is the most recognized quality management system in the world. ISO 9001 is based on a set of scalable best practices that help run leaner, more efficient operations without sacrificing quality.

ISO 14001: Sustainability is of critical importance to governments around the world. Based on a continuous improvement cycle, it delivers ongoing efficiency gains, making firms leaner and more cost-effective overall, while setting a positive example by bringing day-to-day operations in line with official priorities.

ISO 27001: provides tools to protect against cybercrime, vandalism, and online threats. Since it is technology and vendor neutral, it can be implemented, regardless of what infrastructure and systems are in place. In defense, aerospace, and healthcare, a data breach damages reputations and jeopardizes regulatory compliance.

ISO 45001 addresses occupational health and safety policies; it reduces the risk of job accidents. ISO 45001 is based on ISO 9001 and ISO 14001.

ISO 15489 addresses the effective management of records and documents; it guides business to have secure and efficient recordkeeping and records management processes to satisfy regulatory compliance, safety management, data privacy protection, and continuous improvement initiatives.

There are tens of thousands of standards that systems engineers use to assure themselves of a viable result. Unfortunately, government has discovered and abuse them as well. National institute of Standards (NIST) list 2700 standards associated with operation of government agencies in their task of regulating every aspect of American business. My question is: who protects citizens from federal agencies and its use of 2700 standards?

Contemporary philosophical conceptions of democracy often referred to in Rousseau's book: *The Social Contract*. He argues that in order for democracy to work, the law must be derived from the general will of its people where it comes from all and applies to all. For this to be true, however, it has to be the case that the situation of citizens is substantially similar to one another. In a state where citizens enjoy a wide diversity of lifestyles and occupations, or where there is a great deal of cultural diversity, or where there is a high degree of economic inequality, it will not generally be the case that the impact of the laws will be the same for everyone. Europeans solve their diversity problem by establishing a new country every 500 miles.

USA legislators, on the other hand, solve our diversity problems by wallowing in a cesspool of ever-expanding legislative lunacy. Even worse, this lunacy is magnified by four million federal bureaucrats who favor candidates that provide the best chance for them to keep getting paid. To see where we may be headed refer to Reflection 53: Demise of Democracy.

39

CHRISTMAS 2015

39th Epistle of Jim

My happy demeanor was interrupted again by reflecting before Christmas and concluding that I'm getting really old. Geriatric words come to mind like geezer, elderly, spry, senior, aged, retiree, oldster, pensioner, fogey, golden-ager, patriarch and Judy's innovation: "top-of-the-go next-list." My body systems still mostly work but working out an hour a day inhibits the 'out-of-shape' delusion while confirming the "decline-into-decrepitude" reality.

On the bright side, Judy and I have minimal material for geezer cocktail party medical procedure conversations. Our minor skin cancers were inadequate cocktail topics. This year I had a quarter sized, quarter inch deep chunk scooped out of my face by our dermatologist. Later, I complained: "the scar is barely noticeable; I expected something more manly." He promised to use staples next time. I imagined stories involving bear, alligator, shark, and epee, but with this scar, it's a ho hum geezer conversation footnote.

Judy's topic is better: wildly oscillating blood pressure and racing heart. 12 hours after a steroid shot for a heel spur, her blood pressure was 220/120 with a heart rate of 110. After two trips to the Beaver Island Health Center, four visits to our regular doctor and one to a nephrologist, six medications with varied dosages, one air ambulance ride, two trips to the hospital emergency room, over 500 recorded and plotted BPs, and 66 pages of test results documenting her "perfect" health, the nephrologist recommended that she see a cardiologist. Instead, we went to the Mayo Clinic. After driving 11 hours and staying 3 nights, a doctor at this prestigious institution talked to her for 45 minutes and told her to keep doing what she was doing, but don't take your BP so much. We paid extra for this erudite insight!!?? In the Keys her BP is now managed on half dosages of two drugs. Steroids were the catalyst; but, the *@#!&% cause remains a mystery.

Judy continues to paint but knitting was replaced with blood pressure monitoring and analysis. She SELLS her paintings and was commissioned to do others; she still paints birds and friends' pets.

Judy's BP adventure gave me the opportunity to observe medical organizations in action. Holy mother of Pandora! Medical personnel and patients were frustrated by hospital/medical billing systems that must have been designed by accountants to bill insurance companies. When I pointed this out to our doctor during my annual physical exam, as he keyed in one of 144,000 billing codes on his laptop computer, he responded: "tell me about it." The supporting information systems and processes looked much like they did in the 1980's in manufacturing. After spending four months researching blood pressure causes and medication, and hospital systems and billing codes, I think I know how to fix the inappropriate use of technology in medical systems. As I lamented earlier, I am old; therefore, I must find someone less aged to work with me to fix it. I'll keep you informed if I don't "go next."

As I plan ways to reduce travel, our travel escalates. Our return to the Keys involved a 3200-mile trip through Upper Michigan to the Mayo Clinic in Rochester Minnesota, then to New York City to see Lauren, John's family and Jeff who was visiting from Australia and on to the Keys. We are also flying from Miami to LA to see Jamison and family at Christmas. We tried unsuccessfully to sell our Beaver Island home this summer as we both now favor Fernandina, FL; also, the Jacksonville Mayo Clinic is near.

In addition to the Pope, I sent the 31st draft of my book, "Faith and Reason," to three Jesuits at the University of Detroit. I received two underwhelming replies thanking me for my effort. My book was selected by the park book club in the Keys and will be discussed in February. We'll see what befuddlement transpires.

Further exacerbating my go-next-induced anxiety was Rick's death, Judy's sister Janet's husband (5 years younger than us). Rick's passing 6 days before Thanksgiving made us less thankful but gave us an opportunity to celebrate his life on that day with his family on Beaver Island. Rick's funeral was an extraordinary celebration of his life, complete with a flag folding ceremony by two airmen. A somber procession turned celebratory when they played Rick's favorite song: "Drop kick me Jesus through the goal posts of life."

If you behold the spirit of death, open your heart unto the body of life. For life and death are one, even as the river and the sea are one....
And what is it to cease breathing, but to free breath from its restless tides, that it may rise and expand and seek God unencumbered? - Kahlil Gibran

Reflection 39: Process Flow and Community

Based on our personal experience, I conclude that while we may have some of the best medical facilities in the USA, our medical community is dysfunctional and in need of a system redesign.

Professional Communities are populated by individuals who have acquired and used knowledge and skills to support critical areas of society and also serve to critique the idea-to-novel artifacts of its members. Scientific revelations (theories) are validated by experiments, predicted observations, and/or confirmation of mathematical derivations. In a scientific or engineering community most revelation is viewed skeptically, especially if it invalidates established theories.

Within the medical community the "artifact" is the delivery of medical services. Medical practitioners operate more like an ancient guild than a modern professional community.

A guild (ref: www.masterartisan.com) is an association of people of the same trade or pursuits (with a similar skill or craft), formed to protect mutual interests and maintain standards of workmanship and ethical conduct. A guild is a trade union, since each crafter was a self-employed individual artisan or part of a small shop.

Guilds (ref: www.britannica.com) became possible in Europe with the appearance and growth of towns in the 10th century. Craft guilds arose soon after merchant guilds. Craftsmen banded together to regulate competition among themselves. They agreed on basic rules governing their trade and set quality standards to form the first craft guilds. Guilds shaped labor, production, and trade; they had strong controls over instructional capital, and progression from apprentice to craftsman, journeyman, master, and grandmaster. All guild structures were similar: a governing body with a leader and deputies, assistants, and the members' assembly.

Engineering societies evolved from craftsmen's guilds. To become a junior engineer, one must first be educated in a university with an accredited engineering program. However, having the knowledge acquired at such an institution is not enough. All engineers subscribe to the adage: if you build it, it must work. Many apprentice engineers work for a corporation where they become part of a guild-like engineering community. Apprentice engineers learn how to design, validate, and build things that work. Critical skills apply to specific disciplines (e.g. mechanical, electronic, etc), but also require putting in place well designed systems.

When a system is correctly designed, a human user can employ it in a deliberate manner to deliver desired outcomes at the desired time. At this abstract level, technical systems can be described through a black box that shows inputs and outputs.

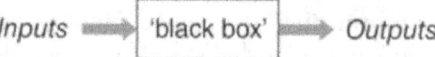

This black box approach is used to manifest the first abstract representation of the system to be designed. The representation is then broken down into inherent actions or technical processes that transform the given inputs into the final output. Combining all relevant operations into a causal, logical chain, in which the output of one serves as input for the next, establishes the functional structure of the system. This structure then serves as a coherent representation of the inherent mechanisms, processes, transformations, and their relations of how the system functions, e.g., how it operates, to establish causal relation between inputs and outputs.

Functions enable engineers to gradually comprehend the central operations that are necessary in the system under development.

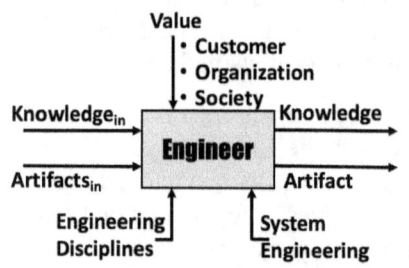

Artifact is an object deliberately made for a human being. It can take the form of a product, digital system, service, or any assembly. It is part of every design process; artifacts have a dual nature. On the one hand, it is an object or service used to accomplish a specific goal; on the other, it is a service, whose function has meaning within the context of a goal-oriented human activity.

Appendix B illustrates an Enterprise System Model that applies to any business, but manufacturing and hospitals are compared throughout that appendix. The model uses process models to capture the facts to measure, manage and improve processes. Many hospitals (including the Mayo Clinic) are hiring systems engineers to lower the cost of healthcare and provide insights into improving the patient care result while doing no harm. Improving individual and community health and senior care will lead to better quality of life and the expectation that we can depend on each other for improving the welfare of people in the community. The benefit of this approach is that while increasing the quality of health and senior care, it will significantly reduce the cost.

After medical school, doctors must become interns where they learn their skills in a hospital in isolation from other hospitals. This system can benefit greatly from the black box analytical approach and model described above.

A way to coordinate engineering (and medical practice) among different disciplines being used within a project as well as medical treatment of patients with similar maladies is a Community of Practice (CoP) where disparate teams can share information, insight, experience, and tools about an area specific to their problem. They facilitate internal and external communication to determine best practices and transfer organizational knowledge within and across disciplines. CoPs create an environment for socialization in which knowledge is created, validated, and shared.

In his book, *The Structure of Scientific Revolutions*, **Thomas Kuhn** points to the importance of acquired skills: "Tacit knowledge" results from learning by doing science (and medicine and engineering) and has the following characteristics:

Symbolic Generalizations
deployed without dissent, can be cast in a logical or symbolic form (e.g., $f=ma$). A science's power increases with the number of symbolic generalizations.
Beliefs
supply preferred or permissible models of shared analogies or metaphors (e.g. heat is the kinetic energy of the constituent parts of bodies)
Values judge whole theories or predictions
permit puzzle-formulation and solution.
are simple, self-consistent, plausible and compatible with other theories
assure accuracy: quantitative are preferable to qualitative predictions
identify margins of permissible error that should be consistently satisfied
Exemplars provide concrete problems-solutions which
are found in periodical literature
are encountered by students in laboratories, on exams, and in texts
allow students to see a variety of situations as alike
allow scientists to solve puzzles by modeling them on previous puzzle-solutions,
allow scientists to see the same things when confronted with the same stimuli (e.g., physicists recognize tracks of alpha particles)
provide empirical content for laws/theories a student has previously learned.
provide symbolic generalizations (e.g. in Newton's 2nd Law of Motion is a law-schema; $f=ma$ in free fall becomes $mg=d^2s/d^2t$)

40

CHRISTMAS 2016
40th Epistle of Jim

My unbearably "wonderful" demeanor, usually interrupted by pathological holiday grumpiness, has been replaced this year by moderate disassociation disorder; Psychology provides a definition: mild disassociation is like daydreaming, getting "lost" in a book, or when you drive down a familiar stretch of road and don't remember the last several miles. That's me most of the time. Last year's events have elevated my disorder from mild to moderate.

I have claimed my body systems mostly work, but this year Judy and I discovered that our vision was being significantly obstructed by cataracts. Friends assured me that cataract surgery was NO BIG DEAL! Holy crap. Someone sticks a knife in my eye, mashes the lens to hamburger (phacoemulsification), sucks out the debris and sticks in a plastic lens. Or, someone could do a similar thing with a computer-controlled laser. Keep in mind lasers can cut through steel or the back of my head. In order to allay my fears, I was assured, this surgery works MOST OF THE TIME! Aaaaaaagh! Yet another indication of aging, Judy and I had a cataract surgery date. You may remember our colonoscopy date several years ago. Needless to say, anyone about to have surgery didn't appreciate my knife in the eye description. All that whining and everything turned out almost OK. What a wimp. However, observing my surgery through the eye being operated on while watching the surgeon through the other eye intensified my disassociation disorder.

I see distance in both eyes just fine, but one eye was supposed to be for reading. I do, however, relive both eye surgeries clearly. Judy wanted a distance eye but got a reading eye; no 2nd eye surgery yet.

Judy and I still contribute little to cocktail party medical procedure conversations since most couples have at least one cataract surgery and joint replacement between them. You remember last year I had a big scoop of cheek that left a "barely noticeable" scar; good news, it bumped up a little to something manly: shark tooth nick.

Once again as I plan to reduce travel, it escalates. In late April, we drove to Brunswick GA for my cousin's son's wedding. They had a pre-wedding party on my 75th birthday so, of course, I thanked the mother of the bride for thoughtfully arranging a party for my birthday; 200 people sang happy birthday to me. Once we got to Beaver Island in May, Jeff came from Australia on an Indian Motorcycle to store in our basement. He magnanimously said I could ride it anytime, but not on dirt. And where is that!?!.

Coming back to the Keys, we left our car during the October hurricane at a motel in Ft. Lauderdale and flew to LA to see son Jamison perform Macbeth. We, of course, saw his brilliant performance three times. Although Macbeth is not 'fun', the 2nd performance was very fun, when Jamison's brother Jeff sat three feet from the stage but failed to distract him as Macbeth.

Building on the disassociation syndrome, I have a new sociological term, which occurs when family members locate far from the central family unit: familial disassociation. The farther members are dispersed the more disassociation. Our family is significantly disassociated with two of us alternating between Beaver Island and The Keys and three sons and families in NYC, LA, and Oz.

Never deterred by ignorance, I know I can solve medical conundrums where others have failed. Doctors deal with complex biological systems with consciousness and emotions designed and evolved by a higher power. Medical diagnosis requires a complex adaptive system methodology: intuit the cause from poorly communicated patient symptoms, test to refine suspicions, intuit, evolve and test a theory, identify the potential interventions; do something; maybe start over. Engineers deal with complex systems that they design and build but won't improve medical diagnosis until they leverage physician intuition in teams.

My moderate disassociation disorder allows me to observe my life's theater of comedy from the audience. Aging has not shaken my confidence in being a skilled thinker despite the fact that it takes me longer to remember what I already know I know. I continue not to be deterred by the breadth and depth of my own ignorance as I try to convince people that I'm smarter than I look. Nobody's buying it so far. Good news (???): my comedy continues as my body deteriorates with my brain (or delusions) intact.

We wish for you this holiday season, minimal disassociation and tragedies and more humor in your theater of life.

Reflection 40: Panentheism

To explain a higher power that evolved complex biological systems with consciousness consider Harvard Professor Alfred North Whitehead's Panentheistic view of God in *Process and Reality*. It is a renaissance of theological thought comparable to Darwin's and Einstein's theories and seeks to restore the authority of religion and God in a way that embraces the sciences, but atheists fail to recognize or acknowledge it (Faith and Reason, 2017).

Eastern gurus assert that science, psychology, sociology, ethics, aesthetics, and human consciousness fall under the umbrella of philosophy and that such a philosophy must embrace a concept of God. Alfred North Whitehead's[6] Theory of Organism provides such a foundation while science alone does not. His *panentheism*, combines concepts of Eastern and Western philosophy, understands God and the world to be interrelated with the world being in God and God being in the world.

Panentheism's concept of God has been used by theologians to develop a rational view for all major world religions and provides a theological framework to guide religions toward a set of universal human values. Whitehead's panentheism argues against atheism and agnosticism.

In his book, *Panentheism: The Other God of the Philosophers*, John Cooper gives a detailed account of the history of panentheism in all major religions.[7] Whitehead's panentheism provides a framework for a philosophy of science and an ecumenical interpretation of the major world religions. It was continued in Hartshorne's process theology, where without God, the world would be a static, unchanging existence radically different from the

---

[6] Whitehead taught mathematics at Trinity College Cambridge, physics and philosophy at Imperial College London and philosophy at Harvard.

[7] Evidence of panentheism was present in Ikhnaton (1358 BCE), the monotheist Egyptian pharaoh; the Upanishads; in Lao-Tsu (4th century BCE); in Judeo-Christian scriptures; in Plato's (400 BCE) concept of Forms and the World; in Plotinus' (270 CE) identification of God with the world; in Proclus (485 CE); and in Pseudo-Dionysus (6th century) drawing upon Plotinus.
In the Middle Ages, evidence of panentheism was present in Eriugena (877), Eckhart (1328), Nicholas of Cusa (1464), Boehme (1624), Bruno (1600) and Spinoza (1677). Later 17th century thinkers such as Edwards (1758), and Schleiermacher (1834). Karl Krause (1832) created the term 'panentheism.' Hegel (1800) and Schelling (1831) sought to unify reality in dialectic thought with process philosophy's where God is affected by the world.

actual world of experience. An eternal and temporal God provides possibilities to change and develop the world.

Whitehead defines God as imminent and primordial in the universe and the purveyor of all knowledge in the form of eternal objects (ingredients that make up real/actual entities and objects). Humans interpret this knowledge in various ways: e.g. physics, genetics, Hamlet, Bohemian Rhapsody, etc...

Whitehead says that creativity is *novelty of instance*. Novelty of instance is a new result derived from previously actualized old data; *novelty of kind* introduces new data into the stream of process. God influences novelty of instance in all things identified by 'descriptive words' such as 'yellow' and 'car.' There are two of an infinite number of these eternal objects.[8]

Eternal objects 'exist' but are activated only when an occasion realizes a particular combination of objects. An observer prehends in a mode of causal efficacy to anticipate the appearance of "a yellow car" in his stream of consciousness. Upon perceiving a vehicle in the mode of presentational immediacy, he limits the occasion with his subjective aim[9]: model and color. The 'satisfaction'[10] of the subjective aim in the mode of symbolic reference imposed upon the prehensions is a 'yellow car.' A broader aim might include brand and style.

For example, consider two different projections of the same reality: husband and wife walk together in the woods. The man walks for

---

[8] **Plato's Theory of Forms** asserts that non-material abstract forms (or ideas), and not the material world of change known to us from sensation, possess the highest and most fundamental reality. To Plato, Forms are the only true objects of study that can provide genuine knowledge. Whitehead's eternal objects are the application to process reality of Plato's Forms.

[9] **Subjective Aim**: Most prehensions (concrete modes of analysis) of the world focus on the past. They are the feeling and analysis of the entire world for that occasion, but they do not complete that occasion by themselves. From prehending data and admittance of new possibilities comes a unified ideal for the end result: subjective aim--a projected concrete form in which to resolve the diversity of feelings of the primary phases of the process.

[10] **Satisfaction** achieves the unity proposed in the subjective aim. The process is finished - all felt aspects have been reconciled in a unity of feeling or 'negative prehension'- denial of access into the satisfaction. With the satisfaction, the occasion is 'done'- fixed form of resultant unity. The satisfied occasion loses its actuality as it passes into history as fixed data.

contemplation and fitness and his wife walks to be with her "plant and wildlife friends." The husband walks briskly for aerobic fitness while contemplating transcendence. His wife wanders while contemplating trees, birds, flora, and fauna. Their subjective aims and fields of consciousness are vastly different. The husband limits his perception of external reality while directing his focus internally. The wife limits her internal focus and maximizes her external awareness of the natural environment. Note that the wife may interrupt her husband's field of consciousness by pointing to an eagle in a treetop while the husband may interrupt his wife's external awareness with an arcane description of transcendence.

Both husband and wife are immersed in the same reality but will recall it with very different perspectives. He will tell you how many miles they walked and relate some aphorism that he conjured up during the walk. She will tell you about eagles, dwarf iris, trees, trash, road texture, and wetlands. Both experienced the same reality in space and time, but it resulted in different 'Occasions.' Both walkers used a different field of consciousness and subjective aim.

Subjective aim affects their experience differently. The husband's perception is severely restricted because his field of consciousness is directed inward toward an abstract problem. His novelty of instance may be to discover a new way to explain perception.

The wife's subjective aim was to reduce her prehension in the mode of causal efficacy so that she could experience more in the mode of presentational immediacy in her natural environment. Her use of symbolic reference may be to identify an endangered plant not known to the area.

This explanation frames issues associated with the past, present, and future purposes of religious systems. Finding yellow cars and walking in the woods are simple examples to illustrate concepts of perception and thought. This view of perception is important in arguments where communities reinforce their wrongly believed perceived projections of reality.

The infinity of the eternal objects to be considered represents God's primordial nature. In His consequent nature, God participates in harmonizing physical and conceptual prehensions, and the subjective aim of every occasion. God's consequent nature conceptualizes all possibilities.

CHRISTMAS 2017

41st Epistle of Jim

The first two-thirds of this year were good while the last third felt like the end of days. Hurricane Irma, LA fires, a tragic death and tooth removal increased my stress and anxiety beyond being aged (growing old is mandatory, growing up is optional), my normal paranoia and consternation about Christmas commercialization.

First, the happy two thirds: Jeff and fiancée Kristina came to visit in February on a rented Harley. Judy went to California to be with Lisa and family shortly thereafter. John, Patty, and Kate visited in April in a Mustang convertible. Seeing a picture of John driving, Jamison observed: mid-life crisis. No mid-life crisis for Jeff as his crises have been continuous. Judy and I went to Chris's college graduation where we got to see Dan and Kate, Patty and John once again. A college graduate grandchild is a signpost of agedness.

Jeff married Kristina in August in Melbourne Australia. Air travel was brutal, but the wedding was great fun and Jeff seemed to enjoy basking in the euphoria of his adoring mother while putting me to work writing a white paper and giving a presentation on optimizing the healthcare process. He thinks I could be a cash cow (I prefer bull) but has yet to figure how to get me engaged for revenue and profit. Being aged, he'd better hurry.

We visited Jamie, Lisa, Ian and Oliver for four days in LA when we came back from Australia. Ian and Oliver go to high school, which is actually called the zoo. It specializes in the study of animal species as opposed to political science. Have any of you flown anywhere lately? It really is consternating. Being aged, I'm ordering a wheelchair next time. Flying from Traverse City via Chicago and LA to Melbourne and back accelerated agedness.

Other significant events: Patty & John and Jamison & Lisa both celebrated their 25th anniversaries this year. Jeff's son Aidan and his fiancée Lauren reproduced our first great granddaughter, Aria, Children celebrating 25th anniversaries and a great grandchild are yet another confirmation of agedness.

Judy spent much of the summer with plants and pictures gardening at home and at our healthcare center interrupted by scanning in and archiving another 5000 pictures. I recently tripled the storage space and doubled the memory in her computer to accommodate her documentation of our family history. Judy is retro, NOT aged.

I finally published Faith and Reason: The Universality of God and Fallacy of Atheism. Judy edited revisions 37-38. I'm not sure how to promote it and to whom. I received a collective ho hum from three Jesuits and a thank you note from the Pope, who didn't read it, but surprisingly several protestant ministers read and liked it.

Hurricane Irma trashed our park on Cudjoe Key in September: 100 homes destroyed, 550 damaged and 9 (including us) with little damage. Having survivor guilt, we endeavored to help neighbors. After removing 826 truckloads of debris, the park looks the worse for wear rather than a war zone. 130mph wind with gusts to 160 didn't just blow homes over, they exploded sending pieces everywhere. Irma spawned 25 tornadoes with winds exceeding 200mph. I love wind, but if it's over 60mph, I start sucking my thumb. And, as of this writing fires continue to burn near LA.

A most tragic event touched us in the fall. After a serious automobile accident our niece Rebecca gave birth to a beautiful 8lb 14oz baby who died a few days later. Rest in peace Wyatt Lee, son of Dennis: "Good night, sweet prince, and flights of angels sing thee to thy rest." - *Hamlet*. Go with God Wyatt Lee.

Since I am distressingly aged, I hope to fix the sorry state of senior care before I have to use it. The World Health Organization rates the US 37th in healthcare at a cost of 17% of our GDP (double most other countries). By 2050, the aged over 85 will increase from 6 to 15 million while significantly increasing the national debt with Medicare costs. As I am rewriting my process quality book unencumbered by experience in healthcare, I look forward to several consulting assignments with healthcare organizations before I claim expert knowledge in a published book.

We wish for you a joyous Christmas and imperceptible aging absent trauma.

Reflection 41: Not Atheism

From THE BOOK, I assert: no god is not provable, but many atheists have tried. In my opinion, the most coherent argument for atheism comes from Physicist Victor J. Stenger's book, *God: The Failed Hypothesis*. He states that if particular attributes of God fail to agree with the data, it would be irrational to use it as a guide for a religion. He defines God:

1] God is the creator and preserver of the universe.

2] God is the architect of the structure of the universe and the author of the laws of nature.

3] God is the source of morality and other human values such as freedom, justice, and democracy.

4] God steps in when he wishes to change the course of events.

5] God creates and preserves life and humanity, where human beings are special in relation to other life forms.

6] God endowed humans with immaterial, eternal souls that... carry a person's character and selfhood.

7] God has revealed truths in scriptures and by communicating directly to selected individuals...

8] God does not deliberately hide from any human being who is open to finding evidence for his presence.

Stenger's scientific argument against the existence of God is a modified form of the lack-of-evidence argument:
- Hypothesize a God who plays an important role in the universe.
- Look for evidence of a God with specific attributes to provide objective evidence for his existence.
- If such evidence is found, conclude that God may exist.
- If not found conclude a God with these properties does not exist.

Stenger summarizes each chapter in his conclusion, which is presented here with a hypothetical rebuttal. In accordance with Whitehead's view of God, the rebuttals presume God's consequent nature in influencing every event and His primordial nature embodied in eternal objects. This would remove from
1] 'creator,' and change 4] to 'God participates in every event.

The Illusion of Design: A God who is responsible for the complex structure of the world, especially living things, fails to agree with the empirical fact that this structure can be understood to arise from simple natural processes and shows none of the expected signs of design; the universe looks as it should look absent design.

Rebuttal: A God, responsible for the complex structure of the world, especially living things, agrees with the empirical fact that very complex structures can arise from simple natural algorithms. The biologically complex structures that arose on earth from a vast empty universe affirm an elegant complex adaptive system.

Searching for a World beyond Matter: A God who has given humans immortal souls fails to agree with the empirical facts that human memories and personalities are determined by physical processes, that no nonphysical or extra-physical powers of the mind can be found, and that no evidence exists for an afterlife.

Rebuttal: A God, who gave humans the capacity for consciousness and self-awareness, did indeed give them souls. The ability to conceptualize and perceive oneself is the essence of soul whether in words (literature), motion (dance) or science (mathematics). The human soul rests in God's primordial nature (Whitehead): "my immediate occasion of experience, at the present moment, is only one among a stream of occasions which constitutes my soul."

Cosmic Evidence: A God whose interactions with humans, including miraculous interventions, reported in scriptures, is contradicted by the lack of independent evidence that these miraculous events took place and the fact that physical evidence so convincingly demonstrates that some of the most important biblical narratives, such as Exodus, never took place.

Rebuttal: A God who lures human action toward beauty and good is supported by the historical facts of sacred and secular texts. Some sacred writings are myths that convey revealing truths about culture; e.g. The Good Samaritan.

The Uncongenial Universe: A God who fine-tuned the laws and constants of physics for life, in particular human life, fails to agree with the fact that the universe is not congenial to human life, being tremendously wasteful of time, space, and matter from the human perspective. It also fails to agree with the fact that the universe is mostly composed of particles in random motion, with complex structures such as galaxies forming less than 4% of the mass and less than one particle out of billions.

Rebuttal: A God whose eternal objects are approximated by the laws of physics and genetics agrees with the fact that earth is congenial to human life. Dr. Francis Collins, head of the Human Genome Project, found "genomes to be elegant evidence of the relatedness of all living things and came to see this as the master plan of the same Almighty who caused the universe to come into being and set its physical parameters just precisely right to allow the creation of stars, planets, heavy elements and life itself."

The Failures of Revelation: A God who communicates directly with humans by means of revelation fails to agree with the fact that no claimed revelation has ever been confirmed, while many have been falsified. No claimed revelation contains information that could not have been already in the person's head making the claim.

Rebuttal: A God who communicates with individuals by means of revelation agrees with the fact that science itself is represented by one amazing, confirmed revelation after another; referring again to Whitehead: "(Science) must come from the medieval insistence on the rationality of God, conceived with the personal energy of Jehovah and with the rationality of a Greek philosopher."

Do Our Values Come from God: A God who is the source of morality and human values does not exist since the evidence shows that humans define morals and values for themselves. Believers and nonbelievers alike agree on a common set of morals and values. Nonbelievers behave no less morally than believers.

Rebuttal: A God who is the source of morality and human values from the dawn of primitive man has always been imagined by man to exist and whose eternal objects and consequent nature have provided the foundation for all morality and human values. If nonbelievers are no less moral than believers, it shows that religious influence benefits all members of society.

The Argument from Evil: The existence of evil, in particular, gratuitous suffering, is logically inconsistent with an omniscient, omnibenevolent, omnipotent God (standard problem of evil).

Rebuttal: Process and change are carried out by agents of free will. Self-determination is in everything, not just humans. God guides the exercise of free will by offering possibilities. God has a will in everything, but not everything is God's will (God is not evil).

Since both Stenger's and the author's arguments are contradictory at least one or both of us have committed narrative fallacies (BS), probably him. A philosophy of science attempting to see natural truth is inadequate to explain 'no god' since belief in a god is about value. A theology of engineering addresses value where 'novelty' is revealed by God.

42

CHRISTMAS 2018

42nd Epistle of Jim

Once again, I approach the gravity of the season with trepidation. Last year's Hurricane Irma tragedy is overshadowed by the Monroe County Building Department who exhibit no compassion for homeowners rebuilding their homes.

Judy continues her art. She has gotten particularly good at painting animals. Part of her unique style is to paint animal eyes as if something is going on in its brain. Her birds are especially interesting because if you reproduce their eyes correctly, it is clear nothing is going on except maybe in parrots. She might consider doing my portrait, with emphasis on the eyes, to reflect more brain activity. Judy also spends quite a bit of time in her gardens nurturing plants whose primary purpose appears to be feeding wildlife.

Jamison filmed a movie on the Leelanau Peninsula, north of Traverse City and 30 miles south of us (over water). The movie is shot in presumably warm weather. The directors did not foresee that Michigan has short 40^0F nights in May. Jamison, acting warm, in shorts and t-shirt in 40^0F was a testament to his professional acting skills. Lisa came to watch as well. We saw them again in LA at Ian's high school graduation. Ian will study Molecular Biology in college and Oliver is studying Cinematic Arts in high school. Lauren is visuals editor at Vanity Fair in NYC.

John has a new job as a partner and head of a creative design group at PwC. Patty started her own counseling business for college students. Dan continues at his music theater college in Philly. Chris is getting his band going in upstate New York. Kate is enjoying high school. We hope to see them this winter in the Keys.

Jeff and Kristina came to visit us in Key West in February and on Beaver Island in September partly to see us and partly to arrange for his Indian motorcycle to be shipped to Australia. Jeff's Aidan and fiancée Lauren recent reproduction of our great granddaughter, Aria, reminds me of how blessed and ancient we are. WARNING: only the young may see humor in some of what follows.

Medline says: You change naturally as you age: the spinal column compresses, foot arches become flatter, arm and leg bones become more brittle, joints become stiffer and less flexible, cartilage rubs together and wears away, hip and knee and finger joints lose cartilage and the bones thicken slightly, lean body mass decreases, fat is deposited in muscle tissue, muscles are less toned, even with regular exercise (gravity is not your friend). AAAAUUUUGH!

The benefit of losing five teeth is that I lost 30 pounds. Unfortunately, gravity and age have created disturbing sags everywhere. At my current weight 20 years ago, my chest was 3 inches bigger, and waist was 3 inches smaller. Also, I am one inch shorter partly because my high arches have sunk to flat fleet. Gravity, a great grandchild, sagging dimensions and passing male life expectancy age are motivators to quickly finish another book.

As we age, medical intervention looms (a euphemism for hack, chop, replace and drug). Equally distressing is the gravity of the state of medicine. Relative to an engineer or mechanic, I am surprised that medicine is a disjointed patchwork of guessers. If you have unexplained symptoms, your best chance is a team of best guessers at a top ten hospital. Part of the consultancy is to enable a patchwork of guessers in a virtual team aided by artificial intelligence.

Barrister and wag, Sir John Mortimer once quipped: There is no pleasure worth forgoing just for an extra three years in the geriatric ward. Rest easy, my mission is to define how to provide exceptional senior HOME care before I need it.

The first draft of The Document Methodology Version III with 100 new pages on health care and 50 pages of revisions is being reviewed by people who won't be shy if they think something needs more work. Unfortunately, my own review suggests 50 pages require revision. Finishing a comprehensive health system process model and the BOOK has me pondering the gravity of aging on brain activity. However, my desire to be famous posthumously prevails.

We wish you good health in a joyous New Year.

Reflection 42: Theology of Engineering

This reflection is derived from THE BOOK and a (rejected) fPET2023 paper (forum on Philosophy of Engineering). Deeply religious people may tell you that they bring their problems to God in prayer. As an engineer, I had a business relationship with God. I'd struggle with a difficult problem for weeks and then wake up one morning with the answer.

A neurological explanation provides insight into how this might work. Research defined five categories of brain waves:
- Delta: produced at 0.5-4Hz in deep dreamless sleep.
- Theta: produced at 4-8Hz in light sleep between.
- Alpha: produced at 8-12Hz when calm, awake, and unfocused.
- Beta: produced at 12-35Hz when a awake, alert, and focused on activities of daily living and making decisions.
- Gamma: produced above 35Hz when actively involved in processing information, learning. and solving problems.

Brain researchers might suggest that I struggle with a problem at 50Hz and divine a solution at 4-12Hz. So, God operates at 4-12Hz. Psalm 46:10 - "Be still and know that I am God."

Engineers have produced so much novel technology in the last 150 years that it is precipitating a decline in confidence of society's administrative functions, institutions, and leadership. This crisis must be resolved with even more novel artifacts (e.g., batteries).

Martin Heidegger, in his book, *Being and Time*, claims technological thinking confuses us by 'revealing' everything to us as a resource available as a means to an end. He calls this 'enframing:' to see everything in this framework as means, ends, causes, and effects. Heidegger maintains that human thinking alone is not able to solve problems presented by technology. He believes that "only God can save us", even if god is taken as a secularized notion of the sacred... "for in the face of the god who is absent, we [fail]."

Alfred North Whitehead's book, *Process and Reality*, answers Heidegger's requirement for a secular god. Whitehead's panentheism (Reflection 40) understands the Absolute being in the universe and the universe being in the Absolute. His God's primordial and consequent nature elegantly supports his explanation of 'reality' as process.

Jürgen Habermas, in his book, *Legitimation Crisis*, claims as societies evolve, they are in danger of entering a state of crisis;

crises arise when the structure of a social system cannot solve the problems required for its continued existence. These crises are not produced by external changes, but through internal incompatible system-imperatives that cannot be integrated. Societies disintegrate when citizens feel their social identity threatened. He defines:
- Social integration as related to the systems of institutions in which people are socially related;
- System integration as related to institutions with steering performances of self-regulated systems; and
- Social systems as life-worlds that are symbolically structured and maintain their boundaries and continued existence by mastering the complexity of a changing environment.

In modern capitalistic societies, political systems are subordinate to the socio-cultural and economic systems:
- Socio-cultural subsystems structures include a status system and sub-cultural forms of life with underlying categories that include distribution of rewards and disposition rights.
- Political subsystems structures include political institutions (state) with underlying categories that include distribution of legitimate power and available organizational rationality.
- Economic subsystems structures include economic institutions (production) with underlying categories that include distribution of economic power and available forces of production.

Key to resolving societies' sustainability and crises is for engineers to engage in global discourse (rather than avoiding 'normal' people) to prevent governments and activist initiatives 'unintended consequences' from simplified views of reality. To this end, value discussions must be guided by rationality, sustainability, ethics, and viable alternatives as well as (the normal forms being) power, hysteria, recreation, comfort, and security. An engineering theology can reframe societies by going beyond existing knowledge to promote a system constrained by moral guidance and sustainability to:
- Benefit individual well-being,
- Precipitate and validate innovation and novelty,
- Increase participation to define solutions that societies value,
- Provide a foundation for creation of high-value artifacts.

Scientific thought is based on deriving a theory (induction) and subsequently trying to disprove it (deduction).

Carl Sanders Peirce claims scientific perspective requires a third perspective: 'abduction' that considers a new possibility; a 'state' of experience in the absolute present. It may emanate from (6 Hz) ideas that may be considered for a new category of inquiry (Whitehead's God's primordial nature of Plato's Forms).

Since artifacts created by engineers within the socio-cultural system have been a major contributor to this crisis, engineers must be engaged in all aspects of the solution including defining the problem, developing the requirements, and proposing solutions within a strategy and portfolio of programs and projects.

Engineering Theology embraces a concept of god necessary to guide society to a universal value system. Human life, institutions and all disciplines are driven by value which engineering embraces; science does not, since it is a search for truth not value. Up to 1000 years ago theology was a continuously evolving search for god's truth to explain everything. Since most people believe in a god and engineering purports to deliver value to humanity, philosophy must embrace god that acts as a necessary (but not necessarily sufficient) condition to get beyond Heidegger's enframing.

Theology of Engineering concepts are based on KNOWLEDGE FLOW TO VALUE, defining elements of engineering and societal communities and finally describing the engineering process which establishes how:
- An engineer's observation leads to the leaps of faith required for implementing tangible improvement from novelty (revelation).
- A design engineering team validates revelation and delivers a prototype to validate its design.
- A production engineering team validates a prototype and constructs situations where capability delivers it.

CHRISTMAS 2019

43rd Epistle of Jim

Here I sit penning yet another epistle. I have decided to enjoy the Christmas season in the Florida Keys, because it meets my criteria for happy winter holidays: NOT snow and NOT freezing. As a NOT snow reminder, we encountered -20^0F when we flew to Detroit in January where I had six holes drilled in my jaw for tooth implants: pain and freezing. AAAUUUGH!

We are saddened that our favorite animals are now in canine heaven: big boy Oscar in LA; energetic girl Flynn in NYC; R.I.P.

Judy will try anything and surprises herself with her art but prefers to give away her paintings rather than sell them. She is happy to be in the Keys with her art pals and continues to adorn our house/art gallery with new creations.

John continues as a partner and head of a creative design group at PwC. Patty's counseling business for students is progressing nicely. Dan wrote and starred in a musical in Philadelphia. Chris migrated from NYC to Philly to continue with his music. Kate is now a junior in high school and is in a dance troupe.

Our grandson Aidan's Lauren just had second daughter Ava to go with Aria. We now have two great granddaughters. THAT moves me from aged to way aged. I am still trying to collaborate with Jeff to build a consultancy focused on healthcare. We are getting close to finding several clients. With my luck, we'll get business in a -20^0F climate or an E.coli India climate.

Despite regular exercise, my aged body parts don't work as well as they did. We depend on our doctor to explain how to mitigate this degradation. Clearly, doctors don't have the same grasp of our body systems that an engineer has of automotive systems. Several encounters with the medical community have left me with: AAUUGH! More alarming is knowing that we have the best medicine and medical personnel in the world and paradoxically one of the worst national health care systems; remember medical gouging represents 18% of GDP; yup, that's $3.3 TRILLION.

People ask me, if you see so much wrong, how can you be happy? "The world is screwed up and I'm a consultant."

Our year might be summed up as trippy. After our return to Beaver Island in late April, we flew off island and drove round trip to Detroit for a May 22 impressions tooth appointment followed by a June 14 appointment to get my bad-ass bone crunching teeth. At our 56th Rowe Inn anniversary dinner I pulverized a steak.

We now fly between Florida and Michigan; the aged shouldn't drive long distances. Demonstrating that my actions deviate from the sensible, our third trip was an 18-hour drive to Sioux Falls SD, followed by a 16-hour drive to Chautauqua NY, and an 8-hour return to Charlevoix MI. In Sioux Falls, I gave an underwhelming speech at a senior healthcare conference. In Chautauqua, we saw Jamison play the lead role as a minister in "The Christians" where he bewildered his flock preaching God told him there is no Hell.

There is still more trippin'. Trip four was to the Traverse City Film Festival. Last year, Jamison filmed a movie in the area called "The Wretched." Jamison insisted that we see its debut at midnight on August 2nd. The theater was full because many locals were extras. After, we drove to Detroit to see if my teeth were still bad-ass; yup.

Trip five in late September was to Detroit for Judy's 60th high school reunion at the Grosse Pointe Yacht Club; I attended with much trepidation; it was OK. Concurrently, the Club ran a sailing-racing-drinking meeting where I reminisced with people that I had raced against. At the reunion, Judy had a great time talking to her old classmates. A retired Doctor husband of Judy's old HS friend lectured me on everything that has gone wrong with medicine; he spoke to the content of my latest book (to be published soon?).

Trip six took us on a snow bedeviled drive to Detroit in November for a Ft. Lauderdale flight. For non-islanders, a four-hour trip to Detroit may appear insignificant, au contraire. Whereas NYC or LA transit time can vary between one and four hours, a trip (off-island) can vary from 1/3rd to 48 hours where low clouds mean no flights and high wind means no boat. AAAUUUGH!

After a fun sail on our catamaran, my aged and aching body parts had me whining about physiological degradation. An aged person reproached me with "old age is a privilege experienced by few."

We wish for you remission of physiological degradation and superlative health in the New Year

Reflection 43: Transforming Healthcare

Healthcare Portfolio Vision: Model the enterprise to deliver integrated, transparent, accountable, quality, cost effective sustainable services to eventually heal patients.

To fix healthcare within a region (as experienced by us and others) will require a portfolio, program, project management strategy. Projects and Programs are continuously monitored and measured against KPIs (key performance indicators) defined by the Portfolio. Each program has its own KPIs with which to assess performance of the projects within the portfolio. Evaluation occurs in a Tollgate Review where subject experts make judgments as to a program's performance. Activities associated with Programs are ongoing and build collaborative medical knowledge and continuously review project operations and results.

Background

To sustain a "healthy" community healthcare and wellness groups can be guided by Intermountain Healthcare in Utah which has the healthiest population at the lowest per-capita health care costs. Utah's per-capita costs is $5,013 versus $9,278 of equally healthy Massachusetts. Brent James, MD, executive director at Intermountain Institute for Health Care Leadership, says that 60% of the state's 3 million people follow the Mormon church's dietary and behavioral restrictions. It excludes tobacco, recreational drugs, and alcohol. The faith encourages large families and strong social networks, both of which provide support when people get sick.

Since there is no comprehensive, complete, "proven" method to guaranteed wellness, it is necessary to establish guidelines for good health in a generic way. There must also be a way to validate that some, part, or all of the guidelines are relevant to wellness. The general approach must treat the health system's community as a (but not randomized) clinical trial.

Five Dimensions of the Medical Environment

- Culture makes information meaningful in terms of interpreting staff's experience and helping them decide how to act.
- Process represents the tasks that staff perform to create value for the patient. It must support measurement.
- Policy provides guidelines and allocates budgets by arbitrating effective and efficient operations with adaptive change to improve health outcomes and insure government compliance.

- Document/content is focused on presenting information to invoke desirable behaviors in the information consumer (e.g. medical staff: quicker diagnosis, ER).
- Infrastructure using global information networks, collaboration technologies and the web is deployed to ensure knowledge flow to improved population health at reduced cost.

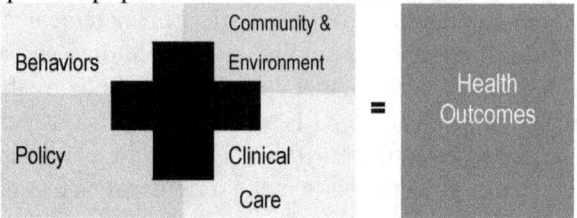

To mitigate the consequence of healthcare costs going beyond 20% of U.S. GDP, a healthcare system model includes institutions and the community and enumerates possibilities for technology improvement and the ways healthcare is delivered. The model quantifies and qualifies targets for capability development and continuous improvement using technologies for telehealth and telemedicine, air services and other transport facilities and disseminating best practices, R&D and innovation.

The metrics described are defined in the context of specific projects and those projects metrics and benefits must support the program KPIs which will be evaluated in terms of the portfolio KPIs.

Set of Key Performance Indicators

Critical to judging whether projects and actions being performed are achieving enterprise goals and objectives is to monitor and report on programs with respect to **Key Performance Indicators**. Sample KPIs are:
- Increased profit
- Increased quality patient health outcomes
- Reduced cost per capita for Population Health
- Explicitly defined Governance policy and procedures
- Delighted patients with experience of care
- Reduced time-to-complete patient-centered solutions
- Increased number of patents
- Improved staff competency and capability
- Improved collaboration / workgroup performance
- Improved access to and quality of records (EHR)

Best Practice will:
- Coordinate community wellness where hospitals create a community health network of acute care, GPs, community, mental health and social care services.
- Determine policy, culture, content, process, and infrastructure necessary to reduce per capita cost of population health.
- Determine the transformations required to create an improved patient experience and positive outcomes.
- Set guidelines to insure wellness, reduce cost of care, minimize patient risk and maximize positive outcomes.
- Educate the community in a language to communicate symptoms, illness, habits, and history.
- Validate everything in the EHR (Electronic Health Record) assuring quality of records compliance (ISO 15489).
- Revise the records framework into a structure that will make it better for analysis by artificial intelligence algorithms.
- Track cost per patient and cost to promote community wellness.
- Initiate Health Fairs to communicate healthy behaviors and how to identify symptoms that are indicators of medical problems.
- Use the EHR system to accelerate patient and knowledge flow to positive outcomes at lower cost.
- Install a Clinical Diagnosis System (CDS) to leverage recording of patient and community data and physician team diagnosis.
- Use an ERP system (Enterprise Resource Planning) to manage staff/resources/facilities/finance.
- Support the above objectives with IT, IoT, and telemedicine.

Programs:
- Program 1 - Inventory and preserve knowledge: create taxonomy, identify records, and define retention schedule.
- Program 2 - Define viable operating environment: record patient. information, define patient projects, Manage facilities/resources.
- Program 3 - Improve workforce competency and utilization.
- Program 4 - Leverage current and existing support systems EHR/ERP/CDS software, Telemedicine, HRM, Finance, Legal.
- Program 5 - Establish/coordinate population health region: health fairs, social outreach, regional tech services, solicitation.
- Program 6 – Coordinate out-of-hospital services.
- Program 7 - Perform Medical Research.

CHRISTMAS 2020

44th Epistle of Jim

Merry Christmas (at Thanksgiving). This epistle is a little short on humor. Happily, we are in the Florida Keys where unseasonably cold is 60 degrees. We sold our house on Beaver Island on Dec. 2nd in freezing temperatures in the middle of the COVID outbreak. We generated fifty 40-gallon bags of trash and put 50 boxes of books and 120 tubs of stuff in our nephew's warehouse on the island. We flew from Traverse City to Key West on December 7th and self-incarcerated for the 7 days. We are unsettlingly settled as "homesteaded" Florida Keys residents not snowbirds.

Judy found moving to be blood pressure elevating but dealing with me moving was the stuff of nightmares. She sorted through 60 years of memories in boxes, like 3rd grade papers and every letter ever sent her. I found a happy place for the insignificant stuff: 17' foot daysailer, Hobie 16', '99 Bonneville, ATV, upright piano, Nordic track, and elliptical trainer. My mother's upright piano is now residing in the island pub; my dad would be pleased.

In LA, a female Shepard/Husky pup, Opel, is filling a gap left by big boy Oscar, now in canine heaven. Emmy, Jamison's small mutt is not happy. When Opel is 3 times bigger, we hope Emmy is her best friend and not her chew toy. Oliver, Ian, Lauren and her fiancé Peter are all in lock-down with Lisa and Jamison. Never has bandwidth on the Internet been more important.

John's working for PwC, Patty's counseling business and Kate's schooling are being accomplished at home. Dan and Chris are in Philadelphia continuing with their music. Since Flynn passed away, the family now has two very cute small dogs: Luna and Sasha.

Jeff and Kristina's family have just been released from enforced 9-month incarceration with the three girls, a boyfriend, three cats, and two chocolate labs. Jeff and Kristina are rebuilding their business with a consultancy focused on healthcare and remote employment.

Because I regularly exercise, my aged body parts are surviving the move and the pandemic, so far so good; like a guy said as he passed the 43rd floor after jumping off the empire state building. Recent physical examinations have validated Judy and I are OK for our age; maybe we're only at the 23rd floor.

We sequestered at home while the news stoked pandemic fears. 300,000 people or 1% of the 30 million known cases have died. 210,000 or 4% were from the 50 million people over 65. 90,000 of the 280 million people under 65 that died represent 0.03% of the population. Lockdowns left 90 million unemployed, degraded our economy and required $trillion$ to be printed. Recently a newscaster described a politician as a "tiny, brained lunatic." That assessment applies to at least half of our politicians. Incarcerate us old people; everyone else go to work or school.

When I forgot a Saturday in early January, it was far more stressful for Judy than me. I did not believe we spent 90 minutes moving our boat from one canal to another until she showed me the boat, prompting a trip to Key West. If you want to see rapid response, tell the person at the ER desk: I think I'm having a stroke. I had a CT brain scan within ten minutes. Good news, I had a brain with no clot or bleeding. In a telemedicine consult, a neurologist said I had Transient Global Amnesia. Age is not a factor, and it goes away in 24 hours. They kept me overnight and released me. Then I got the bill: $19,000, which almost caused a stroke! In a surreal talk with a "hospital financial counselor," she implied it was no problem for me because: "Medicare took care of $16,000 and my supplemental insurance would take care of the rest." Medicare allows them to gouge because of their remoteness (not quality).

In his book, The Price We Pay, Dr. Marty Makary writes: "Healthcare officials confessed that they inflate bills more and more each year to generate more revenue since their insurance companies pay only part of their sticker prices. Insurers confessed they demand bigger and bigger discounts in their contracts with hospitals in order to keep up. Both acknowledged they pass on higher bills to the public… Hospitals markup 2 to 23 times what Medicare would pay." Healthcare is $3.3 TRILLION (18% of GDP) and climbing. Consequently, my book on transforming healthcare that I thought was done was delayed until I rewrote parts of it and added an appendix to propose what to do about the unnecessary cost of insurance, administration, and gouging.

Not getting vaccinated, does all of us a great disservice. Being aged, I have ceased to agree to disagree, but I am resigned to just let people be wrong. So, get vaccinated and hug all your friends.

Reflection 44: A Cure for USA Healthcare

Hospital's current price gouging will soon bankrupt the USA. Healthcare is $4.1 TRILLION (20% of GDP) and climbing. In a centuries old medical tradition, doctors charge rich people enough to cover poor people's treatment. Good insurance now equals rich.

190 million people in the USA have private health care. Insurers protect us from price gouging hospitals, but constant renegotiation adds significant expense. Insurers getting 20% for administration seems exorbitant, but pales in comparison to 500% hospital mark ups. Legislation has been inadequate: "Hospital list prices are set at exorbitant levels to extract higher reimbursements from insurance companies. ....no one knowledgeable about billing would agree to pay [hospital's listed prices]." (thehill.com/opinion/healthcare/414294-congress-should-broaden-legislation-to-curb-medical-price-gouging)

SOAP note (Subjective, Objective, Assessment, Plan) documents the way health care providers write notes in a patient's chart. What follows is a SOAP note to fix for USA healthcare.

Subject Component documents the Chief Complaint (CC)
1] USA healthcare expenditures are 20% of GDP; $4.1 trillion.
2] 5% of the population accounts for 50% of medical expenditures.
3] 30 million people have no insurance.
4] Many rural and remote communities have inadequate healthcare.
5] Bills to patients are usually between 2 to 23 times actual cost.
6] USA drug prices are 30% higher than in Europe.
7] Medical debt puts 20% of Americans into bankruptcy.
8] Medical error may be the leading cause of death in the USA.
9] All legislation continues to not "fix" these problems.

Objective Component documents information from observations and interpretation of cause from symptoms.

1] Patients sign an agreement to pay all bills with no knowledge of cost until after treatment leaving them no recourse to gouging.
2] Operating cost of many medical facilities is more than can be reasonably billed to its patients resulting in gouging or poor care.
3] Some medical staff regularly perform unnecessary procedures.
4] High medical usage patients include seniors with multiple maladies and patients with chronic conditions or drug addictions.
5] Outcomes are poorly measured for diagnosis/intervention/rehab.
6] Insurers and medical facilities are inappropriately regulated.
7] Remote area infrastructure is inadequate to support telemedicine.
8] Telemedical consult invoices are sometimes denied by insurers.

Assessment **Component** documents a (medical) diagnosis.
Congress must pass legislation to require:
1] CMS to publish a recommended and standard average price list with standard DRGs and WHO coded items.
2] Medical facilities must publish their price for the same items.
3] All insurance will be in a Medicare framework varying only in deductible/copay based on age/gender/health.
4] All medical facilities and insurance companies to become ISO 9001 compliant to assure quality and transparency of process.
5] Health care providers to revise their patient payment contact to read: " *I, <patient>, agree to pay for treatment in billing that is not more than <xx>% over the CMS standard prices.*"
6] All disputes go to binding arbitration with payout maximums.
7] Big Pharma offers best drug price relative to foreign contracts.

Plan **Component** documents treatment of USA Healthcare system.
Step 1] Regulate the healthcare and insurance markets effectively:
- Employers may purchase group base and supplemental plans for their employees in a Medicare insurance framework.
- Insurers can offer family plans where each family member may have different deductibles and copays.
- Community programs will provide free exams, promote healthy behaviors, and coordinate with social programs.
- **H**igh **U**sage/**R**isk **P**ool (>$500K in medical costs qualifies) to provides stringent oversight for high medical service use/abuse.
- CMS will partially fund HURP insurance pools for private insurers to reduce the risk for other group insurers.
- Malpractice and/or excessive billing claims go to arbitration.
- All healthcare facilities and insurers must be ISO9001 certified.
- Initiate a national telemedicine program with adequate telecom.

Step 2] Create a proof-of-concept model that delivers integrated, transparent, accountable healthcare.
- Penalize any healthcare facility or insurer that fails to be ISO 9001 compliant and properly publish prices (transparency).
- Provide a policy and procedure manual for a region leveraging telemedicine to integrate EMS, medical facilities and social services and specify a regional disaster plan.
- Institute a community paramedic program with broadest scope and number of procedures performed in the home by EMS personnel that assures Advanced Life Support EMS everywhere.
- Provide Community Paramedic and Physician Assistant certification education for nurses and EMTs.

- Insure major hospitals have ER staff and telemedicine to support rural (remote) healthcare in their region.
- Make major hospital support systems available to the region (e.g., EHR, IT, finance, HR, ERM).
- Develop elder-driven care plans based on quality-of-life goals.
- Assist elders and their family caregivers to get in-home support.

Step 3] Use CMS[11] insurance regions plus one to transition to single payer private insurance and healthcare.
- There will be one insurance policy framework, Medicare with its supplements and variants adopted from Obamacare as follows:
- Bronze= Medicare: $1000 Deductible/40% Copay.
- Silver= Medicare: $500 Deductible/30% Copay.
- Gold = Medicare (after age 65): $200 Deductible/20% Copay.
- Platinum = Veteran; No Pay.
- CMS will issue an RFP for one MAC to insure HURP with Federal government subsidies in the USA.
- CMS will issue an RFP for insurers as MACs to bid a fixed price for one insurer to provide Medicare in a CMS region.
- CMS will provide a Business Plan template to guide non-profit regional insurance organization start-ups.
- CMS pays MACs monthly negotiating overrun compensation.
- Insurers offer supplemental plans: prices may vary with age, gender, lifestyle, previous usage, and preconditions.
- Subsidies for the poor are provided as defined in Obamacare.
- CHIPS and IHS would be modified to qualify under Medicaid.

Step 4] Transition the Federal government from providing healthcare to regulating, paying and auditing insurers:
- Require all MACs, insurers and medical facilities to be ISO 9001 (or ISO 13485) certified by the FDA.
- Privatize VA, DOD and Indian medical facilities: sell facilities but, require services unique to its community.
- Hospitals bill CMS (MACs) and supplemental insurers with FDA oversight and audits.
- Insurers negotiate payments to hospitals from supplemental insurance premiums and Medicare.
- Patients pay the remainder based on their deductibles/copays and supplemental insurance agreement.
- As hospital service costs decline, MACs will be able to lower deductibles and copays.

---

[11] *A Medicare Administrative Contractor (MAC) is a private health care insurer that has been awarded a contract to administer multi-state Medicare claims in one of ten geographic regions.*

CHRISTMAS 2021
45th Epistle of Jim

This Epistle is full of minor tragedies and chaos which are funny but leaves me disoriented. We are back in the Florida Keys. Our commute from our new home near Jacksonville, FL is 8 hours not 30 from up north. After selling our home in December on Beaver Island in the pandemic, I watched with dismay in January while 150 homes in our price range were sold in two weeks. We rashly purchased a home unseen and unbuilt on January 29th. What could possibly go wrong? It was my least-worst investment. Our tiny lot appears bigger because a retaining pond with a fountain abuts our backyard. On the other side is farmland with cows! The 50 other versions of our house are now being sold for $$$$$$ more than we paid. My best investments have always been accidental.

In July, Judy and I flew to Beaver Island to see old friends and visit our stuff in anticipation of getting it shipped in August. Judy again found moving and me to be blood pressure elevating. We discarded many things previously but had 150 boxes of stuff to go through. Getting the stuff to our new home required A $$$$ ransom. The movers should have been jailed for stuffnapping; capitalism at its finest. I registered a complaint with two Federal agencies and got my anticipated response: zip. Our government tax dollars at work.

Judy and I now have one vehicle: a new Chevrolet Colorado truck. It took 100 hours of research to choose this little sweetie. I paid $$$$ less than the cost of a used 3-year-old same model truck. But the Pembroke Pines dealer ripped me off for $$$$ on my trade-in and sold it for twice what they paid me. Capitalism at its finest.

Judy and I celebrated our 80th birthdays this year. She asked me: we're not that old are we? I reassured her that we were not; we are really really old. However, on a positive note neither of us apparently look THAT old. At our granddaughter Lauren and Peter's Houdini Estate $$$$$$ wedding this year, Lisa said everyone thought we looked young: maybe 79. It was great to see John, Patty, Jamison, Lisa and six of nine grandchildren: Lauren, Ian, Oliver, Christopher, Daniel and Kate.

Jamison's female white Shepard puppy, Opel, is now 3 times bigger than Emmy. Emmy is now the older sister but still gets dragged around by a rope-in-mouth by Opel until an exhausted Emmy withdraws to the couch.

Kate and Oliver were accepted at Parsons in NYC for big $$$$$. Both started in the fall. Patty and John are close by for weekend meals and laundry. Their dogs, Luna, and Sasha are doing well. Dan and Chris are in Philadelphia continuing music. Ian will finish his Microbiology degree in December and has published a paper.

Do all dog lovers need two? Jeff and family have two brown labs and three cats. I wonder if they qualify for some kind of zoo subsidy. Jeff and Kristina were unable to attend the wedding since Australia keeps enforcing draconian COVID measures. They continue trying to rebuild their business while in lockdown. To bolster quarantine inflicted diminished revenues, Jeff has taken a position as head of a business incubation unit at La Trobe University in Melbourne. Capitalism at its finest.

Judy is now exercising regularly partly because she feels the need to be fit to put (not keep) up with me without elevated BP. Judy is also back to painting and is adding sailboats to her repertoire of animals, and seascapes. She's having fun which is good for me. "When the queen is happy, all is well in the realm." I am making very slow progress on several intellectually perplexing issues. E.g., Why: Delta and Omicron COVID? Why not: Zeta, or Eta?

Western civilization is now in a state of utter chaos. Bureaucracies were a quagmire of nonsensical automatic phone responses before the pandemic. Now it seems every company has implemented an artificial (non) intelligence system to prevent me from accomplishing anything. Moving, phone and utility companies and local, county and state governments and medical facilities all seem to have devolved to minimize effective communication that precipitate erroneous conclusions to maximize revenues with minimum employee involvement and effort. Capitalism at its finest.

With the pandemic lockdowns, last year I asked: could healthcare rise to 30% of GDP? Good news it went down. Bad news: it went down because major potentially life extending medical interventions were postponed. As befuddled but responsible citizens in our quasi-democracy, we exercised our freedom of choice to get two COVID vaccinations and booster. We hope you got yours so that everyone can hug their friends and family.

Reflection 45: Muddling

Throughout this book I have identified a variety of problems and suggested solutions that I think will solve them. Why am I confident that I (ego) can solve them. I'm a muddler.

In the preface, I introduced the concept of muddling to give you some idea about how to think about solving a problem that you have no idea how to solve. In an earlier Reflection Carl Sanders Peirce's idea of abduction (intuition) was introduced which formulates something from nothing to create a novel and never thought of before idea. If no one in a group has any idea how to solve a problem, you give it to the best muddler. A muddler isn't necessarily the smartest but one who is not intimidated by the breadth and depth of his ignorance. It also requires some system engineering skills which I hope I have communicated. Brain wave at 6Hz is muddling; 50Hz is intense rational or irrational thought.

Some people (me) have solved problems and communicated their solution when people who were measurably smarter than the problem solver (me) could not. Measurably smarter means IQ. Some people think IQ is unimportant; not true. Consider someone with a 200 IQ versus a 150 IQ. IQ is a logarithmic scale. This means $10^2 / 10^{1.5} = 10^{0.5} = 3.16$. So, a person with a 200 IQ learns three times faster than a person with a 150 IQ and 10 times faster than a person with 100 IQ. Obviously, learning is a key element since it is the input to analysis, which subsequently produces an artifact of a thought process.

Remember from Reflection 40, Whitehead, divides thinking into causal efficacy, presentational immediacy, and symbolic reference. Causal efficacy is the rate, bandwidth and content of stuff that is passing through a brain at any given moment. Presentational immediacy is what is absorbed by the brain's causal efficacy filter. Symbolic reference is what is applied from the storage capacity of the brain to the absorbed information. Higher IQ provides broader bandwidth in all three, but not necessarily better filters for problem-solving.

Someone who is really good at engineering is heavily invested in their discipline and will usually filter their bandwidth and content of causal efficacy to those presentational immediacy patterns within their discipline and hence, may not see the real problem or a framework for its solution. People with no engineering skills frequently don't have structures imbedded in their memory to conjure up a framework that will solve a problem in the mode of symbolic reference. Furthermore, without a sophisticated problem-solving background, they will not know the symbolic references to determine a solution.

This brings us to muddling. If one has a broad background and experience in engineering and mathematics as well as a familiarity with other disciplines, it becomes possible to muddle productively. A key aspect of creative thinking has been called thinking out of the box but thinking too far out the box without the requisite skills in problem solving disciplines will result in a cacophony of ideas and no viable solutions (e.g., The Green New Deal, Ethanol). If you have been to see a doctor lately with symptoms of something you don't understand, observe how a good general practitioner muddles through to a cause.

Part of solving wicked problems is attitude, not being limited by your ignorance, and being aware of what you don't know. There are plenty of smart people who don't solve problems because they can't face their own ignorance. Part of muddling is talking to people who tell you how hard and unsolvable a particular problem is but may also provide hints as to why they aren't producing a solution. Systems engineering considers people, processes, systems (technology) and knowledge in many different disciplines.

Two key elements in formal muddling are Stafford Beer's Viable Systems model and IDEF0 hierarchical process modeling. VSM provides a (multi-level isomorphism) framework for understanding, predicting behaviors, and managing individuals, workgroups, and organizations. IDEF0 provides a graphic methodology for illustrating ANY knowledge flow through ANY set of processes with ANY supporting technology. VSM and IDEF0 do not solve problems, they provide a powerful framework within which complex group, organizational and societal problems can be identified and subsequently solved.

I identified this approach to muddling to solve for complex problems as in Reflections 36 and 39.

CHRISTMAS 2022

46th Epistle of Jim

This Christmas finds us still disoriented from our Michigan move. The traffic in Jacksonville will take more getting used to after Beaver Island where imminent traffic danger was turkeys and deer.

Judy and I had our 59th wedding anniversary; kudos to me condolences to her. We are now both 81 which is a really cool number since it's 3^4. 82 will be boring but 83 is a prime and 84 is interesting as it is 3x4 x (3+4) and 89 is also a prime. Actuarily speaking, I may make it to 84 but maybe not 89.

Judy and my travel this year was limited to driving the length of Florida several times and wandering from one medical appointment to another. Each appointment required us to sign more than ten forms promising not to sue for malpractice and agreeing to pay whatever they felt like charging. People who think capitalism benefits healthcare need to experience medicine in Florida. Medical practitioners were OK but administrative and finance staff did their best to bankrupt us and failed, so far. Fortunately, we have Medicare and a supplemental insurance to protect us from medical bankruptcy. We are now ensconced in the Baptist Health System of Northern Florida which, absent bankrupting forms and promises of unlimited payments, is OK. As an aside, healthcare cost has now risen to 20% of GDP and the COVID virus got smarter; it just makes you sick thereby requiring more healthcare.

I finally talked myself into allowing someone to invade my person with a knife; actually, three probes from a robot to install a mesh over a hernia. I was fascinated by the idea of robotic surgery until I was rolled into surgery and spied what looked like a giant arachnid with four-foot legs (not eight) waiting to feed. If they hadn't clamped a mask on me, I was ready to run screaming out of there. All went well and I am now back to my exercise program with the hope that I will live to a cool number like 5^3 or at least $5^2 x 2^2$.

All three sons, Lisa, and Patty came to visit us this year in Green Cove Springs (SW of Jacksonville). Jeff came first in June to eat, cook, and drink. John and Patty came in July. Patty got to visit her friend in St. Augustine. We also celebrated Judy's 81st birthday before they flew back to New York. Lisa got us passes for the Harry Potter venue in Orlando. Jamison walked us around in the venue in late August. We went to a wizard stick store, but I wasn't selected to get one; disappointing because no one recognized me as the wizard that I am. We also celebrated their 30th wedding anniversary at a beach restaurant in St. Augustine.

John came to look after us in September when I had hernia surgery which was much appreciated. I am no fun to look after. Judy and John ganged up on me to obey the Doctor: no running, no heavy lifting, and walking only. I recovered with only a few hysterical moments, one involving a black and blue part. I think he and his brothers, came to check us for dementia or other age-related infirmities. We don't have dementia, but I can't remember symptoms.

We went to a way cool event in November: Van Gogh Immersion. His art was displayed on 60'x60'x12' walls which were covered with multiple paintings that kept refreshing with new canvasses. There were also fanciful animations with spinning windmills, blinking eyes, falling blossoms, and flying black birds.

I love our truck almost as much as people love their pets. And it takes us places and although it needs gas, we don't have to feed it, poop it or walk it. When not in use, it doesn't need attention.

Kate and Oliver are sophomores at Parsons in NYC, so John and Jamison continue depleting wealth. Dan and Chris moved from Philadelphia to the New York area to continue with their music. Chris is now working on a master's in music. Ian is taking time off from school but is investigating graduate programs. Lauren and Peter are now consolidating in wedded bliss in Brooklyn.

Judy exercises sporadically and attends yoga. She is happy to be in the Keys where she paints with her pals and instructor. We foresee a geezer community so Green Cove Springs may be transitional. I still struggle with intellectually befuddling issues: e.g., why not engineering theology instead of engineering philosophy?

Western civilization is in a state of utter chaos. At least the House and Senate are now controlled by different parties, so they may not get anything done. Doing nothing is better than government doing anything where dysfunction rules; we really need term limits.

Now that we are free from pandemic lockdowns, we wish you a less dysfunctional and exploratory 2023.

Reflection 46: Science Rant

What disturbs me is that few seem to understand the fundamentals, values, and use of science. This includes scientists and engineers but most especially politicians, environmental evangelists, and anyone with a liberal arts degree or no degree. Science is not exact and conclusions from a science have widely varying degrees of certainty. Physicists' conclusions are the most reliable when they are predicting physical events in our world and solar system. A chemist can predict chemical reactions. Biologists, sociologists, ecologists, and psychologists can predict little with any reliable accuracy. You are in trouble when scientists "vote" on the conclusions as in the IPCC report on causes of "climate change."

Biology may have been further along by now if they hadn't wedded themselves to Darwin's Evolution. Not all of it, just the part that genes "randomly" mutate and are not governed by some obscure recursive algorithm as suggested by Stephen Wolfram in *A New Kind of Science*. Biology and chemistry are now evolving more quickly since being invaded by quantum physicists.

Medicine is also becoming more of a science than an art as it has been invaded by quantum physicists in neurology and engineers in medical practices. There may even be hope for sociology and psychology as they too have been invaded by physicists and engineers.

Ecology is not bad science, but ecologists are still trying to figure out what elements in human and cyclic climate behaviors are causing destructive planet issues: e.g., soil erosion, nutrient depletion, hurricanes, tornados, land and water pollution, coral reef destruction, ocean rise, and air pollution. This must be constrained by the fact that robust economies require energy that is now supported mostly by fossil and nuclear fuels.

Some ecological causes are obvious: land pollution from trash and soil/food/nutrient depletion from over farming, fishing, and foresting. Denigrating Genetically Modified Organisms makes no sense, when it may be the only thing that will rebuild the soil and increase its yield to feed an increasing world population. Organically grown non-GMO food won't feed the world (yet).

Some solutions to ecology problems that are not so obvious lie in temperature rise and ocean rise and acidification. Also, reducing CO_2 (not a pollutant) by eliminating fossil fuel plants and natural gas pipelines may destroy Western economies in the short term before any benefits can be realized in the long-term. Temperature rise is usually good for humans, but ocean rise and acidification, and habitat destruction are definitely not good. What is really really bad is people who don't understand the risks and varying degrees of uncertainty in scientific conclusions about how to fix problems when they have no knowledge of science, engineering, economic systems, and complex adaptive systems. Future solutions to "fix" the environment should be engineered so as not to destroy western capitalism's economies and possibly kill most of their inhabitants.

From Yale Professor F. S. C. Northrop in *The Logic of the Sciences and Humanities*, consider how sciences evolve.

The 1st stage of scientific inquiry is what one directly perceives: relevant facts from a stream of consciousness. Pure fact is a continuum of aesthetic qualities, not an external material object. Scientific objects are theoretical objects; not immediately apprehended facts. Science requires an objective public world with its scientific objects to be the same for all observers. All one knows as pure fact is what one's senses convey that are intermittent aesthetic qualities for each person; they convey neither substance nor causality in the sense of a public world. Ecology which is in the process of determining the relevant elements in climate change is a science in the 1st stage.

The 2nd stage of scientific inquiry are concepts of intuition whose complete meaning must be found in factors, which can be immediately apprehended in the Whitehead's modes of causal efficacy and presentational immediacy. The 2nd stage of the scientific method inspects the relevant facts designated by the first stage of inquiry. The second stage begins with immediately apprehended fact and ends with described fact in the mode of symbolic reference. Since methods of the 2nd stage of inquiry are inductive involving 1] observation, 2] description and 3] classification, concepts are descriptive and qualitative in character. Biology with its classification of genera and species constructed in terms of observable characteristics is a science in the 2nd stage.

Unobservable objects of the 3rd stage are concepts by postulation or intuition (abduction). They are constructed in a deductively formulated system that designates explicitly what is proposed to exist. To this hypothesis, formal logic deduces theorems (induction) that define experiments to be performed. If all experiments give the result called for by the theorems, the hypothesis is confirmed and its entities and relations are said to exist. Physics (and Engineering) which can be predictive is a science in the 3rd stage.

CHRISTMAS 2023

47th Epistle of Jim

This Christmas I submerged early into my usual holiday dread since it's early November. I am writing this now to put this letter in Version II of "Reflections for My Grandchildren" published in 2007. I want prepublications to take to LA for Christmas where I will ambush my adult grandchildren with questions about it. Version II has an additional 30 Reflections. I've been busy.

After avoiding COVID for two years Judy and I got it in February. A gift from her friend that came to the Keys from Maine. Judy was pretty sick for five days; PAXLOVID medication kept her out of the hospital. If Judy hadn't tested positive, I wouldn't have taken the COVID test. With no symptoms, I may have been a distributer.

In April the web telescope came online with surprising results. From webtelescope.org: "Webb is able to observe some of the first galaxies, which formed a few hundred million years after the big bang. The big bang, the beginning of the universe, is currently estimated to have occurred roughly 13.8 billion years ago." The early universe is showing some galaxies which may or may not contradict the Big Bang Theory that formed our universe. Surprise, the more we know, the more we know that we don't know. Maybe we're just in a Black Hole of another universe. Feeling tiny?

Judy and I are now both 82 which is a really boring number but next year is a prime: 83. We had our 60th wedding anniversary in July (holy marital blessificity). Sons Jeff and John with wife Patty came to celebrate. 60 years is a really really looooooong time.

Because of Judy's fascination with mummies and Egyptology, on her birthday, we saw the National Geographic's Beyond King Tut exhibit in Jacksonville. The immersive experience featured nine projection mapped-driven rooms, with objects and reading displays interwoven. This was way cool, especially since, along with 1,349,795 other visitors, we had gone to the King Tut exhibit at Field Museum of Natural History in downtown Chicago in 1977. Its 55 objects were discovered in King Tutankhamun's tomb.

That was waaaaaay coooool. There was no way Egypt was going to do that again so in 2023 we got an "immersive experience." King Tut, was pharaoh of the 18th Dynasty of ancient Egypt (1341-1323 BC). His death ended the dynasty's royal line. He reigned from age nine until his death at age nineteen. His tomb is one of our greatest archaeological discoveries.

Judy spent quite a bit of time gardening, reading while even doing some knitting and painting. One of her reads was proofreading THE BOOK where she found six pages of mistakes while getting a little weepy over memories in past Christmas letters. She is also pulling together her diary of 20 years entitled "Everything Changes." When she is ready, I will format it into a book with a color cover of her paintings for a family reading.

I spent the first half of the year putting a healthcare model into a modeler which had so many bugs that I decided to quit after getting the first three levels of its hierarchy into it. The good news is that I finally showed how all 12 models in a network communicated with each other. BORING but it really illustrated the complexity.

From September to November, I spent eight hours a day working on THE BOOK. I really like it. The big question is will anybody else. Fifteen of the new Reflections are philosophical, theological, and engineerical (new word). I hope to convey the importance of both. The letters of course communicate the comedy that was, is and hopefully will continue to be our life.

You know that you're getting old when much of your email is associated with quality-low-cost cremation, a place for Mom, Medicare Advantage plans and telemarketing calls for pain medication and type II diabetes. Judy is also writing a sympathy card every other week. Maybe she could get a job with Hallmark. I remind myself that "old age is a privilege denied to many."

From Beneath a Scarlet Sky by Mark T. Sullivan: "…We never know what will happen next, what we will see, and what important person will come into our life, or what important person we will lose. Life is change, constant change, and unless we are lucky enough to find comedy in it, change is nearly always a drama, if not a tragedy. But after everything, and even when the skies turn scarlet and threatening, I still believe that if we are lucky enough to be alive, we must give thanks for the miracle of every moment of every day, no matter how flawed. And we must have faith in God, and in the Universe, and in a better tomorrow…"

We wish for you a miracle of every moment of every day.

Reflection 47: Purpose

The Quest for the Holy Grail has captured the imagination of people throughout the ages. Many of us seekers need a Holy Grail. Scientists' Holy Grail is Truth; Engineers' Holy Grail is Value. Religion was once about seeking Truth and delivering Value; now it's mostly about power and defense of dogma.

As I get older, I would like to look back on my life and think it had some purpose. Grandma and I did some fine work in the area of procreation. I solved some difficult problems which did not really benefit anyone much. I developed a unique ability to solve problems but solved no problems of real consequence.

I wrote five books that few people read, but some people who did read them changed their way of problem solving. Not good enough for a Holy Grail. Although this book may not qualify either, it does chronicle several quests. Maybe the next book on transforming environments will qualify as my Holy Grail.

Money is no substitute for Grail, but if I had more money, it might make the quest a little easier. On the other hand, maybe I would just worry about losing it or making more.

What constitutes your Holy Grail? When you look back on your life what do you want to be able to say about it? Will you seek truth or just earn money and consume?

My purpose with this book is to make some sense out of events that touched you and me and to provide insights for you. I also published a book about theology and the nonsense of atheism, but with a name like mine, I should have used a pseudonym.

I, like millions of others before me, would like to know why we are given the gift of consciousness and desire to know God and know what God thinks (the rest are details).

One seemingly inconsequential purpose was to write Christmas letters. As I look back on things that I have done, most of what I did of consequence was accidental.

Fathering children was no accident, but doing the right thing often enough so that our sons turned into good fathers and decent human beings was an accidental consequence of a few of my and many of my wife's actions. My one skill was thinking up creative consequences for delinquent behavior.

The people around me came out quite good because of or despite their association with me. So, relationships have been one purpose.

Yet another purpose was to become an exceptional thinker. Sadly, I am 30 IQ points short of exceptional. My FIVE books demonstrated that few people were interested in what I thought.

One of those books: *Faith and Reason* represented my quest to insert reason into religions and especially Christianity. I liked it. Once again, few were interested, but I wasn't stoned for heresy.

Although they may shudder at the thought, Richard Dawkins and Douglas Hofstadter have crystallized my idea about how God worked to create the Universe and us. We talked about Dawkins, but Hofstadter has been equally important.

Hofstadter has written several books; "Gödel, Escher and Bach" explored the idea of paradox in mathematics, art, and music. As I mentioned before, Taoism talks about God as the Mother of All Things paradoxically. In another book: "I am a Strange Loop," Hofstadter describes consciousness and soul. He sums up:

"Poised midway between the unvisualizable cosmic vastness of curved space-time and the dubious, shadowy flickerings of charged quanta, we human beings, more like rainbows and mirages than like raindrops or boulders, are unpredictable self-writing poems - vague, metaphorical, ambiguous, and sometimes exceedingly beautiful."

The reality we perceive is driven by flickerings of charged quanta in a cosmic curved space time which we comprehend only with mathematics and imagination.

Repeating the line from Dylan Thomas: "Do not go gentle into that good night, rage, rage against the dying of the light." I am not going gentle into that good night; I will keep writing books in the hope that one of them burns brightly long after I am gone.

So, live your life with purpose. To be sure, you need to have fun, but consciousness is too great a gift to squander. Have an answer when asked: Tell me why you are here, who you are, how you are going to contribute and what is your relationship to God, yourself, other people, the world, and the Universe.

Summary

Reflection	Thoughts to ponder.
Introduction	Who are you? What do you intend to do about it?
Stress/Health	Stress causes illness if you're not mentally/physically prepared.
Wine	Terroir - land, soil slope, elevation, climate produce fine wines.
CAD & Scientific Method	Great science predicts something that has not been observed.
Culture Shock	Culture should balance diversity with homogeneity.
Family – Child Psychology	Negative feedback teaches teenagers freedom requires restraint.
Bureaucracy	Inept bureaucracies underlie many of this century's problems.
Education & USMA	Education must teach problem solving and love of Democracy.
International Business	Capitalism has been good for economies and bad for the planet.
God, Morality, Law	What does it mean to live a religious, ethical, and moral life?
Communication & Memes	A party celebrates life and memes are elements of discourse.
Mobility & Energy	Mobility enriches lives of us few while impoverishing the planet.
Environment & Sun	Sun & wind provides energy options that don't consume or pollute.
Nursing/ Medicine	Medical Bureaucracy inhibits hospital care and increases costs.
Education	Education must cultivate effective discriminating habits.
War	War: after winning on the battlefield, how is order restored?
Generations and Genes	Genes bring a measure of immortality in the next generations.
Galaxies	Milky Way is our Galaxy: Let's at least colonize our solar system.
Internet	Internet provides pearls of knowledge in a sea of disinformation.
Fine Arts	Art, music, literature & theater provide insight into life & science.
History & 1421 Charts	Innovative analysis by one person can change everything.
Reflection & Philosophy	Training prepares for a career. Education expands our world.
Wind & Navigation	Wind is power, wind is motion, wind fills sails. I love wind.
Flow of Knowledge	Decisions must be based on knowledge not on data or noise.
Counting	Most people's knowledge of math requires an emergency upgrade.
Islamic Terrorism	Not facing Militant Islam may make a future fix impossible.
Ships & Seas	Past designs and accidents guide new rules for seaworthiness.
Christianity & Reason	Religion requires faith to search for God's undiscovered laws.
Australia	Australia is a showcase of plant and animal diversity.
Islands	Beaver Island to Manhattan, two diverse ways of life.
Architecture	Build from an Architect's drawing and a project plan.
1434 & Renaissance	The Renaissance was precipitated by the Chinese.
Black Holes	A marble size black hole has the same mass as earth.
Quantum Physics	Invades all aspects of our lives.
Permaculture	Edible Gardens.
Knowledge from Noise	New ideas are derived from incomprehensible noise of life.
Value from Flow	Artifacts that humans value come from engineering flow of knowledge.
Engineering Philosophy	Engineers go beyond induction and deductions to Abduction.
Legislative Lunacy	We are now governed by bureaucrats not elected officials.
Process Flow	Process flow of knowledge is what precipitates value.
Panentheism	God is in everything, and everything is in God.
Not Atheism	Atheism requires too much belief absent reason.
Engineering Theology	Engineers divine new artifacts.
Transforming Healthcare	Transforming healthcare will require interventions by engineers.
A Cure for USA Healthcare	Politicians, lawyers, and insurers prevent curing USA healthcare.
Muddling	How to think.
Science Rant	No One understands Computing.
The Information	Outline of history of Evolution.
5 Generations of Computing	20th Century Evolution of Computing.

USA EPA MPGe	*Reducing carbon footprint requires rational not activists' solutions.*
How to Get Old	*Exercise and take supplements.*
Habitat Sustainability	*Habitat destruction and trash should be our focus not CO_2.*
Demise of a Democracy	*Five reasons why Rome fell (analogous to USA now).*
Finite Planet	*Unsustainable Socio-ecological and economic cycles.*

We have reflected on these ideas big and small. Some of what was said was fact, some were established scientific theories and tested beliefs, some were assertions, guesses and opinions. Many people cannot tell one from the other. It is my fondest hope that after your education and life experiences, you are able to tell the difference.

What's your list of topics that's worth writing three pages on? Is there a structure to all of this? In Appendix C, there are eight pages of topics to study – Which one interests you? Do you know enough about those topics so that you know how much you don't know?

Questions to Ponder
What constitutes a valid argument?
What represents a statistically sound analysis?
What is knowledge, information, data, and noise?
How will you define and manage a project?
How do you systematically solve a problem? Can you count?
How will you communicate orally and in writing effectively?
How will you participate in the Arts?
What do you need to know about science?
How will you become a good parent, citizen, and friend?
How will you relate to yourself, others, Universe, and God?
What is your future job definition? How will you prepare?
What will you do to function effectively in a bureaucracy?
What is your religion and what do you believe?
What is your code of ethics? What is your Holy Grail?
Why and what must you learn about history?
How do we protect people, Earth, our country, and way of life?
When should government go to war? How do we conduct it?
How should government serve us and how do we pay for it?
What is democracy and how do we protect it?
What is law and how should it be administered?
What will you say about yourself in 50 years?
How much don't you know that you don't know you don't know?

BIBLIOGRAPHY

- American Bureau of Shipping, Rules for Conditions of Classification, 2018
- Andrews, Evans, 8 Reasons Why Rome Fell, history.com, Jan 2014
- Anonymous, Imperial Hubris, Brassey's, Inc., 2004
- Audi, Robert, Epistemology, Routledge, 1998
- Baker, James A. and Hamilton, Lee H., The Iraq Study Report, First Vintage Books, 2006
- Bateson, William, Mendel's Principles of Heredity, Cambridge University Press, July 2009
- Beaver Island Historical Society, Beaver Island Journal # I-V, 2002
- Beer, Stafford, The Heart of Enterprise, John Wiley, 1979
- Berkeley, George, The Principles of Human Knowledge, 1710
- Blackmore, Susan, The Meme Machine, Oxford Univ. Press, 1999
- Brennan, Sheilah O'Flynn, Perception and Causality: Whitehead and Aristotle, Process Studies, pp. 273-284, Vol. 3, # 4, Winter, 1973
- Bryson, Bill, In a Sunburned Country, Broadway Books, 2000
- Carnegie Mellon, People Capability Maturity Model SEI, July 2001
- Clark, Manning, History of Australia, Melbourne Univ. Publishing, May 1997
- Cooper, John, Panentheism: The Other God of the Philosophers, Baker Academic, November 2006
- Crichton, Michael, State of Fear, HarperCollins Books, 2004.
- Darwin, Charles and Huxley, Julian: The Origin of Species Sep 2003
- Dawkins, Richard, The God Delusion, Houghton Mifflin Co., 2006
- Dawkins, Richard, The Selfish Gene, Oxford Univ. Press, 1976
- Dennis, Jerry, The Living Great Lakes, St. Martin's Press, 2003
- Dewey, John, How We Think, Dover, 1910
- Descartes, Rene, Rules for the Direction of the Mind, 1629, translation E.S. Haldane/G.R.T. Ross, Cambridge Univ. Press, 1937
- Farmelo, Graham, The Strangest Man (Dirac), Basic Books, 2011
- Frenay, Robert, Pulse, Farrar, Stratus and Giroux, 2006
- Gibran, Kahlil, The Prophet, 7 Hills Book Distributers, 1995
- Gleick, James, The Information, Pantheon, March 2011
- Gore, Al, An Inconvenient Truth, Melcher Media, 2006
- Hardy, Ralph, Teach Yourself Weather, Hodder & Stoughton, 1996
- Hesse, Herman, Glass Bead Game, Holt, Rinehart & Winston 1943
- Holmgren, David, Permaculture: Principles and Pathways beyond Sustainability, December 2002
- Holzer, Sep, Sep Holzer's Permaculture, Chelsea Green, April 2011
- Hughes, Robert, The Fatal Shore, Vintage, 1986

- Hofstadter, Douglas, I Am a Strange Loop, Perseus Books, 2007
- International Standards Organization: 9001, 14001, 45001, 15489
- IPCC Synthesis Report for the 6th Assessment Report, 58th Session, Interlaken, Switzerland March 2023
- James, William, The Varieties of Religious Experience, Gifford Lectures, 1902
- Jefferson, Thomas, The Jefferson Bible, Beacon Press, 1989
- Jones, Jim I. The Document Methodology, 1999, version II 2007, version III 2019
- Jones, Jim I., Faith and Reason 2017
- Jones, Jim I. and Jones, Jeffrey I., Optimizing Healthcare, IEEE HEALTHCOM, China, March 2022
- Kant, Immanuel, The Science of Right, 1800, translated by W. Hastie, T & T Clark, 1887
- Kerwin and Furlong, Legislation: Administrative Procedure Act (APA), 1946
- Lynn, J., MD, *Medicaring Communities,* Createspace, June 2016
- Kipling, Rudyard, Letters of Travel, Amereon Ltd, July 1995
- Kuhn, Thomas S., The Structure of Scientific Revolutions, The University of Chicago Press, 1962, 1970, 1996
- Locke, John, Concerning Human Understanding, Holt, 1690
- Mac Neil, Karen, The Wine Bible, Workman Publishers Co, 2001.
- Machiavelli, Niccolo, The Prince, Oxford Univ. Press, 1935
- Menzies, Gavin, 1421 in 2003, 1434 in 2008, Harper
- Menzies, Gavin, The Lost Empire of Atlantis, Harper, 2011
- Montesquieu, Charles-Louis, "The Spirit of Laws", 1748, (Translator: Thomas Nugent), digireads.com, January 2010
- Nagel, Ernest and Newman, James R., Godëls Proof, New York University Press, 1958
- NASA , Black Hole Math (for high school seniors), February 2019
- Noonan, David, Neuro-, Simon & Schuster, January 1989
- Northrop, F. S. C., The Logic of the Sciences and Humanities, Ox Bow, Jan 1983
- Obama, Barack, Legislation: Affordable Care Act, Mar 2010
- Pagels, Elaine, Beyond Belief, HarperCollins Publishers, 2003
- Panek, Richard, Out There, NY Times Magazine, Mar 11, 2007
- Peirce, Carl Sanders, Philosophical Writings of Peirce, Dover Publications, March 2011
- Pirsig, Robert, Lila - An Inquiry into Morals, Bantam, 1991
- Plato, Dialogues of Plato, Meno and Theaetetus, 387 B.C., translated by Benjamin Jowett, London, Sphere, 1970

- Polkinghorne, John, Faith of a Physicist, First Fortress Press, 1996
- Putnam, Robert, Scandinavian Political Studies Journal, June 2007
- Porter, Michael E., Competitive Advantage, The Free Press, Macmillan, 1985
- Project Management Inst., Portfolio, Program & Project Standards
- Pyzdek, Thomas, The Six Sigma Handbook IV, McGraw Hill, 2014
- Richards, Chet, Certain to Win John Boyd's Strategy in the 21st Century, J. Addams & Partners, Inc., March 2005
- Ross, Douglas, An Introduction to SADT Structured Analysis and Design Technique, SofTech, 1976
- Rousseau, Jean-Jacques, The Social Contract & Discourses (G. D. H. Cole- Translator, February, 2017
- Schreiber, Ronnie, Is the EPA Fudging EV MPGe Figures?, thetruthaboutcars.com, June 2012
- Singer, S. Fred and Avery, Dennis T., Unstoppable Global Warming, Rowman and Littlefield Publishers, Inc., 2007
- Smith, Adam, An Inquiry into the Wealth of Nations, 1780, Thomas Dobson, 1796
- Sparrow, Giles, Cosmos, Quercus, 2005
- Stenger, V. J., God: The Failed Hypothesis. Prometheus, April 2008
- Sterling, Michael, So You Think You Can Count, Philsak
- Sun Tzu, The Art of War, Shambhala Publications, 1988
- Taylor, Charles, A Secular Age, Harvard University Press, 2007
- Thomas, Dylan, "The Poems of Dylan Thomas, New Directions Publishing Corp, 1946
- Tsu, Lao, The Way of Life, 600 B.C., translated by Witter Bynner, Lyrebird, 1972
- Tsu, Lao, Tao Te Ching, 600 B.C., translated by Gia-Fu Feng and Jane English, Random House 1972
- Twain, Mark, Following the Equator, American Publishing Co. 1897
- Wynn, Charles M. and Wiggins, Arthur W., The Five Biggest Ideas in Science, John Wiley and Sons, 1997
- USA constitution
- USMA, 21st century core curriculum in the form of learning models
- World Economic Federation, Global Competitiveness Report, 2019
- Whitehead, Alfred North, Religion in the Making, 1926
- Whitehead, Alfred North, Process and Reality, 1929
- Wolfram, Stephen, A New Kind of Science, Wolfram Media 2002
- 9/11 Commission Report, W. W. Norton, 2003

APPENDIX A: ADDITIONAL REFLECTIONS
Reflection 48: The Information

I am a fan of James Gleick's writing and recommend that everyone read his book, *The Information (published in 2012)*. It is an amazing compendium of "information." However, it is neither comprehensive nor complete. Gleick concludes his book with a return to the Library of Babel quote: "What good are the precious books that cannot be found?" The library will endure; it is the universe. As for us, everything has not been written; we are not turning into phantoms. We walk the corridors searching the shelves and rearranging them, looking for lines of meaning amid *leagues of cacophony and incoherence*, reading the history of the past and of the future, collecting our thoughts and collecting the thoughts of others, and every so often glimpsing in mirrors, in which we may recognize creatures of the information.

Every reviewer (but me) extolled James Gleick's capabilities as a writer and his broad understanding of science and his ability to convey it in a coherent format. I would have preferred less depth on tangential and biographical topics and more on the development of the framework that now supports the Internet. Also, because of digressions, it is difficult to see a coherent timeline.

This is a book about foundational technologies, mechanisms, philosophies, and theories. The ones after 1950 that resulted in the Internet are given short shrift:
1] Program computers with assembly, high level, "C" computer languages;
2] One user, one program evolve to multi-user operating systems (OS) and text;
4] Scripting language to allow general use of programs on any computer or OS;
5] Systems security that allows secure handling of transactions;
6] Library Science and Databases manage the Web's information;
7] Formal and symbolic logic create taxonomies and ontologies for finding and validating the authenticity, reliability and completeness of information.

Without their inclusion, one concludes that the Web is a Library of Babel. This is partially true but these technologies, methodologies, taxonomies, and ontologies can still find lines of meaning amid cacophony and incoherence.

Readers will only find a partial rendering of an in-depth enumeration of the relevant theories and underlying systems of the Internet that have generated today's tsunami of information. Because of its many flaws, I wrote my own history of information in three basic periods that follow.

A. The Premechanical Age: 3000 B.C. - 1450 A.D.

Writing and Alphabets--communication.
- First humans communicated only through speaking and picture drawings.
- 3000 B.C., the Sumerians in Mesopotamia (south Iraq) devised cuneiform
- 2600 B.C., the Egyptians write on the papyrus plant.
- Around 2000 B.C., Phoenicians created symbols.
- 800 BC Hebrew/Aramaic/Greek/Latin derived from Phoenician alphabet.

Books and Libraries: Permanent Storage Devices.
- Religious leaders in Mesopotamia kept the earliest "books."
- The Egyptians kept scrolls.
- 700 BC library of an Assyrian ruler from Nineveh, his capital city.
- 600 BC Greeks began to fold and bind sheets of papyrus.
- 400 BC First public library; the private library was more prevalent.
- 323 BC Library of Alexandria for scholars held 750K scrolls (destroyed).
- 245 BC Callimachus, the first bibliographer, organized his library by authors and subjects. Pinakes ("tables") was the first ever library catalogue.
- 200 BC Rome libraries expanded from war to include Aristotle's collection.

The First Numbering Systems.
- Egypt:1-9/vertical lines, 10/circle, 100/coiled rope, and 1,000/lotus blossom.
- 150 AD Hindus invented nine-digit numbering systems similar to today.
- 875 AD the concept of zero was developed.
- The First Calculators: Abacus. 1st info processors in Persia 600 B.C.

Libraries evolved and books were invented.
- **2nd century**, Codex, stacked, bound wooden boards record literature, science, and technical info is replaced by parchment and form modern day books.
- **350** A catalog of Rome's buildings from 350CE enumerated 29 libraries.
- **500** Egypt's Pachomius established a monastery insisting on monks' literacy.
- **529** Benedict established a monastery in Monte Cassino and mandated how monks would live including reading two hours daily.
- **700** Charlemagne had a robust library in Aachen; ordered one for all schools.
- **800**: Library catalogues are introduced in House of Wisdom and other medieval Islamic libraries organizing books into genres and categories.
- **1400** Vatican Library opened. Accompanying growth of universities was development of university libraries; many were founded from personal donations. Duke of Gloucester gave books to Oxford in 1400s.

1000 AD African Talking Drums whose pitch can be regulated to the extent that it "talks" traced back to the Ghana Empire (830-1235).

B. The Mechanical Age: 1450 – 1840 (alphabet 800 B.C., '0' 875 A.D.)

The First Information Explosion.
- 1450 Gutenberg Invented movable metal-type printing press.
- Developed book indexes and the widespread use of page numbers.

Slide Rules, the Pascaline and Leibniz's Machine.
- Slide Rule. Early 1600s, by William Oughtred, an English clergyman.
- The Pascaline. Early example of an analog computer Blaise Pascal (1623-62).
- One of the first mechanical computing machines, around 1642.

- Infinity, ∞, invented by mathematician John Wallis in 1655 is unlimited, endless, without bound: mathematical, physical, and metaphysical (god).
- Leibniz's Machine (The Reckoner). Gottfried Wilhelm von Leibniz (1646-1716), German mathematician and philosopher.

Babbage's Engines: Charles Babbage (1792-1871), English mathematician.
- The Difference Engine created in 1822: "method of differences".
- The Analytical Engine, Joseph Marie Jacquard's loom during 1830s.
- Parts remarkably similar to modern-day computers. store/mill/punch cards.
- Punch card idea came from Joseph Marie Jacquard's (1752-1834) loom.
- Introduced in 1801. Binary logic fixed program operating in real time.
- Augusta Ada Byron (1815-52). The first programmer.

C. The Electromechanical Age: 1800 - 1942.

Electricity was discovered. Information is converted into electrical impulses.

1] The Beginnings of Telecommunication.
- 1800 Alessandro Volta's battery.
- 1804 Optical Telegraph.
- 1820 Recognition of electromagnetism, H. Ørsted and A. Ampère.
- 1821 Electric motor. Michael Faraday.
- 1827 Mathematical analysis of electrical circuits, Georg Ohm.
- 1832 Electromagnetic Telegraph. Pavel Schilling.
- 1835 Morse Code. Samuel Morse dots and dashes.
- 1876 Melvil Dewey developed the Dewey Decimal Classification.
- 1876 Telephone Alexander Graham Bell. Bell Labs founded.
- 1894 Radio, Guglielmo Marconi 1894 after discovery that electrical waves. travel through space can produce an effect remote from transmission point.
- 1862-1895 Electrical engineering makes electricity ubiquitous.

2] Electromechanical Computing.
- 1880 Punch cards for census. Herman Hollerith.
- 1890 International Business Machines Corporation (IBM) founded.
- 1942 Mark 1. Paper tape stored data and program instructions (8' tall, 51' long, 2' thick, 5 tons, 750K parts). Howard Aiken, a Ph.D. student at Harvard.

Reflection 49: Five Generations of Digital Computing

Note: I've been told that I left some really important stuff out. So be it.

Introduction: The Electronic Age: 1942 – 1951 (Author was born in 1941).
- 1943 Alan Turing defines a way with symbolic logic to 'program' a universal computing machine; developed a code breaking algorithm/machine.
- First Tries. Early 1940s. Electronic vacuum tubes.
- Eckert & Mauchly. First High-Speed, General-Purpose Computer: ENIAC.
- Electronic Numerical Integrator and Computer (ENIAC) 1946.
- Used vacuum tubes to do its calculations, but it could not store its programs was developed by John Mauchly, physicist, J. Prosper Eckert, engineer at the Moore School of Electrical Engineering, University of Pennsylvania.
- 1949 Claude Shannon Bell Labs: Mathematical Theory of Communication
- 1st *Stored-Program* Computer(s)Manchester University Mark I (prototype).
- EDVAC - Electronic Discreet Variable Computer (Mauchly & Eckert 1940s).
- John von Neumann's influential "Report on the EDVAC" in June1945.
- Max Newman at Manchester University, *England outpaced the Americans*.
- 1949 Maurice Wilkes at Cambridge University completed EDSAC (Electronic Delay Storage Automatic Calculator) 2 yrs before EDVAC.
- EDSAC became the first stored-program computer in general use.
- 1951 Eckert & Mauchly at Remington Rand developed the 1st General-Purpose Computer **UNIVAC**: UNIVersal Automatic Computer.
- LEO (Lyons Electronic Office) became the world's first commercial computer (a few months before UNIVAC).

The First Generation (1951-1958).
- Vacuum tubes as their main logic elements.
- Punch cards to input and *externally* store data.
- Rotating magnetic drums for *internal* storage of data and programs.
- Programs written in Machine and Assembly languages require **a compiler**.

The Second Generation (1959-1963).
- Vacuum tubes replaced by transistors as main logic element.
- AT&T's Bell Laboratories, in the 1940s.
- Semiconductors, crystalline mineral materials, allow transistors.

The Third Generation (1964-1979).
- **Jim Jones** wrote CAD algorithms in 1964 in FORTRAN (IBM 7094).
- Magnetic tape and disks replace punched cards as external storage.
- High-level programming languages E.g., FORTRAN and COBOL.
- Individual transistors were replaced by integrated circuits.
- Magnetic tape & disks replace punch cards as storage devices.
- Magnetic core *internal* memories gave way to metal oxide semiconductor (MOS) memory, which, like integrated circuits, used silicon-backed chips.

- Operating systems.
- Large scale time-sharing systems.
- Advanced programming languages like BASIC developed.
- **Jim Jones** received his Dr. of Engr. for work in Computer Graphics (1970).
- Bill Gates' started Microsoft in 1975.

The Fourth Generation (1979 - 1990).
1] Large-scale (LSI) and very large-scale (VLSICs) integrated circuits.
2] Microprocessors that contained memory, logic, and control circuits (an entire
3] **CPU** = (Central Processing Unit) on a single chip.

Allowed for personal computers like Apple II, Mac, and IBM PC.
- Apple II released to public in 1977, by Wozniak and Jobs.
- Initially sold for $1,195 (without a monitor); had 16k RAM.
- IBM PC introduced in 1981 with MS-DOS (Microsoft Disk OS).
- **Jim Jones** debugged first UNIX CAD/CAM workstation with icons (1982).
- UNIX Engineering workstations from DOD Multics secure-time OS.
- MS Windows debuts in 1983 but is quite a clunker.
- Apple Mac with icons debuts in 1984.
- 4th generation language software products: Lotus 1-2-3, dBase, MS Word, etc.
- Graphical User Interfaces (GUI) for PCs arrive in early 1980s.
- Email commercialized about 1984.
- NSFNET connects universities in 1985 evolved from DOD Arpanet.

The Fifth Generation (1990 - 2000).
- Icon driven User Interfaces commonplace.
- HTML scripts developed for Internet Web pages.
- NSFNET is commercialized as Internet in 1995.
- Windows 95 finally debuts in 1995 with icons.
- XML, Java Scripts, Web 2 introduced by 2000.
- Sophisticated Internet Search Engines: e.g. Google.
- **Jim Jones** published his first book: *The Document Methodology in 1999.*

The Internet becomes *"leagues of cacophony and incoherence."* **(2000-2023).**
- Surveillance Capitalism arises with Google, Facebook, Twitter and TikTok.
- **Jim Jones** published: The Document Methodology v.2 in 2007, v.3 in 2019.
- Android and iPhones track your every move and disinformation dominates.

Reflection 50: USA EPA MPGe

USA EPA MPGe ratings are overstated by over 50%.
https://www.thetruthaboutcars.com/2012/06/is-the-epa-fudging-ev-mpge-figures/

USA EPA calculates MPG ratings based on energy at point of delivery; it ignores the energy costs of drilling, pumping, refining, and transporting gasoline to the corner gas station. When calculating miles per gallon equivalent (MPGe) ratings used to evaluate fuel costs for electric vehicles and hybrids, the EPA also ignores the energy costs of producing and transmitting electricity and the energy costs of transforming transmission line voltage to 110/220 VAC and then losses in converting to the Direct Current needed to charge batteries. The EPA also assumes that EV batteries have a charge/discharge efficiency of 100%. Essentially the EPA is treating EVs as though electricity is 100% efficient until it gets to the vehicles' motors. You could say the same for gasoline, by not looking at total energy costs of getting that fuel to market. **The EPA mileage tests EVs, dividing electricity consumed by an energy conversion factor of 33.7 KWhs per gallon of gasoline to arrive at MPGe ratings.**

There are extraction, processing, and transportation energy costs for all fuels, including the coal, natural gas, gasoline, and uranium used to generate electricity. Drilling, pumping, and refining crude oil plus trucking and dispensing gasoline consumes the equivalent of about 10% of the energy in the crude oil. That 10% energy cost is comparable to the 90% efficiency of electrical transmission lines and local distribution systems, or the 90% efficiency of AC/DC conversion and battery charge/discharge cycles. ~~90% efficiencies together yield an 81% efficiency. With gasoline,10% energy cost is all that's involved. Most energy in the near term, not generated from coal will be generated from natural gas, not wind and solar power (with their own energy costs).~~

Essentially, to run an electric vehicle, a chemical is converted into heat then into electricity. Turning chemical energy into heat into power involves waste heat. Average energy efficiency of electrical power plants is about **42.5%** (this is a fair number). ~~Multiplying all efficiencies in electricity generation to be charged into your car's battery pack 42.5% x 0.81= 34.4%.~~
https://www.eia.gov/todayinenergy/detail.php?id=44436 >60% utility energy loss.
https://propane.com/for-my-business/fleet-vehicles/propane-autogas-emissions-data/

- EV Honda Fit's EPA rating of 118 MPGe x .[425] ~~.344~~= 50 MPGe (actual).

- EV Fit as 29% more fuel-efficient than the gasoline version; much less than MPGe.

According to Honda Insight HEV to Fit EV table, HEV is more efficient than the Fit EV.

Honda	Insight HEV	Fit EV	Fit ICE	Note:
MPG	54	50 mpg	35mpg	Insight
Length	183.6 in	161.4 in		is bigger
Width	71.6 in	67 in		than Fit

EV's 1000lb battery requires 30lbs of cobalt, 25lbs of lithium, 200 of lbs copper 400 lbs of aluminum extracted from 250 tons of ore!!!

HEV battery weight < 250lbs (more efficient HEV batteries result in higher mpg)

https://www.eia.gov/energyexplained/electricity/electricity-in-the-us.php

Fossil Fuel Energy: Natural gas 38% / Coal 22% / Petroleum < 1%.

Renewables: 20%: wind 9.2% / hydro 6.3% / solar 2.8% / biomass 1.3%; Nuclear 19%.

Note: 40,000 coal industry employees will need to be retrained for another occupation or the US can ship coal to China as does Australia who burns no coal.

Ford has a Qualified Vehicle Modifier (QVM) program to convert trucks to dual fuel (LP). Preparing natural gas for use is simpler, cheaper, and less polluting than refining petroleum.

Reflection 51: How to Get Old

From David Noonan's book, *Neuro-*: "Sitting in the doctor's waiting room, the patient faces the fact that his body may not be working right. Feeling at odds with one's own body is an understandable reaction to sickness, and it's one of the things that make doctors' waiting rooms such weird places. In the grip of a kind of psychological dismemberment, the patient sits there feeling betrayed by his own [body]."

I am in pretty good shape for a person over 80. However, I feel at odds with my own body as it ever so certainly degenerates. My biggest asset in sports was the intensity I brought to mediocre athletic skills to win when competing against better athletes. My grandson won't even shoot baskets with me for fear I'll seriously injure myself. I need to avoid sports that require quickness of movement because my brain demands movement of a 20-year-old.

Aging is being "in the grip of a kind of psychological dismemberment." Working feels like being "betrayed by [my] own body." Now I don't feel sorry for me, and I don't expect anyone else to. My very old body works much better than most other very old bodies and many would-be bodies my age aren't working at all. However, lifting heavy objects in the sun, getting dehydrated, and climbing up high ladders isn't such a good idea as Judy continuously reminds me. I am still operationally useful, but I did forget an entire day after working outside replacing all the flooring on our front deck. Transient Global Amnesia lasts 24 hours and 'usually' never returns but I felt "betrayed by my own body."

Now that I'm done whining, being 82 years old is a privilege not afforded to many. I will now speculate on how to live longer.

It breaks down into several areas in order of priority:

1. Weight / Cholesterol
2. Supplements/ breakfast drink
3. No smoking or drugs
4. Moderate Alcohol consumption
5. Exercise
6. Food / Diet
7. Genetics
8. Medicine

My Unsubstantiated Opinion: You are in charge of your health. Spend time thinking about and researching what is best for you in terms of exercise, sleep, supplements, food, socialization, sports, lifestyle, religion, and your emotional well-being. Fear and stress are good things if it motivates accomplishment. Not being able to sleep can be good if it does not negatively impact your waking hours. Enjoy the extra hours rather than stressing out about not sleeping or just take a nap later (like me in my old age).

Exercise: 12-ounce curls don't count. My personal experience is by exercising 30-60 minutes a day, I need 2 hours less sleep. Arguing with a woman who said that I was taking years off my life by not getting 8 hours sleep, I responded that I already spent 12 waking adult years longer than she had ($\approx$360x2hrs/60yrs). I make the first hour of my day about body preservation with exercise and supplements while ignoring my body for the next 17 hours except for an occasional beard trim and shower and some food of course. Try to avoid colliding with something big or having major collision incidents (cycling into cars), crashing a vehicle (e.g., car, bike, ATV, skateboard, motorcycle) and falling from heights.

Supplements: Vitamin E helps me recover more quickly from a workout and vitamin B helps mitigate the physical effects of stress. I discovered steak helped me recover from a weight workout but made running the next day a misery. I also found that wine consumption helped my next day run (not a recommendation to guzzle large quantities of alcohol). I also take a multi-vitamin and other stuff not worth mentioning because I think half of them help but I'm not sure which half. I also have my high-powered morning drink: V8 Fusion, blueberries, banana, green superfood, beet and protein powder and Greek yogurt. Brewer's yeast is good, but it makes me a hot air balloon; I generate enough gas without it.

No Smoking or Drugs and Alcohol in Moderation: You are really shortening your life if you do either drugs or smokes. If you must abuse yourself, alcohol will take longer to kill your liver than smoking will to kill your lungs. Keep in mind, excessive drinking can result in collisions. Drugs including prescription drugs can do damage everywhere. Take drugs, if you must, to restore body function but take as little as possible.

Weight/Cholesterol: If you can be fat and healthy more power to you. I found as I got older fat became debilitating. High cholesterol will eventually cause major blood vessel blockages. FYI: you need your blood to circulate. Keep monitoring your blood, it can identify problems early that you are unaware of. "Every pound of weight we put on is 5 miles of blood vessels. If your heart beats 100K times a day, that's 500K miles a day for one pound of fat," says Dr. Kopecky at Mayo Clinic. Also, it puts more stress on all your joints below the waist. I have fatted myself up to a right knee problem and now row instead of run.

Food/Diet: Feel free to ignore all of this. Spend all the time you like preparing and over-eating whatever you like but do include some vegetables, fruit, and meat. If you must eat really right, eat like Mormons or Kosher Jews; both groups outlive the average American by 5 years. Feel free to ignore whatever food pseudo-experts tell you but watch your weight. You might even try vegetable and fruit pills and ice cream for protein and fat. Being over-weight might be OK but being obese and morbidly obese will probably kill you early.

I eat-to-live as opposed to live-to-eat. I put food at the bottom of my priority list. Eating right can be extremely time consuming. If left to my own devices, I would eat steak and bean salad and the supplements above. Enjoy your desserts and whatever else that you want to eat while you can but clogged arteries and type II diabetes are really really bad.

Genetics may be the most important factor in longevity, but we don't get to pick our parents. Maybe in the future you'll be able to splice in anti-fat, anti-aging, and superpower immune system genes, but not today. Don't underestimate the value of a good immune system. My "Genghis Khan" of immune systems that annihilates any wayward virus is more important than an athletic muscular body. My body type is the well-known mister-potato-head shape: oversized ovoid body and stubby limbs.

Medicine: To assess your health, know your blood chemistry. When something goes wrong consult a medical doctor not an alternative health pseudo-doctor. Spend all the time you like with dieticians and alternative medicine people to stay healthy and bolster your immune system, but if you're not well, a medical doctor is the only rational choice (e.g., cancer, broken bones, disease, tumors, etc.). However, remember what the medical student who graduates last in his class is called: Doctor. Find a good one (it's not easy). If you must see a specialist, research, and pick the best hospital for your malady. US News and Medicare rank hospitals. E.g., Mayo Clinic for diagnosis, Cleveland Clinic for heart, M.D. Anderson for cancer, Bascom Palmer for cataracts. If you need a surgeon, hand-eye coordination is important not published papers.

The more accurate the description of symptoms, the better chance a doctor has to make the right diagnosis. Your body is a complex adaptive system that doctors don't quite understand, but they know 100 times more than you, so bear with them while they guess. Find a good guesser.

Reflection 52: Habitat Sustainability

To support its adaptive management[12] approach an Island Sustainability Task Force (ISTF) defined and managed a portfolio[13] of programs which in turn contain multiple projects intended to preserve natural resources and promote ecotourism.

An Island Portfolio of Programs and Project charters communicate the breadth and depth of activities necessary for the sustainability of an island is outlined here. The portfolio is continuously evaluated in Tollgate reviews in terms of key performance indicators to determine the success and set priorities for its various programs and projects.

Project and Portfolios are continuously monitored and measured against the KPIs[14] defined within the portfolio. Each program has a different subset of KPIs with which to assess the performance of the projects within the portfolio. This evaluation is performed in a Tollgate Review where subject experts make judgments.

Programs: Activities associated with Programs are ongoing and are intended to build ecological and tourism knowledge and continuously review operations and resultant artifacts of projects within that program. The five programs (includes 20 projects) are:

1] Inventory and Conserve Habitat

2} Manage Animal Species

3] Protect Problem (endangered and invasive) Plant Species

4] Promote Tourism: Hunting, Fishing, Wildlife Viewing, Natural Resources

5] Seek funding and recognition

Currently KPIs and goals require expert critique and approval:
- Number of visitor days per season; average dollars per day spent

---

[12] **Adaptive management** is a structured, iterative process of optimal decision making in the face of uncertainty, aimed at reducing uncertainty over time via system monitoring.

[13] **A portfolio** is defined by the Project Management Institute as a collection of projects, programs and other work that are grouped together to facilitate effective management and meet strategic business objectives. Components of a portfolio are quantifiable; they can be measured, ranked and prioritized. Program management's goal is 'doing the right work'; project management's goal is 'doing the work right'.

[14] **KPIs:** Critical to judging whether the projects and actions being performed by the ISTF are improving the Island's natural assets and economy is monitoring and reporting on programs with respect to Key Performance Indicators (KPIs).

- $s of funding from academic and government sources
- $ value of real estate sales (including land); ratio of value
- $ value of commercial and residential buildings built/remodeled
- % Knowledge of natural habitat inventories
- Acres of Invasive Species / less than 2 acres
- % of archipelago assessed for threats to biodiversity, habitat and species and mitigated / 100%[15]
- % acreage of submerged vegetation for fish spawning recorded
- % of wetlands and shoreline documented for pollution and species at risk and mitigated / 100%
- Level of Pollution and species at risk (level 1 to 6; best = 1, high =5; not known = 6) / level 1

Threats to the biological diversity of the Island were identified: water flow manipulation, landscape fragmentation, invasive exotic species, pollution of all kinds, forestry, and moderate conservation ethics in the human population. The wetland natural communities of the region have been reduced in many cases to small, isolated fragments that harbor exotic species and have lost some of their integrity. The lakes, ponds, rivers, and streams that define this ecoregion are compromised by pollution. Deer, raccoons, and groundhogs have been introduced to the ecosystem. Restoration of ecological systems, forests and their component species will be vital to success in conserving forest, wetlands, and aquatic features.

Influencing public local, state, and federal policy in the areas of water management, forestry, and deer management will be crucial. Deep and committed partnerships in all these endeavors will be important to be successful in achieving the goals of this plan.

Islanders understand the relationship and value of wildlife and habitat to their health, social and economic well-being. Citizens, NGOs, and government agencies must partner to insure responsible recreation, forests, habitats, endangered species, and native wildlife populations are more robust, self-sustaining, and in an appreciably better condition than they are today.

The island's economy is heavily dependent on eco-tourism. Understanding what residents and tourists value is a critical part of identifying what to preserve. ISTF must inventory natural resource and habitat assets and define projects for their restoration.

---

[15] For KPIs 7 and 8 level 1-6 will be defined in detail. Mitigated means a risk mitigation plan and actions have commenced.

Threats by Program:

Program 1: Lack of inventories and information to assist with appropriate planning.

Program 2: Proliferation of game species. Loss of bird and migratory habitat.

Program 3: Endangered species loss; proliferating invasive species.

Program 4: Not enough tourists. Destructive human interaction with natural resources.

Program 5: Inadequate private, local, state, and academic planning, resources, and funding for restoration of public lands.

Portfolio, Program and Project Reviews

There are two primary developments resulting from planning:

1. A set of programs for Eco-tourism, Tollgate Reviews and Project Management. These can be used to implement and guide work on the Island in the context of Portfolio Management
2. A table of outputs from these generalized processes that define specific document titles, and data capture descriptions as well as a summary of the associated template structures:

Island Programs	Tollgate/Portfolio Review Procedures	Project Management
Inventory and Conserve Habitat	*Assess Work Result*	*Propose*
	Assess Work Process	*Initiate*
Manage Animal Species (QDM)	*Determine Alignment with Goals*	*Plan*
		Execute
Inventory and Manage Problem Plant Species	*Prioritise Projects and Balance Portfolio*	*Control*
		Close
Promote Tourism	*Decide: Stop, Hold, Go*	
Seek Recognition & Funds	*Approve, Record, Deploy.*	

Monitoring and evaluation of progress is dependent on tollgate reviews by 'qualified' experienced reviewers specific to at least one KPI. Failure to use the right person in a critical review can result in a poor assessment of the portfolio's progress. Clearly defining the experience of reviewers and making sure the selected person for a role or task is qualified will have a major impact on the results of the proposed projects.

Reflection 53: Demise of a Democracy

Philosophy: Why Democracies Fail. See modern parallels?

Plato argues that democracy is inferior to monarchy, aristocracy, and oligarchy because democracy tends to undermine the expertise necessary for proper governance of society. Most people lack the intellectual talents to think well about politically difficult issues. Hence, the state will be guided by poorly worked out ideas because incompetents are good at using manipulation and mass appeal to help themselves win office. Plato argues that the state should be ruled by philosopher-kings or an expert oligarchy (like China) who have the competencies required for effective rule.

Montesquieu states that a necessary condition for the existence of a republic is that the people in whom power is lodged possess the quality of "public virtue," meaning that they are motivated by a desire to achieve the public good. Montesquieu asserts that without strong public virtue, a democratic republic is likely to be destroyed by conflict between various "factions," each pursuing its own narrow interests at the expense of the broader public good. He argues democratic republics must be small to succeed since people must collectively know and trust each other. This suggests homogeneity NOT diversity. Europe supports diversity by establishing a new country every 500 miles or less.

Five Reasons Why Rome Fell. See any modern parallels?

1. Invasions by barbarian tribes
The most common theory for Western Rome's collapse was a string of military losses sustained against outside forces. The Romans weathered a Germanic uprising in the late fourth century, but in 410 the Visigoth King Alaric successfully sacked the city of Rome. From then on, no Roman emperor would ever again rule from a post in Italy, leading many to cite 476 as the year the Western Empire suffered its death blow.

2. Economic troubles and overreliance on slave labor
Rome was also crumbling from within thanks to a severe financial crisis. Constant wars and overspending created significant debt, and oppressive taxation and inflation widened the gap between rich and poor. To avoid a taxman, the wealthy moved to the countryside and set up independent fiefdoms. At the same time, the empire was rocked by a labor deficit. Rome's economy depended on slaves to till its fields and work as craftsmen; its military provided a fresh influx of conquered peoples to work. But when expansion ground

to a halt in the second century, Rome's supply of slaves dried up. In the fifth century, the Vandals claimed North Africa and began disrupting the empire's trade as pirates in the Mediterranean. With its economy, commerce, and agriculture in decline, Rome lost its grip on Europe.

3. The rise of the Eastern Empire

Rome's fate was partially sealed late in the third century, when the Empire was divided in half— Western Empire seated in Milan, and Eastern Empire in Constantinople. The division made the empire easier to govern in the short term, but over time East and West failed to work together to combat outside threats, and the two squabbled over resources and military aid. The Greek Eastern Empire grew in wealth while the Latin-speaking West descended into an economic crisis. The Eastern Empire's strength diverted Barbarian invasions to the West. The Western political structure disintegrated in the fifth century; the Eastern Empire succumbed to the Ottoman Empire in the 1400s.

4. Overexpansion and military overspending

At its height, the Roman Empire stretched from the Atlantic Ocean to the Euphrates River in the Middle East. With such a vast territory to police, the empire faced an administrative and logistical nightmare. Romans were unable to communicate quickly or effectively enough to manage their holdings. Rome struggled to marshal enough troops and resources to defend local rebellions and outside attacks. As more funds were funneled into the military to maintain the empire, Rome's civil infrastructure fell into disrepair.

5. Government corruption and political instability

If Rome's sheer size made it difficult to govern, incompetent leadership only served to magnify the problem. Being the Roman emperor was always a dangerous job, but during the second and third centuries, it was a death sentence. Civil war thrust the empire into chaos, and more than 20 men took the throne in a span of only 75 years. The emperor's own bodyguards assassinated and installed sovereigns at will. The political rot extended to the Roman Senate, which failed to temper emperors' excesses due to its own corruption and incompetence. As the situation worsened, civic pride waned, and many Roman citizens lost trust in their leadership.

Reflection 54: Finite Planet

Predicting the climate and state of the planet in 50 years based on a "consensus" of environmental scientists has been the subject of much justifiable criticism and skepticism. The problem facing us today is that, left to our own unfettered capitalistic "freedoms," we could quite possibly make the planet uninhabitable for humans. Simply put, we need to stop consuming irreplaceable planetary resources and stop generating waste that the planet cannot absorb.

Ecological Model Overview

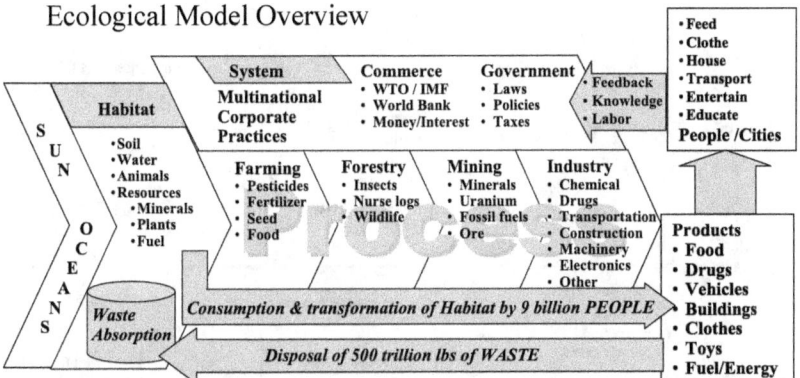

Regulated by government, driven by corporate practices and supported by habitat, processes in farming, forestry, mining and industry generate non-biodegradable waste and consume and transform habitat to produce products for people who support processes and create knowledge to provide feedback to change government, commerce, corporate practices, and habitat usage.

Problem: Volume of waste is too high for habitat to support.

Problem 1: 500 trillion pounds of waste will be generated in the next decade that fouls and can't be absorbed by habitat (earth) fueled by population growth and a waste generating lifestyle.

Problem 2: Consumption of energy, water and biomass fueled by a world population increase from 2 billion to 9 billion people in one hundred years who adopt a waste generating lifestyle.

Problem 3: Government and commerce organizations' policies and multinational corporate practices that systemically export high waste generating industries to third world countries and eliminate jobs from first world economies.

Problem 4: Politicians and environmentalists are not focused on reduction of consumption and waste, but on the "consensus" view that CO_2 reduction will reduce global warming thereby reducing the probability that problems 1, 2, and 3 will be solved.

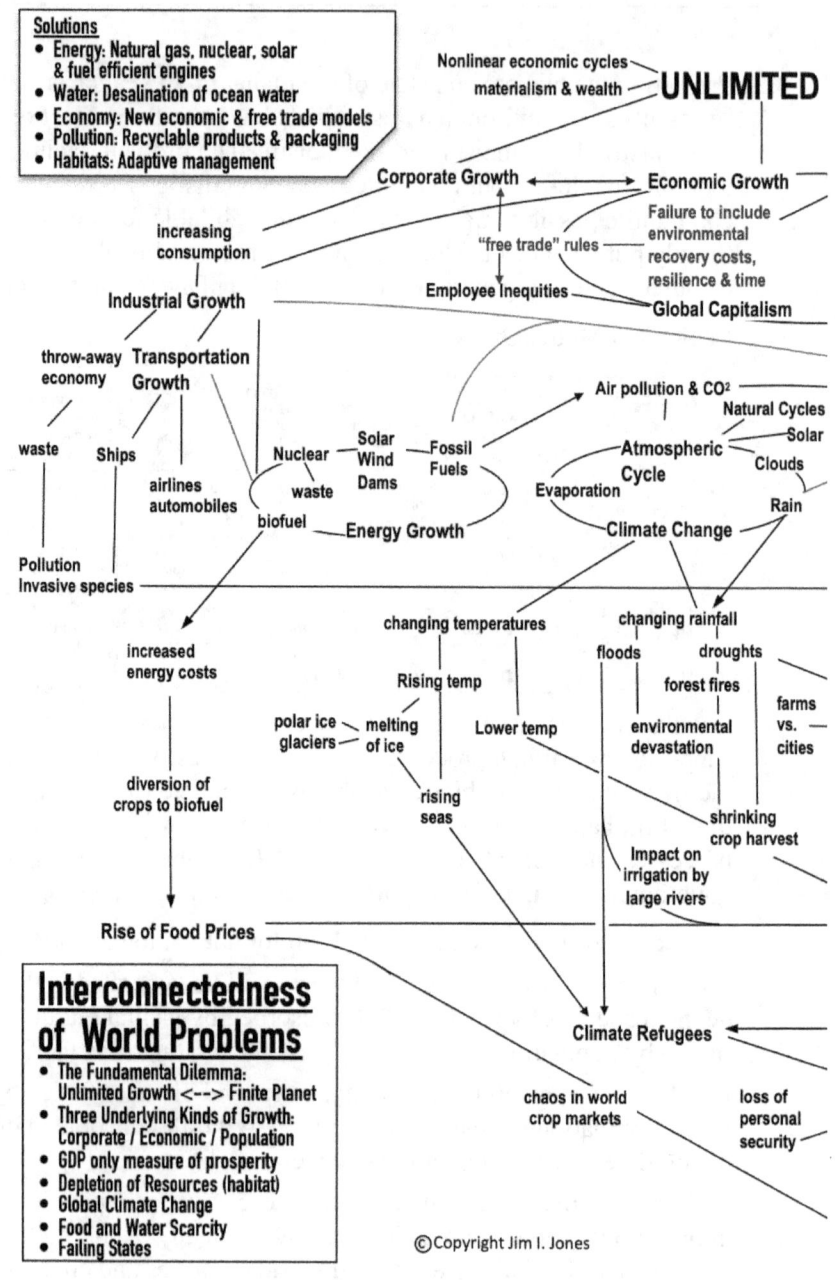

REFLECTION 54

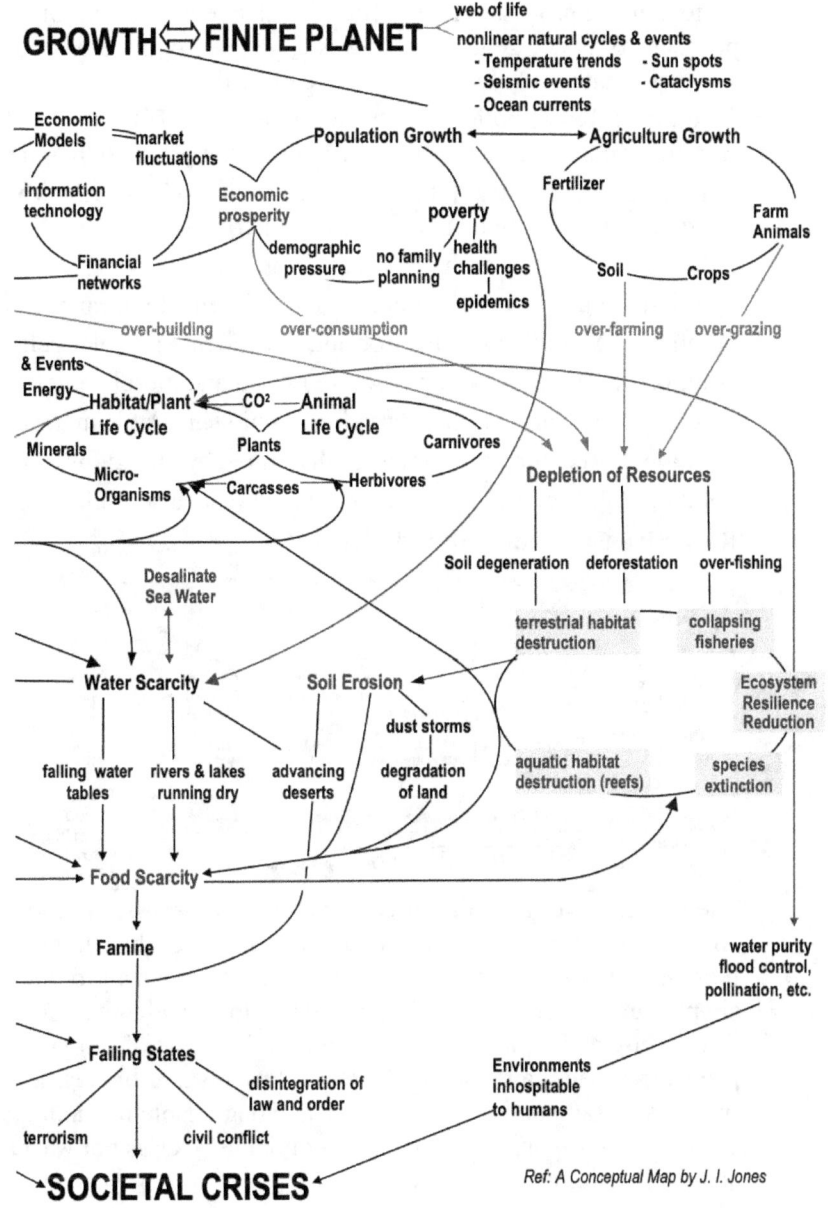

Ref: A Conceptual Map by J. I. Jones

APPENDIX A

Solution: To preserve habitat change policies and practices in the system, make processes more efficient, change the content of products to reduce generation of waste; get energy directly from the sun, desalinate ocean water and stop cutting down trees.

Solution 1: Revise policies of the World Bank, WTO, and IMF to reward corporate reduction waste from product production and use.

Solution 2: Fund research that makes better use of solar, nuclear, hydroelectric, hydrogen, and fossil fuel energy generation.

Solution 3: Fund research to increase crop yield.

Solution 4: Fund research to innovatively desalinate ocean water.

Solution 5: Manufacture steel roofing imbedded with solar cells.

Solution 6: Support developing more hybrid and diesel vehicles.

Solution 7: Reward corporate production biodegradable materials.

Solution 8: Reclaim and reuse heat dissipated by energy plants.

Solution 9: Inflict a gas-guzzler tax on all personal vehicles.

Recursive Environmental Model

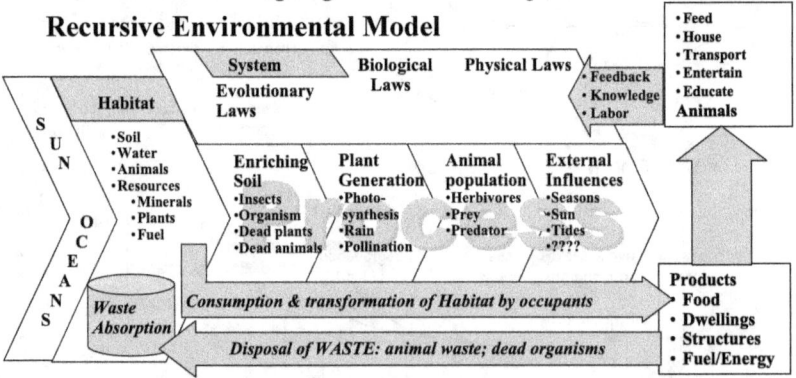

The model serves as a high-level overview for discussion of global issues. It must be revised to "work" at all levels of the habitat process from micro-organisms to world usage. It must provide a simple but recursive view of habitat. Transforming habitat takes the form of use and replacement of resources like minerals, organisms, plants, trees, animals, fuel, and water. Waste is non-biodegradable, like plastic, radioactive material, etc. and degradable like animal waste, paper, rusting metal, carbon monoxide. CO_2 is not waste since it is required by plants.

Europeans seem to enjoy a quality of life equal to Americans with half the consumption and waste generation to habitat. To sustain a Quality of Life to which people have been accustomed in North America, we must eventually have an unlimited supply of fuel (solar, hydroelectric, wind) and fresh water (desalinate sea water) and air/oxygen (stop destroying plants and trees).

APPENDIX B: COFFEE HOUSE CONFERENCES

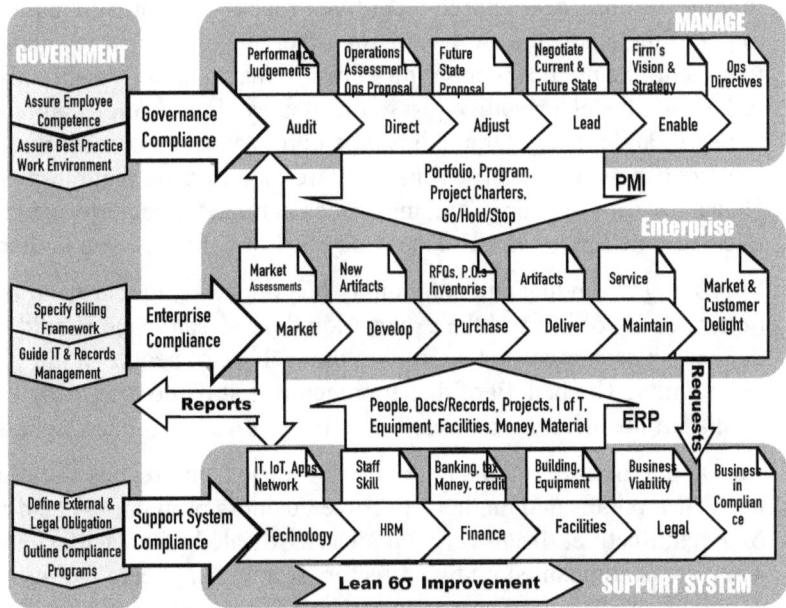

TDM Enterprise System Model Overview

The Document Methodology for Enterprise Analysis and Healthcare Transformation (TDM) is built upon the content, flow, and disposition of documents as the knowledge objects of business processes. It uses process models shown above to provide the facts to measure, manage and improve processes. The Coffee House Conferences ended each chapter, that showed how to lower the cost of healthcare and provided insights into improving healthcare (and manufacturing) with systems, technology, development, and innovation.

TDM was first derived from working in manufacturing environments over 20 years prior to the publication of version I in 1999, TDM has proven to be applicable to a wide range of environments since then; version II was published in 2007. Version III published in 2019 was targeted at healthcare environments. TDM's flexibility results from an axiomatic framework designed to preserve its generality.

Because my experiences have been in manufacturing, that industry is contrasted with healthcare. From a system engineering perspective, a patient is a complex adaptive system that is only partially understood by the medical community. Furthermore, patients with major and multiple problems will require a diagnosis-treatment-rehabilitation program of projects to manage, schedule, and use medical resources.

Each patient and especially the elderly present a challenge that severely inhibits defining a structured repetitive process. Senior care requires much of the medical expertise of any other age group, but in evaluating treatment, the medical community must focus on quality-of-life instead of keeping the elderly alive just to die slower. For example, ambulance transport and intense paramedic and emergency room procedures may be more detrimental to frail seniors' welfare than treating them in-place. Hence, in-residence or in nursing homes paramedicine performed with a telemedicine link to an ER doctor may be critical for "doing no harm."

Improving individual and community health and senior care will lead to better quality of life and the expectation that we can – and should – depend on each other for improving the welfare of people in the community. The benefit of this approach is that while increasing the quality of health and senior care, it will significantly reduce the cost.

This appendix is divided into six Coffeehouse Conferences that illustrate the TDM axioms and methods to solve business problems. The directors of a manufacturer discuss critical ideas associated with each axiom. They are accompanied by two directors from a healthcare facility who comment on the differences between healthcare and manufacturing. Their waitress is a philosophy graduate who provides insight into the work of six philosophers.

Philosophies of Socrates and Lao Tzu are each reviewed in a Coffeehouse Conference because they were the first to explore the elements of knowledge and change. Philosophies of Rene Descartes, Immanuel Kant, John Locke, and Adam Smith are discussed because they provided a philosophical foundation for information, management and manufacturing sciences now used in healthcare.

TDM asserts competing on knowledge is dependent upon an enterprise's (clinic's) ability to explicitly define, monitor and continuously improve knowledge flow-to-value for products and patient services.

Previous Reflections introduce the relationships between noise, data, information, and knowledge flow to value. This raises the question: knowledge flow to what value? Value in manufacturing is primarily driven by competition in the marketplace and can be determined from market analysis and statistics where customers know price, quality, and capability of products from various competitors.

Many economists subscribe to the *Subjective Theory of Value*: economic value comes not from any quality of the good in question, but from the human mind. Nowhere is that more prevalent than in healthcare where prices are frequently not listed. Many people who have insurance think it's free indulging in tests that aren't indicated by their malady opting for unnecessary procedures. Perversely, healthy people devalue insurance until they require major medical attention at which point, they want to purchase insurance at 5% of the cost of the medical intervention. This does not demonstrate the "normal" dynamics of Adam Smith capitalism.

Continuous improvement initiatives emphasize the importance of quality, measurement, and efficiency. They are focused on defining and successfully completing projects, but not on setting policy, goals, and objectives. To set direction managers must know where they are:
- FIRST, know how its knowledge flows to value everywhere.
- NEXT, define POLICY and outline a portfolio to leverage EXISTING skills, operations and technology better.
- THEN, change initiatives can be used with the assurance that its "baby step" projects take the firm in its intended direction.

Important as quality is, design engineers take an abstract concept and produce one (not necessarily quality) prototype. Concept to a prototype vehicle takes two years; manufacturing engineers take two more years to build a quality product every 20 seconds. Two years is about quality while all four years is about knowledge flow to value.

TDM embodies five axioms discussed in Reflections 55 – 60.
- Reflection 55 (Smith) introduces methodology elements.
- Reflection 56 (Socrates) categorizes knowledge as documents. Axiom 1: Documents record enterprise knowledge. Knowing what support systems were used to record and access knowledge in what documents provides a base to create more value.
- Reflection 57 (Descartes) defines process with document milestones. Axiom 2: Documents define enterprise process. Defining projects with document milestones of core processes provides a foundation to monitor and compile statistics on performance.
- Reflection 58 (Locke) guides skilled people in production of value. Axiom 3: Documents provide facts to manage people. Managers use summaries of process statistics to operate and change core processes.
- Reflection 59 (Kant) with the facts to manage and change the business. Axiom 4: Documents structure support systems. Requirements for exceptional access to knowledge and for computation of process statistics frame technology architecture.
- A Reflection 60 (Lao Tzu) introduces innovative change into the firm. Axiom 5: Documents guide enterprise change. Using variance to understand process and relieve bottlenecks provides the facts to simulate, plan and deploy innovative change.

The Example Manufacturing Problem

Monstrotech is a profitable $3 billion first-tier supplier for medical manufacturers, with three divisions: mechanical components, disinfectants / chemicals, and assembly services. It serves the health system industry. Mechanical components were 50% of its revenues.

Improvement initiatives created local efficiencies but had minimal impact on profit. The company has difficulty establishing its vision and the building blocks to achieve it. To achieve objectives, Hiram Powers, CEO, created 7 teams that focused on where the firm was and where it needed to go.

The first two teams are governance teams. One has the responsibility to develop a collaboration strategy that empowers workgroups. This was important because previous re-engineering efforts downsized the company, flattened the management hierarchy and left employees feeling abandoned. The second team was chartered with the IT issue of how to evolve to improve governance, compliance, and performance.

Each of the other five teams dealt with issues focused on its core processes.

Market

This team was to define products and services that "surprise and delight" customers. With no strategic market plan, product innovations were all driven by development's VP.

Consequently, proposals written in response to RFQs were rejected. Marketing was currently trying to make up for these short-comings by "schmoozing" customer management.

Marketing ran test market programs to determine what its customers' want. A statistical software system and library analyzed this data. The results were printed in reports and sent to senior management.

Marketing team reviewed software packages for statistical analysis as well as a proposal system. Purchasing and manufacturing systems were off limits to marketing that needed their data for proposals. Consequently, sales guessed at cost, capacity and schedule data and adding 15% to cost.

Develop

The development team included members from service, purchasing, and manufacturing. The team's goal was to shorten the time to market, thereby reducing suppliers and simplifying assembly. The team needed to rework the existing development process to have product, quality, manufacturing, packaging and maintenance personnel review a detailed product design before its release to manufacturing engineering. The team anticipated this would make the design process more complicated but result in fewer changes as the product moved toward production. Changes late in the process cost millions; changes before release of design cost hundreds. To reach these goals, the team had to define the best use of various application software:

computer-aided engineering for stress analysis, computer-aided design for 50% improvement in design and computer-aided manufacturing for die design and fabrication.

CAD software use had almost no impact on the time-to-market process because management began viewing more design alternatives to fill up the saved time.

Purchase

This team was chartered with forging partnerships with key suppliers and integrating the supply chain. They must regularly audit suppliers to ensure that they were compliant with regulations and standards (e.g. ISO 15489, ISO 9001, EPA, HIPPA, and GAAP). Compliance had cost Monstrotech and its suppliers a great deal of money and eroded margins. Purchasing was now looking at ways to make the interface to its suppliers more transparent without jeopardizing the security of its intellectual capital.

The team had the additional task of resolving issues with bill-of-materials (BOM), which defines product components for purchasing and assembly. The detailed component BOM had been out-sourced to Monstrotech's suppliers. Also, components built at different locations required different assembly BOMs. BOMs, cost information, supplier information and master schedules existed on an antiquated system. All divisions used the system in different ways, so they couldn't share designs.

Deliver

This team focused on two issues: increase inventory turns and reduce time-to-build. To do so, coordinated with the development and purchasing teams. Also, the success of the business rested on the development of proposals, which relied on accurate statistics.

The team looked at installing Enterprise Resource Management to resolve system issues, but concluded that, they had to reengineer processes to use it.

Because scheduling did not consider current production status on the factory floor, specific orders had priority based on how disruptive late delivery would be to customers. It was impossible to optimize fabrication because of interruptions to expedite parts.

As an alternative or precursor to ERP, Hiram thought that applying TDM might help identify problems and help structure a solution.

Maintain

This team was chartered with ensuring repeat customer business. Support not only dealt with the product reliability and maintenance issues and schedules, but also maintained strategic partnerships with customers. The support team was responsible for maintenance and instruction manuals for dealers.

Support offset printed manuals and ordered them far in advance to keep costs down. The team considered on-demand print methods, CD-ROM distribution and an Internet server to provide better service. Also, it was chartered to propose new products to improve its customer's profitability.

Strategy

Hiram knew he was spending money on change and hoped — but didn't know — if it would improve profitability. His teams presented compelling cases for initiatives and technology, but most wouldn't show an ROI for several years.

All seven teams found it difficult to quantify progress. Hi concluded that initiatives conflicted. Documents had been used to control manufacturing for 250 years before the invention of the computer; so, Hi decided to interpret his business through its documents.

From TDM, Hi saw that documents:
- Record an enterprise's knowledge.
- Define an enterprise's processes.
- Provide facts to manage people.
- Structure support systems.
- Guide the process of change.

Subsequently, Hi examined the company's use of resources that revealed more resources had been funneled into changing processes with no immediate payback.

Hiram carefully chose Directors, who would be his Methodology Team:
- Jud Blunt, Manufacturing,
- Ed Block, Engineering,
- Donald Denominator, IT,
- Jason Skywalker, Strategic Planning,
- Priscilla Precise, Programming.

Hi showed them his view of the changes in resource distribution, communicated his misgivings and asked them to take a document view.

Jud saw a similarity between his manufacturing experience and documents flowing through processes. He convinced the team that this approach might resolve conflicts between business teams and reconcile the components of a company vision.

Jason's concern was that the firm provided products and services that sales could sell. He knew that sales guessed critical cost and capacity information. Availability of cost and capacity documents would help.

Ed agreed that a new system for better version control and access to past engineering designs would spare duplication of effort and costly mistakes and could achieve his goal of time and cost savings.

While the other team members gave Document Methodology a vote of confidence, Donald had reservations. He needed to be sure that change didn't disrupt flow in the current system and didn't create setbacks.

The Example Healthcare Problem

Jon Earworthy, CEO Titanmed Clinic, assigned two of his directors to meet with Monstrotech's team:

*Clarence Barton: Director of Nursing
Alice Perry: Director of Engineering*

They are responsible for outlining a strategic plan for the Clinic.

Their clinic follows the TDM high level process model, but the details within each process are very different.

Their view of TDM is represented by the Pentagon.

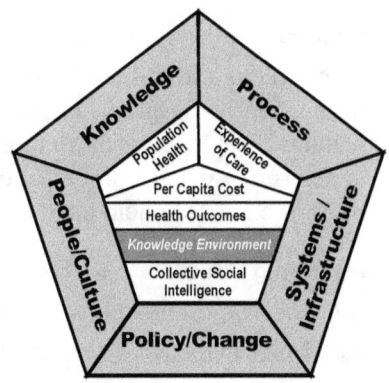

- *Policy provides guidelines and allocates budgets by arbitrating effective and efficient operations with change to improve health outcomes and insure compliance.*
- *Knowledge content is focused on presenting information to invoke desirable behaviors in the information consumer (e.g. medical staff: quicker diagnosis, ER).*
- *Process represents tasks that staff perform to create value for the patient; it supports measurement.*
- *Culture makes information meaningful, in terms of interpreting staff's experience and helping them decide how to act.*
- *Infrastructure uses collaboration technologies, global information networks, and the web to ensure that knowledge flows to a positive care experience, better population health at lower per capita cost.*

Current Value Proposition:
Patients billed for a medical procedure.

Future Value Proposition:
Healthcare is focused on community health, experience of care and per capital cost of community health.

In-/out-patients quality of life improves while doing no harm.

Patients are diagnosed quicker and rehabilitation is focused on both in-hospital and at-home recovery.

Benefits to Patient
- *Mitigate risk of iterative diagnosis*
- *Mitigate risk of return to hospital*
- *Improved staff skills to provide a better patient care experience.*

Benefits to Hospital
- *Increased positive patient outcomes*
- *Better diagnosis methods*
- *Qualify for Medicare bonus*

Initiative Benefit:
- *Deliver Value Faster*
- *Faster and globally assisted diagnosis with less time in a bed*
- *More understandable and up-to-date, WI and Documents*
- *Better management of resources*

Reflection 55: WEALTH (Smith)

Background

Five directors from the Monstrotech Manufacturing and two directors from a nearby hospital, all busy with their corporate initiatives, are reading "The Document Methodology" and classic literature. They hope to determine where corporate conduct and thinking have gone wrong and if the ancients can help them resolve some thornier business issues.

Manufacturing Directors

Edward Block: Director of Engineering

Jud Blunt: Director of Manufacturing

Donald Denominator: Director of IT

Priscilla Precise: Director of Programming

Jason Skywalker: Director of Strategic Planning

Medical Directors

Clarence Barton: Director of Nursing

Alice Perry: Director of Clinical Engineering

Facilitator

Elena Piscopia: Vassar philosophy graduate, waitress quoting: **Adam Smith** (1723 – 1790), Scottish Wealth Expert, studied mathematics and philosophy at the University of Glasgow. He studied philosophy at Oxford for six years. He taught moral philosophy for 12 years at the University of Glasgow. His business contacts outside the university provided him with the insight to write "An Inquiry into the Wealth of Nations" in 1776, the foundation for modern economics.

Concepts

Impact of change, risks, structure of information and process quality are being discussed and their impact on profit and competitiveness now and in the future.

Setting

An empowered workgroup of these five and two directors meet bi-weekly in the local coffee shop, "The Java Beanery." We enter as each sips a Sumatra Roast and discuss issues and non-issues of concern. When they are deep in conversation about the issues, facilitator, Elena quoting Adam Smith, interrupts the discussion. Although the focus of the discussion this week is on wealth, digressions occur.

Overheard at The Java Beanery

Alice: Thank you for allowing us to sit in on this informal meeting to improve effectiveness and efficiency at Monstrotech. It is Clarence and my intent to understand your approach to improvement initiatives and determine if some or all of them apply to healthcare and how we might need to revise them.

Donald: Welcome Alice and Clarence. I hope to understand better what goes on with us as well. To my fellow directors, why all of this emphasis on radical change lately? We're just getting systems configured uniformly, running efficiently and under control.

Jason: The purpose of our business is to build wealth, not to be efficient. Efficient can be bad if it inhibits adaptiveness.

Pris: Wealth is a nice platitude, Jason. Does wealth mean profit?

Elena: Sorry, you're talking so loudly, I couldn't help but overhear your discussion. Ever hear of Adam Smith?

Donald: What does a Scottish soccer player have to do with this?

Elena: Good grief. Smith, the late 1700s Scot, invented modern economics.

Donald: Well, I had the country right; who are you to lecture us on Adam Smith.

Elena: I'm a philosophy graduate. I decided that I could make more money as a waitress, but I reserve my right to think, for even to think wrongly is better than not to think at all.

Jud: Thinking rightly, Smith is the one who said, "productive labor adds value."

Elena: Ah, yes. Are you the one associated with manufacturing?

Jud: Yes, I'm in charge of manufacturing.

Elena: Smith says in his *Inquiry Into the Nature and Causes of the Wealth of Nations* that only you are productive. "Though the manufacturer has his wages advanced to him by his master, he, in reality, costs him no expense. The value of those wages being generally restored, together with a profit, in the improved value of the subject upon which his labor is bestowed. But the maintenance of a menial servant never is restored." I have a photographic memory.

Pris: I see. Enterprise is composed of manufacturing and us menial servants.

Jud: No product, no value. So, you know who's important here.

Jason: What if we're building something no one wants to buy?

Elena: Why on earth would you build it then?

Jason: Markets change faster now. Competition is fiercer. What people will buy can change month to month.

Elena: In Smith's time, the French minister of agriculture proposed that a nation's wealth was solely dependent on agriculture. Now you're saying manufacturing is not the fundamental issue in a nation's wealth, which appears equally ridiculous.

Jason: Because we're competing effectively today doesn't mean we'll even be in business next year.

Elena: People still eat, and require shelter and household goods, do they not?

Ed: Yes, but people spend more than half their income on discretionary goods.

Elena: You mean frivolous expenditures. I like shoes.

Ed: People think of a second means of transportation or a second home as a necessity now. Vacations to relieve stress are considered necessary as well.

Jason: Advertising convinces them that they need it.

Elena: Thanks to the wonderful world of Internet and marketing, it's no longer sufficient to build the best product. You have to convince people that they want to buy it?

Clarence: I'd like to insert a comment and ask a question if I may. The hospital offers a service where the input is a sick person who in the best of circumstances exits as a well one. Doctors in a sense do the repairs, but nurses are the ones who spend the most time to properly care for patients. How should we view 'enterprise' in the context of this narrative?

Jud: In manufacturing we have parts flowing through equipment to create a product. In your environment you have patients flowing through a series of processes from diagnosis to repair to recovery with nurses presiding over the flow. The difference is the flow in manufacturing is predictable, the flow of multiple patients is not, but you still have staff and facilities usage issues requiring sophisticated resource planning.

Alice: Since my responsibility is clinical engineering that seems to be a huge if not insurmountable difference.

Ed: Alice, the processes are fundamentally much different, but you still need to manage staff and resources which is accomplished by an Enterprise Resource Planning system. Be still Donald and Pris lest we digress into a quagmire of information techno-speak. Let's get back to marketing.

Jason: May I remind you if we don't sell something, we don't get paid. Even if our products are the best, cheapest and most necessary, we still have to convince our customers to buy them. Consumers are bombarded with information about products. They usually buy the best *marketed* product.

Elena: How, pray tell, does advertising add value to the product?

Jason: As a supplier, our customers are other manufacturers. If they don't know about our quality, capacity, and capabilities, they won't engage us. Marketing knowledge is just one form of knowledge that the company competes on; others include development, manufacturing, and support knowledge.

Clarence: Marketing for us involves making our community aware of wellness and our capabilities to restore wellness; they need to be aware of our commitment to quality, positive outcomes, areas of specialty and awards. Another aspect of marketing is soliciting donations since we are non-profit where profit goes to more research and better facilities. Communicating our capabilities to the community is key to our survival.

Pris: Companies and hospitals now compete on knowledge.

Elena: Companies always compete on knowledge. So, let's review the fundamentals as Smith originally proposed them. "The general stock of any country divides itself into three portions:

1] That which affords no revenue or profit such as food, clothes, household goods, housing, etc.

2] Fixed capital which includes:
- All useful machines supporting labor.
- Profitable buildings.
- Improvements of land for agriculture.
- Acquired and useful abilities of employees by education, study or apprenticeship."

Jason: This is exhausting. Are you done yet? Coffee please.

Elena: Soon. "3] Circulating capital which divides itself into 4 parts.
- Money.
- Finished goods in the possession of business.
- Materials remaining in the hands of business.
- Finished goods still in the hands of the merchant."

Donald: Up until a few years ago, that's exactly how we assigned value to business.

Elena: So, what's changed?

Jud: Fundamentally, nothing. Materials and finished goods have value, but they're a liability unless they are purchased. It is no longer a foregone conclusion that what is made gets purchased. So, we minimize inventory.

Alice: Our problems are not the same, but the idea of fixed capital is a problem for us as well. We need a certain number of beds occupied to break even.

Elena: That's fundamental. Fixed capital can't yield any revenue but by means of circulating capital.

Ed: Exactly. There seems to be one other issue not emphasized in Smith's explanation of fixed capital associated with knowledge.

Elena: Smith covered that under the last point of 2]: acquired and useful abilities of employees by education, study or apprenticeship.

Ed: But the enterprise *itself* has knowledge.

Elena: Machines enhance the productivity of labor and may be thought of as having knowledge, but it is fixed at the time of purchase.

Alice: The measures of excellence, as evaluated by US News Best Hospitals, is size of patient population, medical technology, process excellence, positive outcomes and risk mitigation.

Ed: Independent of machines, the firm has knowledge residing in documents that define its products and manufacturing processes. Also, computers continuously add to their value by saving, managing and providing access to knowledge.

WEALTH

Clarence: Although patient data resides in electronic health records (EHR), much of the knowledge in healthcare resides with medical staff and physicians. If we want to accelerate patient flow to positive outcomes, we must do a better job of capturing that knowledge in some kind of system and make it available at critical times as the patients flow through processes.

Jason: So, because the market demands new products more quickly, (and demands more positive patient outcomes faster) and there are more competitors, the time to develop, build and sell products (and services) must be significantly less. Therefore, the machines and systems that an enterprise purchases represents a change or increase in enterprise knowledge.

Jud: Also, students of Deming assert that "every system has variation; hence, the information needed to create optimum systems is unknown and unknowable." Therefore, in manufacturing (and medicine), we must always monitor the process to see how to make it better.

Elena: I see. The knowledge of people and systems can no longer be thought of as fixed but must continuously change in order to be competitive. Therefore, we must revise our view of the second portion of the general stock of the country to place more emphasis on knowledge.

Jason: Also, since a significant portion of the cost of a product or service is in sales and advertising, we must expand our view of the product to include educating consumers as to why they should purchase the product.

Pris: So, it isn't just people who touch the part, but also people who *add* value, which in the long term becomes part of what the consumer purchases. If we view the product or process change as a system, Ed and I are in the business of building a system. If the new system we build is used by manufacturing to produce more operating profit, we manufactured a system that has value.

Alice: Similarly, if we view patient flow as part of a system with new processes and technology that delivers better patient outcomes faster, we add value to patient wellness to insure our survival.

Donald: And if IT provides an information service with the knowledge to reduce cost and improve outcomes (product or patients), I increase operating profit and added value.

Elena: It appears wealth is quantified in terms of adding value and that knowledge is a newly added dimension in increasing the "wealth of nations." So: What is Enterprise Knowledge?

To be continued...

Health Knowledge Observation

Alice's problem related to documents were more complex than those in manufacturing. She reasoned that she not only had all of the problems being discussed by the Monstrotech's directors within the hospital but also needed to expand her knowledge base to include 'community wellness.'

She determined that her hospital had to collaborate with "social, clinical and acute care groups" to improve on maintaining a "healthy" community. She was guided by the fact that Intermountain Healthcare in Utah has one of the healthiest populations at the lowest per-capita health care costs. A healthy Utah is just over half the cost of an equally healthy Massachusetts ($5,013 vs. $9,278). A preponderance of Mormons may explain some of Utah's overall edge on health. 60% to 70% of the state's 3 million people identify as Mormon. Most of them follow the behavioral restriction: no tobacco, alcohol, or recreational drugs. The faith also encourages large families and strong social networks, both of which provide support when people get sick.

Clarence observed that since no one associated with medical care had a "proven" methodology to guarantee wellness, The best approach may be to treat the community associated with the health system as a (not randomized) clinical trial. Lastly, he felt that the hospital was farther along with "paperless" since it had to comply with government Health IT standards or face severe penalties.

Alice saw that by following the progress of the EHR as a patient went through various stages of diagnosis, intervention, and recovery that each patient could be characterized as a program of projects flowing through the health systems various departments requiring specific resources.

This is very different than part flow through a series of workstations, since patient flow could be changed with no notice, as the results of tests and interventions are evaluated. Also, this is multiplied as each patient has their own unique continuously modified program. However, seeing this as a program of projects would allow the scheduling of resources in a resource planning system.

Alice and Clarence agreed that documents are ubiquitous to every wellness and healthcare environment and that a document taxonomy must be defined to support such a view of information; their approach must:

- Educate the community in a language to communicate symptoms, illness, habits, and history.
- Validate everything recorded in the EHR complies with ISO 15489.
- Revise the SOAP framework into a structure that will make it better for analysis by AI algorithms.
- Track not only the cost per patient, but the cost to promote wellness within the community.
- Initiate health fairs to communicate healthy behaviors and to identify symptoms of medical problems.
- Make guidelines and framework correspond to national efforts to insure wellness, reduce cost of care, minimize patient risk and maximize positive outcomes.

This could be enabled with information technology and telemedicine. This could lead to the installation of a Clinical Diagnosis System (CDS) to take advantage of rigorously recording patient and community data and physician team diagnosis.

Alice noted that there has been much written about effective, efficient, and quality operation of healthcare systems and the application of manufacturing methodologies such as LEAN and Six Sigma. The results had been mixed at best, partly because manufacturing is a well-defined environment, whereas the practice of medicine is a partially intuitive art form that is applied to patients that are complex adaptive systems.

In mechanical systems (as in manufacturing), one can know and predict in detail what each of the parts will do in response to a given stimulus. Thus, it is possible to study and predict what a system will do in a variety of circumstances. In complex adaptive systems, the "parts" (as humans in health care) have the freedom and ability to respond to stimuli in many ways. These could arise as emergent, surprising, and creative and be interpreted as innovation or error.

Shewhart's PDSA cycle (Plan-Do-Study-Act) was the seminal work associated with analysis and change in manufacturing and subsequently applies to hospitals. However, its philosophy is built to analyze and change manufacturing where process is explicitly defined with stable cycle times and variation.

Rather than PDSA, Alice thought that hospitals should consider fighter pilot instructor's Col. John Boyd's OODA loops (Observe-Orient-Decide-Act) to define doctor/patient relationships. She noted that orientation shapes observation, shapes decision, shapes action, and, in turn, is shaped by the feedback and other phenomena coming into the observation window, which is fundamentally the process of medical diagnosis.

Through medical education and medicine's generic heritage, cultural traditions, and previous experiences, physicians develop an implicit repertoire of diagnostic skills shaped by environments and changes that were previously experienced. Unlike PDSA, many medical diagnoses are shaped by OODA, an unfolding, evolving, uncertain, changing, and unpredictable reality.

An Oxford University team's review of 67 published clinical trials on evidence-based medicine concluded that most were methodologically flawed. So, physicians must also rely both on examination of evidence and on heuristic thinking, which is an unconscious, context-sensitive, associative process (OODA) that rapidly makes connections.

Reflection 56: KNOWLEDGE (Socrates)

Background

Documents record enterprise knowledge and intellectual capital that aid companies to be competitive in a rapidly changing market. Creating a method for understanding business that identifies, structures, categorizes, and tracks documents is critical to explicitly defining processes in sufficient detail to make informed judgments about how to operate and change business processes.

Director Participants

Edward Block: Engineering   *Jud Blunt*: Manufacturing
Donald Denominator: IT   *Priscilla Precise*: Programming
Jason Skywalker: Strategic Planning
Clarence Barton: Nursing   *Alice Perry*: Clinical Engineering

Facilitator: Elena Piscopia: philosopher waitress quotes:

Socrates: (470 – 399 B.C.) Greek philosopher.

We see Socrates through the Dialogues of his student Plato who was the founder of the Academy in Athens in 387 B.C. The frustrating part of these Dialogues is that they rarely come to a specific conclusion about a topic, but in the process of the Dialogue many hypotheses are proposed, discussed and rejected. This method of dialogue has gone on in taverns, coffee shops and boardrooms throughout the world.

Concepts

Enterprise knowledge is to be discussed in terms of an information frame-work, ISO 15489 records management, retention, and core documents.

Setting

The topic of "What is Knowledge" has occupied philosophical thought for the last 2,500 years. Extrapolating these ideas to "enterprise knowledge" becomes the focus for discussion. In the first session, the group concluded competing on knowledge was key to building wealth. Again, the directors are drinking Sumatra at The Java Beanery.

Overheard at The Java Beanery

Pris: Consultants are telling us to compete on knowledge these days. But what are they talking about?

Jason: People have been asking that since Socrates in 400 B.C.

Elena: It's been over 2,000 years since Socrates chugged hemlock. Jason actually reads Socrates? The Dialogue of Plato he refers to is called *Theaetetus,* where he asked you the same question: "What is knowledge?" But maybe you ought to focus on what is *enterprise* knowledge.

Jason: I just read one little dialogue with Theaetetus where Plato hypothesizes and refutes many definitions of knowledge. We don't need 10 definitions of what knowledge isn't.

Elena: One of the fortunate benefits of my overhearing your loud and unfocused discussion is that I already have heard 30 definitions of what your enterprise knowledge isn't. For example, Jud, just look at your daily 400-page factory floor status printout. Very little of your current state leverages knowledge, just incomprehensible chariot loads of data.

Jud: Amen.

Donald: May I suggest a glass of hemlock for our waitress?

Elena: I'll just ignore that remark. Ed, why don't you try to define enterprise knowledge?

Ed: Before we could explicitly define our knowledge, we needed a conceptual framework to categorize it. To do that we considered using TDM's core, support and management processes to guide Monstrotech's document classification.

Alice: Although our core level processes are much different, after talking to Ed, we decided to start there as well.

Ed: Talking about process may seem off topic but having a general idea of process is necessary to frame enterprise knowledge. If we think of Jane Wycoff's mind maps captured in documents, we have a more general view of data – graphics and text – and can also relate skills to processes.

Jud: But, in manufacturing, we write everything down now. Repeatability is an issue. The less people know the more you have to document how tasks are performed. Unfortunately, most engineering education focuses on concept-to-prototype rather than how to manufacture something.

Ed: Personal knowledge is important, but we really need to increase the knowledge of people in workgroups so that we learn from each other. That means we need a formal way to communicate knowledge. In manufacturing engineering, the solution is formalized in process plans.

Alice: In medicine the personal knowledge of the general practitioner has been instrumental in diagnosing the cause from a patient's subjectively defined symptoms. We are migrating to specialist teams orchestrated by the diagnostician, and we are attempting to use artificial intelligence algorithms on EHRs, but those results have been of little help to date.

Donald: Monstrotech uses ISO 15489 standard to guide creating records that are reliable, systematic, managed, auditable and integral to the business. As for your diagnosis problem, Alice, you should consider developing a document model with an ISO 15489 EHR process audit.

Clarence: Patient records are full of nursing's SOAP notes. SOAP is an acronym to guide nurses to record activities associated with a patient. S-Subject: what the patient says; O: data from observation or measurement; A: Analysis from S&O; P: action plan. To be ISO 15489 compliant would represent a lot of auditing.

Alice: Many physicians use SOAP to frame their instructions. I am sure that patient health records lack the accuracy of product specifications and much of the diagnosis is dependent on physician intuition rather well-defined processes. An ISO compliant records process has a cacophony of activities to schedule.

Pris: Alice, I would be happy to sit with you and Clarence to map a way to capture your cacophony of process at a high level.

Donald: To capture our product specifications and the processes to manufacture them, we've purchased and continue to populate and enhance our computer-aided process planning system, or CAPP for short. Computers to the rescue.

Pris: We really need a CAPP system for all business activities.

Jud: Process plans are documents, that tell people how to perform tasks.

Donald: Maybe if we took a document view of information systems, we'd empower people with the information they need.

Jud: Profound thought, Donald. Give people on-demand documents. I'm surprised no one has thought of that before.

Pris: Sarcasm, sarcasm. Jud, maybe you should be scheduling documents as well as parts through the factory.

Donald: That same model would allow scheduling patient flow (as a portfolio of projects) through activities.

Jud: It isn't just about scheduling, we need to empower our production employees within their process to issue part orders, so those parts show up on-demand.

Alice: Empowerment in a clinical sense goes without saying because the only ones who know what's going on with patients are those involved with their well-being.

Elena: May I suggest a dialogue on "Is knowledge freedom?"

Pris: Freedom? What's that got to do with anything here?

Elena: I just heard the word empower. Knowledge is not a sufficient condition, but it is a necessary condition for people to be empowered to work productively.

Donald: Did you learn "necessary and sufficient" from Aristotle?

Elena: Obviously not, I learned that from your loud conversation. In yet another dialog, Plato pointed out to Meno that "the only right guides of man are knowledge and true opinion. But if not by knowledge, the only alternative that remains is that statesmen must have guided states by right opinion."

Pris: Let me see if I have this straight. Fact-based management doesn't automatically mean good management. But without the Socratic divinely acquired "right opinion," a manager must have knowledge of the transaction status to make good business decisions. The problem here is that transaction status is tracked in detail only in manufacturing.

Donald: That's why all business processes should be enabled by a workflow cycle to allow 'effective' fact-based management. Management knowledge then depends on management skills (but not necessarily "right opinion") and transaction facts that get summarized from transaction documents.

Alice: Younger physicians attempt to practice evidence-based medicine except their "evidence" comes from clinical trials, most of which are flawed. So, we are still dependent on intuition from experience as well as facts. I suspect that is also true in the case of non-manufacturing employees.

Ed: Alice makes a good point. Engineering is much more apt to have processes that can vary significantly from engineer to engineer on the same problem based on past experience.

Jud: The workflow cycle generates the shop floor schedule that we were discussing earlier. It's the system that assures that a network of processes generates the right document at the right time or alerts someone if it doesn't. Documents involved in the workflow cycle include project schedules, resource requirements, progress reports and problem reports.

Elena: How does this help Alice?

Jud: Coffee please. Although there is more variation in clinical and engineering processes, these methods could significantly reduce the variation, and the historical statistics generated could aid in the solution of future problems.

Jason: Consider this: Documents are the real user interface. If our computer systems looked like the documents that were already "flowing" around the enterprise, maybe we wouldn't spend so much on education, and maybe the technophobes would relax a little around computers.

Clarence; This is especially true for doctors and nurses. Our new health information technology has initially hindered more than helped. It would be a good idea to look at how we document patient history and patient "repair" plans before systems are installed. Right now, our IT department is more concerned with compliance to government regulation, reliability and security than in improving healthcare.

Elena: Computers are wayyyy cool. The Greeks wouldn't have had to enslave all those people if they had computers. But you all use them so stupidly. Make computers present actionable knowledge not noise to people.

Donald: Where is the hemlock?

Jud: Jason, are you and Elena actually having a practical idea?

Jason: We are allowed to have practical ideas if they're about concepts. And, speaking of concepts, don't we control our value chain represented by our integrated supplier network with the knowledge that resides in engineering drawings and process plans?

Pris: If we're outsourcing more and more, including the design of subsystems, aren't we outsourcing our knowledge as well?

Ed: We have many initiatives to get our products to market faster, which include outsourcing component designs to our suppliers. The only way to ensure that what we asked for is what we get is to demand documents from our suppliers at each step of their design process.

Clarence: The one core process that we have more elements in common with manufacturing is Purchasing. The hospital could potentially reduce cost by optimizing our inventory levels.

Ed: For Clarence and us this makes involving suppliers strategically a critical activity. In our case, to accelerate the time-to-market process, integrating the supply chain is key and a document view is central to the initiative.

Jason: Careful Ed, we outsource knowledge when we outsource the design. Also, we might even outsource knowledge that has strategic value. Like IBM outsourced the design of the operating system for the PC to Microsoft and the computer processor chip to Intel. IBM created two of their most formidable competitors by outsourcing knowledge. It's not a bad idea, but it is a radical change.

Jud: Like radical change means improvement? While we're tossing the corporate cookies in the air and hoping they come down on the table in some recognizable form, where does my paycheck come from?!

Jason: Emotional outbursts only make you the loudest, not the rightest, Jud. We need to compete in tomorrow's market as well as today's. Change is the key to competing tomorrow.

Jud: Nice platitude, Jason. Are you paying college tuition yet? Try this: A paycheck in the hand is worth two in the weeds.

Alice: Your concern about protecting your knowledge really hits home. Our government mandated that all hospitals implement patient electronic health records. These records, while protecting individual security, were supposed to be shared nation-wide so that AI algorithms could be used to develop symptom/cause relationship to help make better diagnoses anytime, anywhere by anybody. IT vendors quickly understood knowledge is power and don't share.

Elena: The Greeks invented competing on knowledge and did more to change mankind than any enterprise. Concepts aren't results; the Greeks were up to their ear lobes in concepts. The Romans engineered and built their concepts while Greeks dialogued.

Pris: Maybe we've just identified the real job of senior managers. Arbitrate the "as is" with the "to be."

Donald: That must be programese for the state of business this year and next year. Arbitrate in this sense seems like another word for judgment where we hope our

Ed: management has good sense. Then, when Jud gets to the weeds with Jason, he might find his two paychecks.

Ed: Leadership could be defined as the judgment required to arbitrate between what and how much to keep doing and what and how much to change. To empower rather than abandon employees, a leader defines the boundaries within which employees can change their business environment.

Donald: We've come up with some pretty specific ideas of knowledge in enterprise, not by inventing something new, but by taking an innovative document view of the capabilities, disciplines and systems that already exist.

Pris: Elena, could you sum up?

Elena: An employee's knowledge can be used by the enterprise but until it is represented in a document that is structured for all employees to make use of, that knowledge belongs to the employee and not the enterprise. Enterprise present value is defined by its ability to produce a product or service that generates revenue. The more knowledge that enterprise retains in documents, the less risk to its ability to add value.

Jason: Value is a pretty vague word. Coffee please.

Elena: Soon. Value is also represented in Jason's future sense by the enterprise's ability to develop a product (or service) that will delight its customers. Both present and future value is supported by the enterprise's ability to acquire and use knowledge, thereby helping it to compete on knowledge.

Clarence: From that analogy, medicine has a long way to go, since medical expertise exists mostly in physician heads, medical and software vendors aren't playing nice and "sharing" their EHR histories and they are not ISO 15489 compliant. Sadly, management seems more concerned with profit than patient outcomes.

Pris: Be that as it may Clarence, the innovation here is that documents are the knowledge objects of business processes. So, a process document model provides an accurate view of our business. Your management must consider policies that reward knowledge sharing rather than knowledge hoarding.

Alice: Without getting into Federal government agency acronyms, EHR system providers are required to share their system knowledge and many don't – knowledge is power. There are now payment penalties for not sharing. I need to coordinate with our IT department to insist that our software vendors comply with government mandate to insure that knowledge precipitated from their EHR systems is shared between all EHR vendors. Eventually this will improve our system's ability to help diagnosis disorders.

Elena: It has been a marginal pleasure speaking with high-powered executive people. You have progressed in your discussion from knowledge to process. Ciao.

To be continued ….

Health Process Observation

Alice saw that model for manufacturing was useful but her core processes were very different from Monstrotech. Also, her DELIVERY was guided by Michael Porter's IPU (Integrated Practice Unit).

Process improvement was a fundamental underlying part of Federal mandates for the hospital. Accountable Care Organizations (ACOs) were specified in the Affordable Care Act (ACA) to improve the efficiency of the networks of hospitals and doctors that deliver services to Medicare patients and thereby lower the government's costs.

"ACOs are groups of doctors, hospitals, and other health care providers, who come together voluntarily to give coordinated high-quality care to Medicare patients. The goal of coordinated care is to ensure that patients get the right care at the right time, while avoiding unnecessary duplication of services and preventing medical errors."

By transforming into a high performing ACO, their patients get better, more coordinated care over time; the patient is the center of care, and patient outcomes and satisfaction are two of the goals.

Alice surmised a document/process view of patient flow could capture their flow through the Delivery process. However, she still needed to consider improving wellness in the entire community. This meant she had to consider that Market and Maintain would require a very new future state definition.

Once again, developing a document/process view would provide the clinical engineering group with the necessary approach and information to identify gaps between the current and desired future state to improve the cost of care per capita.

Alice felt that Porter's IPU concepts would provide a framework to explicitly define patient care and assure the best patient outcomes at the lowest cost. But community wellness improvement would require reaching out to the community with "Health Fairs" to provide free health testing to assess patient wellness, catch potential illnesses early on and to provide extensive education and any other form of encouragement that would encourage healthy habits: e.g., no smoking, few alcoholic drinks, balanced diet and regular exercise.

Her future state model must not only show Market>Develop>Purchase >Deliver>Maintain core process detail, but also, consider support technology and services. The high-level model needed to be developed to the third or fourth levels to provide a clear idea of how the hospital's core functions stress support areas; e.g., laboratories, ORs, beds. rehab centers, beds, kitchen, pharmacy, etc.

Simulations could be used to identify required staff, resources, facilities, drugs, and beds. Simulations would treat each patient as a program of projects scheduled through medical events. That simulation data could then be analyzed and used to improve overall patient process performance.

Reflection 57: PROCESS (Descartes)

Background

The purpose of business is to produce value, not documents. However, documents are the knowledge objects and are records of business processes. Tracking their flow provides a uniform way of understanding enterprise. Documents [verbal or written] initiate, are input to and are output from a process. Documents are either the product or describe the state of a product or service of a successfully completed process. An unsuccessfully completed process usually produces a failure document. By defining documents as products of processes, analysis of flow can be applied to an entire organization.

Director Participants

Edward Block: Engineering   *Jud Blunt*: Manufacturing
Donald Denominator: IT   *Priscilla Precise*: Programming
Jason Skywalker: Strategic Planning
Clarence Barton: Nursing   *Alice Perry*: Clinical Engineering

Facilitator: Elena Piscopia: philosopher waitress quotes:

René Descartes (1596-1650): French process expert

René Descartes remarked that instruction seems to be "increasing the discovery of my own ignorance." He graduated from the University of Poities in France with a Law Degree. His work was all published while in Holland (1629 to 1649). *Rules for the Direction of the Mind* was published in 1629.

Concepts

Core Processes of Market>Develop>Purchase >Build>Maintain and the associated document flow for both healthcare and manufacturing are central to the discussion. Porter's IPU and Medicare are key to healthcare delivery and insurance is key to healthcare support.

Setting

We find the group puzzling over the topic of "Process." Once they had illuminated their thinking on documents as the knowledge objects of business processes, it led them to further investigate business processes. When we left the group in Chapter 2, Pris had concluded that Knowledge exists within the context of Process. The directors are again drinking a Sumatra Roast at The Java Beanery.

Overheard at The Java Beanery

Ed: As we try to understand our business as a network of processes instead of departments in an organization chart, we have accepted The Document Methodology view as Market>Develop>Purchase>Deliver>Maintain. I think this a good start for most business if we include the administrative processes of HRM, Technology, Finance, Facilities, and Legal.

Alice: I agree with Ed that the major areas he described work for healthcare. Furthermore, defining 'Develop' as a Portfolio of projects and 'Purchase' are quite analogous to manufacturing. However, Market, Deliver and Maintain are vastly different for healthcare; I hope to emphasize this later.

Pris: Whether for healthcare or manufacturing, documents provide a useful window through which to analyze business operations. By applying a document view to established process, management, and systems models, they reemerge with a cohesive thread (the document).

In René Descartes 'Rules to Direction the Mind,' he said that study should direct the mind toward correct judgment. TDM may support correct judgment because it considers processes, people and technology.

Elena: Did I hear Descartes name mentioned in that misquote of his work? The essay was entitled: Rules for the Direction of the Mind. What he wrote was: "The end of study should be to direct the mind toward the enunciation of sound and correct judgment on all matters that come before it."

Jud: No surprise about our waitress, but Pris is having a French philosophy discussion with her. Imagine that.

Elena: I read Descartes "properly" in the original French. But we digress. I think his second fundamental rule is much more pertinent here: "Only those objects should engage our attention, to the sure and individual knowledge of which our mental powers seem adequate." Documents may be considered in that context.

Clarence: Let me interject here. One of the problems with IT diagnosis support systems is that they generate so many alternatives that they are useless in identifying causes from symptoms or they generate no causes.

Jud: Elena and Clarence just set the stage for this tiresome monologue. Documents drive every step of a process. They provide the control for initiating, operating and completing processes, and regulate resource acquisition. Engines aren't bolted onto wings on the assembly line without a process sheet that specifies which bolt goes where with how much torque and with what tool. Changes aren't made to an assembly process unless an Engineering Change Notice gives the authorization and information to do so.

Clarence: From diagnosis to intervention to rehabilitation of the patient, documents not only record progress and status, but also direct flow from requests for lab results, to scheduling staff, operating theaters, chemotherapy and therapy and every other step required to achieve patient wellness including monitoring after being released from the hospital.

Pris: Because they are generated at each step of a process, documents reveal the state of the process at any point in time and represent the time-based flow of resources through the process to create products and Clarence has succinctly pointed out healthcare services.

Documents are an excellent comprehensive source of information for modeling all business processes. By looking at the progress of documents through processes, companies can identify where processes are delayed or overloaded and if processes are adequate. By identifying the bottlenecks of a process, document analysis assesses flow of information through the bottlenecks and facilitates change (maximizing the return of the investment in technology). Consider the development of an automobile . . .

Ed: Yes Pris, consider the development of an automobile. Tens of thousands of drawings and hundreds of thousands of revisions can be generated over a three-to-five-year period to build a car. If a part fails or can't be built, millions of dollars may be spent on redesign.

New product documents must flow to key engineering and manufacturing people for review and criticism early on and often in the process before the "final" design release.

Clarence: Pris and Ed, consider managing hundreds of patients simultaneously with all of the documents necessary to chart and schedule their progress through hundreds of processes being performed within the major areas of the hospital.

Jason: You've all been talking about engineering and manufacturing and indirectly purchasing, but you haven't mentioned marketing or maintenance. Since we sell to other manufacturers, marketing is fairly sophisticated involving response to RFQs with proposals that guarantee time-to-delivery from POs in the volumes requested. We also need documents that feature our capabilities and products. In customer service, we must use parts service manuals and scripts to document problems as they relate to our customers. Coffee please, Elena.

Alice: Our marketing and customer support problem is very different. Our documents must not only educate the community in our capabilities, but also instruct them in healthy lifestyles and educate them in how to communicate their symptoms and medical history. Our 'customer' is an insurance company or Medicare with stringent rules not only on how to deliver services, but how we bill for them.

Elena: Soon Jason. That reminds me of my personal favorite, Rule IV. "There is a need of a method for finding out the truth." It seems to me we've discovered a method: understand, schedule, track, analyze and continuously improve documents, which is related to Rule V, which is long.

Jud: Isn't it German not French to have rules for everything?

Elena: Germans learned everything from the French except about food and women. If Descartes' rules were good enough for geometry, they are certainly good enough for your organizational concepts. Speaking of geometry, how do you transmit part geometry around the enterprise?

Pris: We store them as CAD objects, which are tied to computer versions of geometric algorithms. That way we can do things like define a point object as an intersection relationship between two-line objects.

Alice: We have graphic objects with which you're all familiar: X-Rays and EKG plots. Our EHR system stores them so they can be displayed for review. Unlike you, however, our evaluation 'algorithm' is in doctor's heads. Their techniques are learned as interns; your engineers and craftsmen would call them apprentices.

Pris: An EHR system captures patient histories in the rows and columns of a relational database, but part geometry as well as medical images require a different approach. Object-oriented data bases and programming are the way we now develop engineering software. That means we tie software associated with the data together in an object. We can think of and model the enterprise in terms of objects by defining processes with their associated outputs.

Jud: Ugh. Objects, shmobjects. What I want is to talk in terms of documents that are tailored to the way I think about performing my job.

Clarence: So do doctors and nurses.

Pris: Well, commercial software is available to manage document objects and use email to control and monitor work. Besides documents can be considered aggregates of objects.

Jud: Now you're talking. Maybe you'll actually start assembling systems from that commercial document software, so that our computer systems can be delivered and changed in months rather than decades.

Pris: Jud, try manufacturing software on a lathe. Is there any hemlock left for Jud?

Jud: While Elena gets my drink, picture this. Suppose we take a synchronous manufacturing view of the whole business.

In manufacturing, we know that if a particular operation is so busy that it prevents the production of products, the cost of the delay to the entire operation is attributed to that bottleneck. If we view the document as the product of business processes, synchronous manufacturing principles and the associated technology can be applied to all business processes to relieve business bottlenecks.

Donald: Can we use existing manufacturing technology to run the business?

Pris: Not quite, Donald. We can use document and workflow technology to accelerate document flow and time stamp the documents for later analysis. We can also take advantage of manufacturing science to help us understand enterprise. But, some of the assumptions made in simulations and finite scheduling are built around much more certain time durations and variation than are present in many business processes. But we can work those out.

Alice: In medicine, duration and variation in your non-manufacturing processes is magnified ten-fold as patients flow through the hospital system. The initial diagnosis is frequently modified as lab results return and again as a team of

	specialists 'arbitrate' yet another diagnosis. This can change again if the proposed 'repair' fails. Multiply this by several hundred patients and you see a finite capacity schedule that must change every two hours.
Ed:	Could you take that duration/variation conversation offline?
Jason:	Let's dump our current systems and take a document view of information.
Donald:	Hemlock for Jason and coffee for me please, Elena.
Ed:	Donald, Jason, it doesn't have to be disruptive. We can deploy our document view of information in the context of Six Sigma: quality initiative that we're implementing throughout manufacturing.
Pris:	Think of 6σ as a race with many laps. In the first lap, software is put in place, so processes are better controlled, and transactions documented for the next lap. Also, the first several levels of a process model are completed, revealing ways to maximize benefit from existing process.
	In the next lap, more detail is added to the process model, and the simulation of the "highest benefit" processes are performed. This translates into workflows that are used to schedule and manage work in bottleneck areas. As workflows are defined in more areas, they can be used to analyze document flow through core processes.
	Use simulation to ask: "What if' certain processes are changed or eliminated?" Major changes to organizational infrastructure should be made only after lap three or four.
Alice:	In the context of Porter's Integrated Practice Unit (IPU), we're looking at 6σ and Lean; both were derived to improve manufacturing. Because intuition is paramount in diagnosis, we don't see how either or both can be effective without fundamental changes to their methods. An IPU provides focus on one of 14 areas of medicine, but the support areas, non-medical staff and facilities must be 'shared' across disciplines.
Clarence:	Beyond the IPU, we are looking at adopting Lynn's Medicaring to provide much of the care that nurses provide in the hospital to frail elders in their home (to be discussed under "People and Systems").
Elena:	It sounds like you're moving on to the subject of Quality. So, before I leave you, read Descartes Rules for the Direction of the Mind. I will summarize with a set of new Rules for the Direction of the Enterprise.

Rule I: Adopt The Document Methodology for sound and correct judgment of enterprise.

Rule II: Only documents that add value for the customer should engage our attention.

Rule III: In the subjects we propose to investigate, our inquiries should be directed by content, context, format and flow of documents.

Rule IV: There is need of a method for managing with facts based on monitoring flow of knowledge.   To be continued . . .

Healthy People Observation

Clarence and Alice agreed that many of the issues that the TDM team concluded regarding culture were also applicable to health systems.

Clarence proposed that there are very few businesses that are more dependent on the skills of its staff than medicine. While the cost of a physician is two to four times higher than the cost of an engineer, nurses are key to the successful performance of a myriad of processes requested by a physician. Lastly, nurses spend considerably more time with a patient (10x) than the physician.

More importantly, the consequences of incompetence or error can be death or extended debilitation. It is important both nurses and doctors do the right thing and do the thing right. Monitoring, measuring and recording data is key to continuing to improve patient outcomes. Here again, a Document/ Process model along with technology monitoring and staff notes are a critical part in assuring positive patient outcomes.

Information technology can be an enormous help to nurses by providing support from ordering meals, drugs, and supplies and presenting norms and comparing them to patient status statistics. Nurses, from this knowledge, can assure distraught patients that everything is proceeding as expected or can call for a physician if something appears to be wrong. Confident, compassionate, concerned nurses provide assurance and an environment that calms the patient to insure the best outcome.

Clarence concluded that a critical aspect of a nurse's duties must be to continuously observe and improve the patient care environment, which includes providing what the military calls an After-Action Report (AAR). This can be very difficult to initiate because of the real threat of litigation if a mistake is acknowledged. Transparency is touted as a good thing by citizens for their government, but it must be acknowledged that a confidential ARR is necessary for patient care to improve.

Doctors and nurses must have a frank discussion about the successes and failures of specific activities and whether a failure was a mistake, incorrectly defined procedure, the result of the patient's condition, or failure of the patient to follow a prescribed medical protocol (e.g., stop drinking or smoking). This data is collected anonymously and compiled in an AAR database to warn personnel about which defined procedures are inadequate or can be misapplied. This information is used to change Standard Operating Procedures (SOPs). To insure continuously improving competencies at all levels, continuous training is initiated with staff, not only for newly revised clinic procedures but also in the use of technology.

Reflection 58: PEOPLE (Locke)

Background

Documents are the repositories for transactions and strategic information that managers require to improve and direct the enterprise at every level. Stafford Beer's recursive structure of management preserves the autonomy of the business process at every level of the organization. Through W. Edwards Deming's profound knowledge, business processes can continuously be improved and accelerated by reducing complexity of the business processes and documents.

Director Participants

Edward Block: Engineering   *Jud Blunt*: Manufacturing

Donald Denominator: IT   *Priscilla Precise*: Programming

Jason Skywalker: Strategic Planning

Clarence Barton: Nursing   *Alice Perry*: Clinical Engineering

Facilitator: Elena Piscopia: philosopher waitress quotes:

John Locke (1632 – 1704): English Quality Expert

John Locke won a scholarship to Oxford where he received his master's degree and then lectured in Greek and Moral Philosophy. He studied to become a medical doctor but did not receive a degree. Starting in 1667 for sixteen years, he served Lord Chancellor Ashley as physician and general advisor and eventually secretary of the council of trade. While in England, France, and Holland, he worked for over twenty years to publish in 1690, "An Essay Concerning Human Understanding".

Concepts

Quality, Stafford Beer's Viable System Model. Skills, Balanced Score, Metrics, Portfolio of Program are discussed in the context of improving enterprise effectiveness and adaptability.

Setting

Once, they discussed the idea of "Business Processes" in detail, they recognized that the "Quality" of processes was critical. In the third session, they discussed Process and concluded in the current business climate that Quality was a key component in building Wealth. Our directors are again drinking Sumatra at The Java Beanery.

Overheard at The Java Beanery

Ed: Six Sigma (6σ) is our quality initiative to be implemented throughout the enterprise.

Jud: With 6σ, we're teaching every employee to be customer-focused, map the key internal processes, decide what's important to measure, monitor the process, and change it to delight the customer. Much of 6σ is associated with information. The only problem with 6σ is that it has a local not a global, focus.

Pris: That's where Donald's IT people can participate in all local 6σ sessions to provide a global perspective. For example, keeping a design in development longer to get criticism on its manufacturability significantly reduces the cost and time to develop and manufacture it.

Jason: Senior management must set the tone to create a culture of measurement. They must develop a "Balanced Scorecard" that tells the firm what is important for the success of the enterprise. That scorecard will tell how they intend to measure financial strength, employee capability, customer satisfaction and internal business operations.

Alice: We have a similar balanced scorecard where 'customer' is replaced here by patient (not insurer). The World Health Organization has defined 100 metrics with which healthcare organizations can measure and judge their performance. However, our management is concerned about government healthcare reform and mandates, getting paid by Medicare and insurers and only then patient safety and outcomes.

Donald: Whatever goals and metrics management sets, 6σ is telling people to measure themselves. Could their measures ever possibly be poor?

Elena: From Locke's book "Concerning Human Understanding" consider the reasons of how men give their assent contrary to probability:

"Want of proofs - Men want proof who have no opportunity to make experiments nor collect the testimonies of others.

Want of ability to use them - Those who don't have the skill to use those evidences they have of probabilities.

Want of will to see them - Men's thoughts are engaged elsewhere; laziness keeps others from any serious thought.

Wrong measures of probability."

Jud: We're certainly having trouble with a lot of our people in manufacturing. They're used to fighting fires and are having a tough time expanding their view of the job to include measuring and improving it as well. They claim that if they have to analyze their jobs as well as perform them that their productivity will be reduced.

Clarence: At the moment, our only measures for quality are final outcomes after patients have gone through everything. We don't track wrong diagnosis and there may be several before the right diagnosis is 'precipitated.'

Alice: Doctors are loathe to acknowledge mistakes for fear of being sued, which could possibly result in his/her right to practice medicine being revoked. The Emergency Room is always fighting fires where a wrong diagnosis or intervention can kill the patient. Improving quality is key, but acknowledging failure can cost millions in law suits.

Ed: Some of our most productive people (including ER doctors as well) perceive themselves as doers. Many of them have a great deal of difficulty stopping what they are doing to ask: am I doing the right thing versus doing the thing right.

Pris: Part of the problem here is that we continue to measure, and reward people based on a specific task rather than rewarding the empowered behavior that we claim is our paradigm.

Elena: That brings us to Locke's "Wrong measures of probability:"

1] "Propositions that are not in themselves certain and evident.

2] New information that changes old dogma.

3] Predominant passions such as placing probability on one side of a covetous man's reasoning, and money on the other.

4] Giving up of our assent to the common received opinions."

Jason: Boy, nothing changed much. Our whole accounting system was the "authority" by which we built inventories of finished goods. We had to take a $20 million write-off two years ago because finished goods were considered an asset which manufacturing continually delivered to.

Jud: Yes Jason, we all know that. We've gone to a more appropriate system of accounting now and are trying to minimize both finished goods and material inventories.

Pris: But, this is an example of how important "Wrong Measures" are. If we measure and reward behavior which doesn't improve quality and add value, we think we're doing great;, but we're really going out of business.

Alice: In medicine, we have gotten paid for a service rendered rather than results. Also, tests were ordered to validate absence of certain contra-indicated conditions to reduce the risk of being sued if the condition was present. The system 'rewarded" billing as opposed to results.

Donald: Are we getting off the topic of quality?

Jud: Not really. The way we insure a quality product is to insure a quality process. If the process is varying or getting out of control, we fix the process before it affects product quality. But, we have to be sure that what we measure reflects what we must improve and what adds value.

Jud: But, quality is fundamentally about the explicit definition of process that is directly related to our knowledge of it. Coffee please Elena.

Elena: Soon Jud. Locke's thinking was ahead of this team in 1670: "With intuitive knowledge, the mind perceives the agreement or disagreement of two ideas immediately: white is not black. With demonstrative knowledge, the mind cannot so bring ideas together as by their immediate comparison. Demonstration depends on clearly perceived proofs."

Jud: Deming's Profound Knowledge presents the issue of variation of process. To have demonstrated knowledge of the variation, the process must be explicitly defined. When transactions are monitored, variation can be determined.

Ed: A project definition is the demonstrated knowledge of process. This explicit definition must represent the "intuitive" knowledge of the manager and workgroup who are responsible for and operate the process.

Alice: It's good to hear Ed use intuitive. A physician's intuition defines a patient's flow through the hospital system. We discussed earlier that flow could be defined as a portfolio of projects supported by a resource management system.

Pris: Demonstrated knowledge of the process is represented by the fundamental support systems.

Elena: Locke again: "Human Knowledge extends no further than we have ideas and can perceive agreement or disagreement."

Jason: All this talk about quality process is ignoring the most important aspect of quality: people and by extension culture. Management must create an atmosphere of trust in our enterprise system. To do this, we must have clear policies that reward innovative ideas for improving process without trying to find a scapegoat for an existing problem.

Ed: This is one reason why we have adopted The Document Methodology. It recognizes that separate document and management models are necessary and concurrent to our process and change models. The management model, derived from Stafford Beer's Viable System Model (VSM), provides a framework for employees and departments to act as 'viable systems' that not only operate but also adapt their operation as their environment changes.

Pris: In support of VSM, we are much more capable of extending our ideas and perceiving agreement or disagreement. We are not more intelligent, but our sophisticated access to knowledge with technology has provided us with better collective social intelligence. I have access to product and process data worldwide with information systems.

Jud: In manufacturing we have evolved to a much higher level of collective knowledge with continuous improvement methods supported by information technology.

Elena: Locke was a pragmatist; he believed knowledge is about experience in our world. As a rationalist, Descartes believed reason is independent of our world. He defined knowledge as pure and abstract with structures that are abstract from but may be aided by technology. Although Descartes' intuitive certainty is essential for certain axioms, it is still the

Clarence: result of world experiences.

Clarence: Our nursing staff has better access to past charting and physician and nursing notes thanks to our IT systems. Doctors are in charge of "fixing" a patient, but nurses must insure the integrity (or quality) of the hospital system within which the patient transitions from ill to well.

Donald: Our information technology accelerates the rate at which we can "experience" new knowledge by a factor of ten. Modern perception of business is pragmatic. And, I would say that this entire century is characterized by pragmatism.

Jason: Bull! Thanks to theoretical physics' rationalist approach our world now includes the atom and the universe. Your vision of knowledge wouldn't exist without the theoretical vision of the Turing machine. Actually, your vision of knowledge is characterized mostly as "noise." Being bombarded with data doesn't mean that someone knows anything.

Jud: I hate to come to Donald's rescue as the U. S. distributor for noise, but information in manufacturing is being focused on knowledge of process and its variation. Deming says rational prediction requires theory and builds knowledge through systematic revision and extension of the theory based on prediction with observation.

Ed: Yes, but then Deming says without theory, experience has no meaning, one has no questions to ask, and there is no learning. It is difficult to see where the pragmatists view stops, and the rationalists view begins. Computer Aided Design (rationalist) and Statistical Process Control (pragmatist) are critical to our competitiveness.

Pris: If anything, we are overly pragmatic. If an initiative is successful in some remote corner of the business, we try to apply it everywhere with limited success. In management texts, all we see are anecdotal solutions and case studies about business problems. We need a few rationalists to postulate theories of enterprise.

Alice: Point taken Pris. In our hospital we had some success applying 6σ in our ER where one measure of success is wait time. 6σ helped perform triage much better and cut wait time by half. However, half the people have minor ailments and can be sent home. Others can be treated and sent home. If they are really sick, we get them; then, we are back to a patient portfolio of projects flowing through a complex network of processes. 6σ hasn't helped much with that yet. We may need a rationalist to postulate a model of the whole system.

Jason: Maybe we are defining an abstract way to help us think about the entire enterprise from both a rational and pragmatic philosophical viewpoint. For example, in *Managing for the Future*, Peter Drucker observes;

"If we achieve profits at the cost of downgrading productivity or not innovating, they aren't profits. We're destroying capital. On the other hand, if we continue to improve productivity of all key resources and our innovative standing, we are going to be profitable."

Pris: Drucker's productivity and innovation could relate indirectly to our pragmatic and rational philosophies. Furthermore, a pragmatic view of a company subdivides it into: *knowledge, process, people and systems*. We need to innovatively *change* the company and its products using a rational view or theory of the enterprise.

Ed: But isn't that pragmatic. Also, it's quite a stretch to relate rational and pragmatic philosophy to Drucker's management view. Adam Smith's wealth seems more appropriate.

Jason: The ultimate rationalist view is Stafford Beer's VSM; we haven't talked much about the most important quality entity: people. As Beer points out, within his/her area of responsibility, an individual must arbitrate between what to do and what to change. At least minimal 6σ skills are required to view and productively change process.

Clarence: In the hospital, physicians are already empowered to change how they process each individual patient; however, nurses are expected to follow a doctor's instructions to the letter. If a nurse perceives a problem, she/he needs an explicitly defined process to arbitrate a change to a physician's order that involves management and the attending physician.

Pris: Considering Ed's, Clarence's and Jason's opinion, for a company to increase wealth, it must continuously improve (as with 6σ) existing process, products, and structures within a "rational' VSM management framework. We must define and measure what it means to improve and to demonstrate our theory of knowledge (rational) and operation (pragmatic) of enterprise.

Jud: We need to make effective use of systems and technology that measure and report on productivity and innovation as often as we measure and report on profit and growth if we intend to increase the real wealth of the company.

Elena: You have evolved from discussing measurement, quality and empowerment, to John Locke's pragmatic and rational view of enterprise 300 years behind your time. In this view, systems support flexible processes run by people who must measure and continuously improve their individual and collective tasks in ways that add value.

To be continued ...

Health System Observation

Alice observed IT and EHR systems were not a panacea for all her facility's healthcare problems. However, IT presented opportunities for improvement that have not been realized. The first could be to mitigate possible government penalties for not complying with the mandate to make EHR data accessible to all EHR vendors for analysis by artificial intelligence (AI) algorithms to correlate symptoms-causes to aid in medical diagnosis.

Once all of the data is being shared between systems, it becomes possible to provide a better Clinical Support System (CDS) for medical diagnosis. However, critical to that success is developing a framework involving telemedicine that allows a geographical dispersed team of specialists to collaborate in the diagnosis of patients with multiple symptoms propagated by multiple causes. Because this collaboration formally records and categorizes symptoms, causes and critical decision factors, it is then possible to "discover" whether the resultant diagnoses produced positive or negative outcomes. This information resides in a data base, which is continuously evaluated by an AI algorithm (i.e., IBM's Watson) to support a CDS, which subsequently helps improve diagnosis with better "guesses" of causes from symptoms.

Once telemedicine with a CDS is installed in an emergency room (ER), a physician will be able to effectively diagnose patient symptoms in collaboration with an EMS paramedic and begin the correct medical intervention and transfer of a patient to the best and nearest medical facility. This scenario could be repeated all over the region with the proper use of telemedicine.

In yet another telemedicine benefit consider that there are mentally capable frail elders who cannot perform many simple tasks (e.g. bathing, food preparation, shopping, etc.) necessary to maintain their independence. In the past, they would be placed in a nursing home. However, with Medicare's PACE program (Program of All-Inclusive Care for the Elderly), an attending spouse (also frail) with daily visits from qualified care givers and a paramedic communicating with a virtual ER physician, an elder can be cared for at home; thereby, improving quality of life at a lower cost of care. Emergency events can also frequently be handled by a paramedic and virtual ER physician eliminating the need for an expensive, traumatic transport and ER visit.

IT systems, telemedicine, senior care, work instructions derived from a document/process model will make homecare for the elderly possible at a 70% cost reduction over a senior care facility. Home IT/telemedicine and a document/billing framework must be employed to automate and simplify billing cost of care to insurance companies, Medicare and Medicaid. IT systems and Internet along with a document/collaboration model will significantly reduce cost and improve quality of diagnosis resulting in positive patient outcomes.

Although many of the support systems such as resource planning, financial management, human resources, computer network management, project management and officeware were similar to manufacturing, the knowledge associated with patients and communication within the community were vastly different.

Healthcare software must:

- Manage the Electronic EHR.
- Allow patients via the web to manage their medical record, make appointments, check in, ask questions, view test results, order medications, pay bills and print and sign documents.
- Allow nurses to record tasks on mobile devices.
- Provide a CDS capability.
- Provide reporting, workflow tools and dashboards to manage patient census.
- Provide tablets for caregivers to document care.
- Manage ER visits, track OR use, and display room and bed status.
- Manage admissions, discharge and transfer of key information and status of patients.
- Document visits, orders, procedures, results, and send communications to patients.
- Schedule chemotherapy and manage cancer patient visits.
- Report on care decisions, identify trends, manage costs.
- Request and review lab results.
- Write and transmit prescriptions.
- Bring the EKG readings into the medical record.
- Document eye related procedures and write lens prescriptions.
- Manage Inpatient and Outpatient Day Surgery.
- Provide documentation, film tracking, and viewing of Radiology images.
- Document pregnancy episodes and deliveries.

Medical Technology

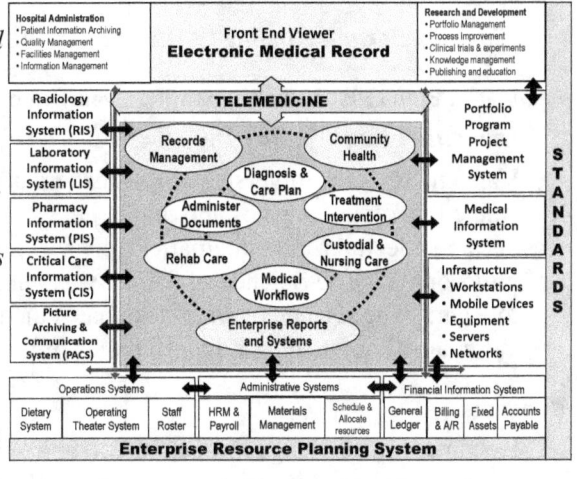

Reflection 59: SYSTEMS (Kant)

Background

Knowledge classification specifies the information architecture to support electronic documents on distributed client/ server heterogeneous computer networks. Document technology provides the foundation to rapidly assemble integrated systems from commercial off-the-shelf software. This approach reduces the complexity of business processes by explicitly defining processes in a workflow system that permits limited access to documents through a document management system.

Director Participants

Edward Block: Engineering   *Jud Blunt*: Manufacturing
Donald Denominator: IT   *Priscilla Precise*: Programming
Jason Skywalker: Strategic Planning
Clarence Barton: Nursing   *Alice Perry*: Clinical Engineering

Facilitator: Elena Piscopia: philosopher waitress quotes:

Immanuel Kant: 1724 - 1804 German Meta Expert

Kant entered the University of Konigsberg at age sixteen where he studied theology, physics and mathematics. He finished his degree and became a lecturer in mathematics, physics, logic, metaphysics and moral philosophy. "The Science of Right" was published in 1788. According to Kant: "The science of right designates the philosophical and systematic knowledge of the principles of natural right."

Concepts

Document, Knowledge, Management, and Workflow cycles along with portfolio and project management and application software are considered in the context of Support Systems.

Setting

We find the group trying to understand the impact of "Systems" on enterprise. Once they discussed quality and management in the fourth session, their discussion concluded that in the current business climate, systems are a key component in creating a competitive advantage and continuously improving quality processes. The directors are again drinking Sumatra at The Java Beanery.

Overheard at The Java Beanery

Donald: Working with computers has taught me about competing on knowledge. Furthermore, we're installing a new $100 million Enterprise Resource Planning (ERP) system that will make us more competitive.

Clarence: We have installed an ERP system as well. It is used to assign staff schedules, track bed status, schedule operating theaters and manage drug, disposable and food inventories. It has been a big help in scheduling staff and managing the facilities necessary for the hospital to function. But the amount of information presented to the nursing staff can be overwhelming.

Jud: Computer systems have been the biggest knowledge inhibitors in the history of modern manufacturing. They generate an avalanche of "useful" data (*makes quotes in the air*) it should be categorized as electronic counter measures.

What I *need* is a one-page schedule at 6:30 a.m. not a 400-page printout at 10:00 a.m. on the status of the industrial marketplace. I could care less whether that schedule is on a computer screen or comes stuffed in a courier's ear.

Pris: This is a great example of how documents also can act as bottlenecks. Finding ways to improve the flow, content and knowledge retention of documents can accelerate processes.

Donald: Who asked you, anyway? We couldn't possibly get that schedule without our finite scheduling system residing on our manufacturing server.

Jud: We don't get the 400-page printout until 10:00 a.m. twice a week. I also don't need to have 350 pages of detail, which gets down to defining the disposition of the toilet paper.

Clarence: For us no toilet paper can be a problem. Making sure patients get food, clean sheets, bed pans, toiletries, and a host of non-medical supplies is important to psychological welfare, especially if they are already stressed with a problem like cancer. We must also see a variety of documents regularly: schedules, lab tests, surgeries, medication, etc.

Donald: Well, as Clarence points out, some of your associates would consider it an emergency if toilet paper isn't available.

You don't know how difficult configuration control, disk management and security can be. That's why we may not have that information at 6:30 a.m.

Jud: If the Japanese had this computer system maybe we could compete with them better. Right now, they schedule their entire factory on 3"x5" cards.

Donald: Maybe we could equip you with 3"x5" screens.

Pris: Donald. Jud. Try to focus on the kinds of systems we need to support people in their creation and use of knowledge.

Donald We should start by listing all of our systems and functionality and see if they meet our present and future needs. Maybe we need a special task force...

Ed: Oops. Our facilitator has arrived.

Elena: It sounds like you could use advice from Immanuel Kant.

Jud.: Kant? We were expecting Isaac Newton from you.

Elena: You need Kant far more than you need Newton.

Donald: This is about technology. What does Kant's metaphysical meandering have to do with systems?

Elena: Everything and nothing. You talk about leveraging enterprise, workgroup and individual performance with information technology. Furthermore, you conclude the key to successful empowerment is document systems supported by computer networks. Maybe you should occasionally think about how to provide systems that protect the rights of individuals, workgroups and enterprise.

Pris: Déjà vu all over again. George Orwell a decade late.

Donald: We have security and access rights on all of our servers.

Elena: Try to focus your attention on the people issues first, and then you can commission as many task forces as you like to confound the technical issues.

Jason: Can our systems assure individual and collective rights under our existing laws of security, accuracy, and privacy of information?

Elena: Jason, let's not worry about that for now. Let's talk about "What is Right?"

Donald: Oh boy. That's of the same genre as "What is Truth?"

Elena: Germans don't dialogue. Germans make right rules. Let me introduce Kant's "The Science of Right."

"All right is accompanied with an implied title or warrant to bring compulsion to bear on anyone who may violate it in fact.

Anything is 'mine' by right, when I am so connected with it, that if any other person should make use of it without my consent, he would do me injury.

This constitutes the right to impose upon all others an obligation to abstain from the use of certain objects in our possession."

Pris: Let me see if I've got this right; pun intended. The Science of Right wants to tell us how to assign information objects to individuals and provides a legal structure to protect individual and collective rights.

Jud: Why do I even have to worry about this rights junk?

Jason: Suppose you're a senior manager. Keep in mind, information is power. Do you assume that every one of your 50K employees is ethical and honest?

Pris: So, what if they're not?

Jason: Since I don't know who needs every piece of information on the network, suppose I give everyone access to all of it; including personnel files.

Donald: Not *my* files.

Alice: We have really BIG security issues. We are bound by law to insure that a patient's electronic health record is secure and can only be divulged by patient consent; so patient data is stored anonymously. Unauthorized release can incur fines and lawsuits.

Jason: Amen Alice. If you're on our Board of Directors, you can be sued as well for fiduciary irresponsibility. Assume only one of our 50,000 employees is dishonest and he gives critical product files to the competition.

This is followed by an unsuccessful product launch because the competition got to market first with our product. The theft of the information comes to light. Does the employee even go to jail? No; who gets sued — the employee? Not likely, but the Board of Directors is financially accountable for the loss of revenue. If I'm going to give you access to critical company data, might I consider investigating your private life to verify your character?

Pris: My private life is *my* business.

Ed: It sounds like The Science of Right is exactly what we need to define a foundation for who has access to information on the network. Furthermore, since I'm in charge of critical product information, I need a legal structure to decide who gets it. I need to define penalties or fines for unauthorized disclosure. Also, I want IT guaranteed protection from unauthorized access.

Pris: We've been talking about empowerment facilitated by unlimited access to information. Absolute insanity.

Donald: Fortunately, on distributed networks, we can partition a server by department and restrict access to people in that department.

Pris: Are we doing that now?

Donald: No, but the good news is that since our systems are so disconnected at this point, it's difficult to access data even if you *should* have access to it.

Pris: Saved by our own technological incompetence.

Elena: Now that Donald has admitted to technical foibles, let's review what security within those cycles means when managing people. Kant says there can be only three external objects of my will:

"1] I can only call a corporeal thing mine if I possess it, even though I don't physically have it.

2] I must be able to assert that I am in possession of the will of the other although the time for the performance of it has not yet come.

3] If I possess them by mere will, provided they exist anywhere in space or time, my possession of them is purely juridical."

Jud: What is a "juridical." Why are we subjecting ourselves to all of this mumbo jumbo? Coffee please.

Pris: Juridical relates to law in general and its administration.

We say that we are empowering our employees, but how do we do that without chaotically going out of business? We've elected to do that with technology. But to do that we must redefine the fundamentals of management.

One speaks to the ownership of information objects.

Two speaks to the obligation of the employee to estimate and subsequently perform a task in the context of a project.

Three speaks to obligation between employee and manager, employee or workgroup to support the goals of the enterprise and protect the information objects in their charge.

Elena: Soon Jud. Outstanding, Pris. I suggest that you review The Science of Right as a foundation for fact-based management and empowered workgroups.

Jud: Thank goodness. I thought you were going to review the whole subject of Metaphysics. Coffee please.

Elena: Soon. Humor is no excuse for the absence of reason. Besides, Pris is the only one who seems to be keeping up. The rest of you clearly need more time.

Alice: This is one of the few areas where healthcare may actually be ahead of manufacturing with regard to systems. HIPPA compliance - I won't explain the acronym - requires exceptional security associated with regard to patients' EHR, which is subject to audit. However, nurses, doctors and patients complain about getting access to patient data when they want it.

Jason: We certainly didn't solve anything in this session. All we've managed to do is identify how disjointed our knowledge of management is from our knowledge of the technology that is supposed to help us manage it.

Donald: Maybe we don't have to know everything about process before we take advantage of our technology. If we take a document view, isolate information by department, and only transfer information between departments — defining it as an output document to the customer of the process — we shouldn't be in any worse shape than we are now, from a privacy and security aspect.

Pris: So, what you're saying is that we need to view technology through the prism of the document. That also means that we should base our method for change on a document methodology. Although there is effort in designing and implementing a good document system, the trade-off is having a haphazard, uncontrolled flow of documents because there will be documents, recognized or informal.

Elena: You've evolved from focusing on technology to empowering your employees rightly. You haven't solved the problem of empowerment, but at least you're examining problems with structures that may actually solve it.

To be continued . . .

Building Enterprise Wealth

How well companies capture and provide access to knowledge that generates value for their customers significantly impacts wealth. Document structure and content provide a foundation for understanding how knowledge facilitates the generation of enterprise wealth. Documents provide a coarse grained but detailed enough view of knowledge in enterprise for analysis. By considering time, knowledge, people, processes, and systems, synchronizing document flow can increase the rate of value generation for customers.

Reuse Knowledge	Present and future wealth in enterprise is captured in its knowledge documents. Providing exceptional management of knowledge in documents maximizes the reuse of enterprise knowledge. It ensures that documents and records have authenticity, reliability, integrity and usability and support good governance.
Accelerate Process	Once the information outputs of process are understood, processes are explicitly defined; workflow monitors the process; subsequent statistics are compiled and provide the facts to accelerate the process by eliminating bottlenecks.
Train People	Process statistics provide the facts to manage people, but people need to be trained in continuous improvement methods and enabling technologies.
Deploy Technology	Document technology supports exceptional access to information; workflow technology provides the ability to explicitly define and monitor process. Transaction statistics are analyzed and used to eliminate bottlenecks.
Guide Change	Once processes are well understood, radical process innovations are made with minimum risk because change is warranted by the facts.
Build Wealth	Profit is realized today by continuous process improvement. Profit is greater in the future by making exceptional use of carry-over knowledge and accelerating the processes by which present and future value is generated.

Health Policy Observations

- *Evaluate policy, culture, content, process, and infrastructure to reduce per capita cost of community health with input from nurses, physicians, engineers, dieticians, management, IT staff and patients.*
- *Identify knowledge flows in healthcare systems to resolve community healthcare, cost and quality issues.*
- *Use current and future state models to determine the transformations that create improved patient care and community health outcomes.*
- *Leverage existing and planned organizational strategic IT, web and telemedicine initiatives.*

- *Network hospitals, clinics, mental, social, GP and acute care services.*
- *Educate the community to communicate symptoms, illness, history.*
- *Initiate health fairs and seminars to communicate positive behaviors & serious medical problem symptoms.*
- *Validate all that is recorded in the EHR for ISO 15489 compliance.*
- *Revise the SOAP framework to support artificial intelligence analysis.*
- *Use EHR system to enable patient flow to wellness at lower cost.*
- *Use technology to manage, monitor and report on patient flow.*
- *Use an ERP system to manage staff, resources, facilities, finance.*

Health Change Observation

Vision: Healthcare Transformation
- *Volume => Value*
- *Fragmentation ===> Integration*
- *One Provider=>Multidisciplinary team*
- *Episode=>Population health*
- *Passive Purchaser=>Consumerism*
- *Buildings=>Health IT & Telemedicine*

The future state of healthcare is heavily dependent on continuously improving the current state to an "idealized" future state. This requires that a current state is defined in sufficient detail to get to a future state. Getting somewhere depends on knowing where you are.

Approaches that take baby steps may show improvement initially but can quickly go nowhere without a clear vision of where we are and where we're going so "baby" steps go in the correct direction. Lamenting that healthcare is too complex to understand, stems from the fact that the methodologies being employed to "fix" healthcare were derived from experiences in manufacturing. Although "intuition" plays a major role in design, manufacturing engineering is characterized by rigid analytical thinking based on facts.

Although evidenced-based medicine "attempts" to diagnose patient symptoms, "intuition" based on past experience is frequently successful.

Introducing collaboration with an experienced diagnostician leading a virtual team discussion of capable specialists provides the best opportunity to produce the right diagnosis in the shortest time.

Plan (Define>Measure)>Analyze>Improve>Maintain) proposes a document/ process model of an entire Medicare ACO that includes all community health related entities as well as at-home frail seniors and EMS. "Plan" starts with a generic hierarchical model. This model is then reworked to reflect the real-world hospital based on 20-30 interviews with key personnel and reviewing key documents used in all areas by the healthcare system. Four levels generate 5x5x5x5=625 processes to capture document and patient flow through the care system.

Further, it proposes collaborative, project, and viable system models and analyzes the gaps in the current system for adequate, appropriate operation. It then proposes a plan with milestones, times and resources to proceed. Because there is a comprehensive process model, it is possible to define a program of local process improvement projects that collectively reinforce the direction toward its ideal future state.

Reflection 60: CHANGE (Lao Tzu)

Background

Knowledge flow to value provides a paradigm to predict what changes will create the most value for business. Explicit definition of processes with document technology allows real-time audits that provide statistical summaries to indicate how to simplify a process and reduce its variation by assuring flexible access to the correct version of documents, Just-In-Time. Process document modeling understands the business environment, document simulation understands the flow, variation and bottlenecks of business processes and document object modeling supports rapid prototyping with commercial software.

Director Participants

Edward Block: Engineering   *Jud Blunt*: Manufacturing
Donald Denominator: IT   *Priscilla Precise*: Programming
Jason Skywalker: Strategic Planning
Clarence Barton: Nursing   *Alice Perry*: Clinical Engineering

Facilitator: Elena Piscopia: philosopher waitress quotes:

Lao Tzu: 6th B.C. Chinese Transition Expert

Lao Tzu was keeper of the imperial archives at Loyang in the Honan province. Lao Tzu is the author of the Tao Te Ching that describes the essence of Taoism. Taoism is concerned with the spiritual level of being. Of far less metaphysical importance, but critical to the change process is the Taoist focus on balance, paradox, and flow.

Concepts

Now that the first four Axioms have been reviewed, the last objective is to discuss how to go about not only changing the enterprise's operating processes, but also its culture.

Setting

Once, they discussed the idea of security and privacy of information in detail in Reflection 59; the group recognized that document systems that support a flexible approach to information management were critical in a rapidly changing autonomous business environment. They discussed systems and concluded that they needed a comprehensive process for change that considered people, processes, and systems. We find our directors again drinking a Sumatra Roast at The Java Beanery.

Overheard at The Java Beanery

Donald: It would seem that we should start by listing all of our systems and functionality and see if they meet our present and future needs.

Pris: You certainly are enamored with your technology Donald. We really need to model the firms 'current state' to propose a 'future state.'

Jason: You certainly are enamored with your models, Pris. How long will this modeling process take?

Pris: We just did an order entry process model; it took 5 people about 6 months.

Donald: That's just great, Pris. That means it will take 30 people three years to define an "current state" model of the business.

Pris: That's job security for us analysts and programmers.

Jason: How does a "current state" model add value to the business?

Pris: We must know where we are before we know where to go.

Ed: At the rate you 'model,' by the time you're done telling us where we are, we won't be there anymore. We need to build a high-level document/process model of the business to set the context of your object/data modeling Pris. We should be able to create high level as-is models for the entire enterprise in three months instead of three years.

Jud: Through 6σ we're already mapping and analyzing business processes. And in the factory, we simulate the factory floor, using a finite capacity scheduler. Why don't we make analysis everyone's job so that we continuously add value, while we collect process data that will help us determine what new processes should look like?

Ed: Jud, 6σ is great, but it generates too much detail initially, like Pris' object model. We need to start with a high-level process model to see how the organizational pieces interact with each other. Then at lower levels of detail, the model can be used to guide simulation.

Alice. Ed, that makes sense to me. We've had 6σ consultants tell us that hospitals are too complex to be modelled across its entire system. Now, I'm beginning to see how we could model our entire hospital system with TDM.

Pris: It just isn't done that way.

Donald: Pris, you're in the business of changing people's work environment. You seem to grasp new concepts as fast as anyone. Why don't you understand that you need to change your approach to analysis?

Pris: Who are you to tell me how to do my job?

Jud: You're always telling us. Now it's our turn.

Elena: Once again, you fail to see the obvious. You misrepresent what was written 2500 years ago by Lao Tzu.

Jason: Oh boy. First, dialogues; then, metaphysics; now, paradox!

Elena: "Knowing ignorance is strength.
Ignoring knowledge is sickness."

Pris: What has that got to do with anything?

Jason: I get it. We're educated in our own disciplines, but we're not learning from each other. Pris, you're not learning from Jud because you think his approach is too simplistic, but he used it to deal with a great deal of complexity on the shop floor. Lastly, no one likes to face the breadth and depth of their own ignorance. By ignoring each other's knowledge, we create sick systems.

Donald: Sick Systems! We give you the systems that you ask for. And, we run them efficiently, securely and reliably.

Elena: Oh boy! You really don't get it.
"Shape clay into a vessel. The space within makes it useful.
Therefore profit comes from what is there; Usefulness from what is not there."

Donald Is this another paradox?

Ed: Not at all. By making sure you're in control and efficient, Donald, you minimize the value of the people who use the network. I can't tell you how many times I've had people sitting idle because your "optimized" network was overloaded. We need a "useful" information utility that comes from underutilized capacity, so that we all can be effective.

Donald: I'm in charge of information. It's my butt if things get screwed up. We also have to deal with the issue of making sure that you're all using the proper version of the software; that's why all programs are on a central server.

Clarence: Donald is echoing the lament of our IT people when we complain about system response or usability. They are so focused on up time, system security, and federal compliance that they have no time to deal with users.

Alice: Sorry Donald. Clarence is frustrated with our IT department; that may NOT apply to your IT department.

Elena: "He who does not trust enough will not be trusted."

Jud: Amen. We at least have to trust each other. Certainly, there are programs like word processors that can exist on each machine. And with all this client-server technology, each department can be in charge of its own data.

Donald: The entire enterprise needs that data. It must be available to everybody.

Pris: Donald is clearly accountable for enterprise information security. However, he needs to arbitrate between departments if the information in one department's partition is required by another.

Jason: Remember *The Science of Right*? We need to define global accountability of information but distribute accountability by department or job classification.

Pris: This also gives us a way to evaluate the autonomy of processes. One criterion for restructuring processes would be to minimize the required documents that have to flow between processes.

Donald: How do we know what anyone needs? Maybe everything!

Jud: That's the problem that we have now. We get everything. We really need to ask a question in a structured way to get exactly what we need.

Jason: Through the Prism of the document.

Donald: So, based on our discussion, let me sketch out how technology and system capabilities can provide secure partitioned access to the enterprise's data.

Some of our systems are monolithic and provide multiple applications within the software to access data. In every case, we can restrict access by job classification of the person logging in. So, an individual – nurse, patient, physician, etc. – has access to certain parts of the system based on how they are identified within the system.

The data will all be in one place (sort of), but the departments' application and user identification will restrict access to data and filter only that data into the documents that the access rights allow.

Alice: We have purchased a monolithic system; it contains all required healthcare apps to manage patient electronic health records and provides enterprise resource planning as well. We picked it because we required exceptional access to the organization's data. But we still need a document/process model to make optimal use of those systems in a clinical environment and to define access restrictions by department and individual.

Pris: Alice, we have not made such a purchase, but we will need a document/process model to tell us how to deploy off-the-shelf software packages that can be assembled into a loosely coupled integrated system or buy a monolithic one.

Donald: Pris is concerned about picking the best of breed software applications while I'm left to provide the information framework that 'looks like' one system and access data from one data base.

Ed: Now that you've identified the alternative support systems, maybe we should discuss how we go about figuring what WE need to be more effective.

Jud: We also need to look at how we transition from old to new systems without putting ourselves out of business.

Jason: None of this makes any sense unless we have a road map of where the business is first and then where it needs to go.

Ed: Jud, you've already discussed quality management. We need to redefine those procedures to include the deployment of computer technology. If everyone participates in the analysis and deployment, they'll be more likely to accept and effectively use new systems.

Jud: This must be a new age where product and process engineers communicate.

Elena: Now, now watch the testosterone: Lao says: "Be gentle and kind.
In speech be true. In ruling be just.
In business, be competent. In action watch the timing."

Jud: Timing is everything. I would suggest to Pris that we already have people with the skills to effectively analyze all business processes, if her department will work with our system engineers. Synchronous manufacturing principles have helped us optimize manufacturing; this approach can also be used to optimize business processes.

Pris: We've been talking about documents representing knowledge flow to value. If we treat them as output objects of business processes, we can optimize business processes by synchronizing document flows.

Ed: If documents are remembered and time-stamped, they create a history and allow history to be repeated — in the form of simulation models which can think ahead to test the validity of suppositions about the future.

Jason: The enterprise's ability to remember and use those documents effectively is a measure of the enterprise's intelligence. The higher its intelligence, the better it competes on knowledge.

Alice: With our new systems we get plenty of screens of information, but we need to do a better job of tracking and structuring nurse and physician notes about the patient, which have been hand-written in the past. We need to make better use of voice recognition software so medical staff can dictate what they are doing and what needs to get done while they are working with a patient. An 'as-is' document process model, along with ideas about better ways to collaborate may help to derive a future state model.

Elena: "Achieve results, because this is the natural way.
Achieve results, but not through violence.
Force is followed by loss of strength."

Pris: What's violence got to do with this process?

Clarence: We have a real problem with 'violence' in a medical sense. Many 'repairs' are extremely traumatic, from surgery to chemotherapy to rehabilitation. These depend on the fact that the patient has the capacity to recover. This may not be the case with frail elders. We in the medical community must abide by the hypocritic oath: 'do no harm.' Fixing the problem (especially with frail elders) may not be possible. In those cases, we must counsel the frail patient on 'quality of life' and reassess medical support in the context of home care.

Alice: Managing frail elders' healthcare in their home or in a nursing home outside the hospital is a way cool problem that involves telemedicine and a host of other technology and coordination of off-site medical personnel and care givers. I can also see how a process model can support. However, I'll stop right now and just say thank for all of the ideas that you have given us that will help in improving the wellness of our entire community; you included.

Jason: Thank you as well Alice. Jud will be very interested in your work with elders.

The current way that we go about change is a pretty violent and disruptive process as well. We attempt to understand processes intellectually through models, but we don't understand them emotionally because we are outside.

By introducing the notion of modeling and analysis through the enhancement of the 6σ process, everyone is naturally involved and participating in change. Also, by forcing change we lose strength, which means we lose profit because people need significant training to adapt to radically new systems.

Jud: Alice if you have a psychiatric IPU, you might be able to help Jason as well. To Jason's point, we know we can do this in manufacturing. Is our management ready?

Jason: Our management is heavily invested in the current state of our business. That means they have financial, emotional and intellectual investments in the status quo.

Ed: Let's not underestimate these people. We all got to where we are based on the business as it currently exists. We're all in this together and we're all finding our way in a fiercely competitive market.

Elena: Humility is the way of the Master:
"Standing on tiptoe a man is not ready,
Striding he has no pace,
Admiring himself brings him no respect.
Pride has never brought a man greatness.
But, brings the ills that make him unfit."

Pris: The truth is, we must change the way we manage and change the business. People at all levels will be asked to adapt. People at all levels will be held accountable for performing their jobs differently. Some won't adapt. We need our Science of Right to reward the new behavior that will be required.

Jason: We need to adapt the planning process so that management is involved at every step. Actually, we need to integrate an assessment and change process into every employee's job. That way, everyone is 'adapting' to change continuously. They can internalize the overall mission and objectives of the enterprise and align their processes accordingly.

Elena: Lao provides the new management paradigm:
"If you can bear issue and nourish its growing,
If you can guide without claim or strife,
If you can lead men without their knowing,
You are at the core of life."

APPENDIX C: COLLEGE CURRICULUM TO REFLECT

How much more don't you know that you don't know you don't know?

I made four starts at writing Reflections version I. When my granddaughter asked: "Why do I need to know…," I had the idea of writing the reflections (loosely) around the central theme of education and the Christmas letters. Life is a learning experience. Proficiency in any discipline requires hard work and experience, but knowledge about something can be acquired by reading or classroom instruction.

What I was trying to do is give grandchildren an idea of how spectacularly much they didn't know. Selecting a group of reflections is best served with a theme in mind. For grandchildren, (and you), education should be our focus for all our years.

With some topics like CAD, knowledge, counting and the Internet, I spent 25 years as a practitioner. On others, like religion and philosophy, I have read more than 50 books (these topics are never ending). I had the qualifications to become a sail designer and was once offered a job at the Bureau of Atmospheric Research. I am comfortable having strong opinions on environment, weather, navigation, mathematics, medical systems, and engineering.

On war and peace, I have read many books, but am certainly not an expert nor am I an expert on culture, architecture, astronomy or wine. They are important to me, so I researched them (at least three books) and wrote about them.

To write a new reflection or rewrite an existing one required reading an average of three books which was probably only enough for an introduction. Occasionally one book documents an entirely new revelation and Reflection, like Menzies' "1421 and 1434."

If you are going to write what you think on a topic for others, you need to verify that you are not totally full of crap. On topics, like Religion and Philosophy, you need to find a subtopic and stick to it if you are going to write a Reflection in two to four pages.

The common theme for dialog between grandparents and grandchildren is not to tell them what to think, but to mentor them in how to challenge what anyone thinks by expanding their world view. We should help build their confidence and encourage them to become an informed and active participant in our capitalistic democracy and to contribute in one of the over 500 curriculum areas that follow.

Mathematics

1] Pure Mathematics
- Algebra / Algebraic Geometry
- Analysis
- Discrete Mathematics
- Statics / Dynamics
- Geometry & Topology
- Harmonic Analysis
- Logic & Foundations
- Number Theory / Set Theory

2] Applied Mathematics
- Control Theory
- Dynamic Systems
- Non-linear Dynamics
- Numerical Analysis & Computation
- Partial Differential Equations
- Differential Equations
- Applied Dynamics

3] Statistics & Probability
- Applied Statistics
- Biostatistics
- Biometry
- Probability
- Statistical Methodology
- Statistical Theory

Biological Sciences

4] Biology, General
- Biochemistry
- Biophysics
- Molecular Biology
- Structural Biology
- Anatomy
- Cell Biology
- Developmental Biology
- Cancer Biology

5] Ecology & Evolutionary Biology
- Behavior & Ethology
- Biogeochemistry
- Botany
- Evolution
- Population Biology
- Terrestrial & Aquatic Ecology

6] Public Health
- Environmental Health
- Epidemiology
- Biostatistics

7] Genetics & Genomics
- Computational Biology
- Genetics
- Genomics
- Molecular genetics

8] Immunology & Infectious Disease
- Immunity
- Immunology of Infectious Disease
- Immunopathology
- Immunoprophylaxis & Therapy
- Pathology

- Parasitology
- Systems Neuroscience
- Biology/Integrated Biomedical Sciences

9] Kinesiology
- Biomechanics
- Exercise Physiology
- Motor Control
- Psychology of Movement

10] Microbiology
- Bacteriology
- Environmental Microbiology & Microbial Ecology
- Microbial Physiology
- Pathogenic Microbiology
- Virology

11] Neuroscience
- Neurobiology
- Cognitive
- Computational
- Developmental
- Molecular & Cellular

12] Environmental Health
- Medicinal Chemistry & Pharmaceutics
- Pharmacology
- Toxicology

13] Physiology
- Cellular & Molecular Physiology
- Comparative & Evolutionary Physiology
- Endocrinology
- Systems & Integrative Physiology

14] Animal Sciences
- Animal Sciences
- Aquaculture & Fisheries
- Dairy Science
- Poultry Science
- Zoology

15] Entomology

16] Food Science
- Food Processing
- Food Microbiology
- Food Chemistry
- Food Biotechnology

17] Forestry & Forest Sciences
- Forest Biology
- Forest Management
- Wood Science & Pulp/Paper Technology

18] Nutrition
- Comparative Nutrition
- Human/Clinical Nutrition
- International & Community Nutrition
- Molecular, Genetic, & Biochemical Nutrition
- Nutritional Epidemiology

19] Plant Sciences
- Agronomy & Crops
- Botany
- Horticulture
- Plant Biology
- Plant Pathology
- Plant Breeding & Genetics

20] Bioinformatics. Biotechnology & Systems Biology

Physical Sciences

21] Astrophysics/Astronomy
- Physical Processes
- Instrumentation
- Sun & Solar System
- Stars, Interstellar & Galaxy
- External Galaxies
- Cosmology

22] Chemistry
- Analytical Chemistry
- Biochemistry
- Environmental Chemistry
- Materials Chemistry
- Inorganic/Organic Chemistry
- Physical/Polymer Chemistry
- Medicinal-Pharma Chemistry

23] Computer Sciences
- Artificial Intelligence
- Robotics
- Complex Adaptive Systems
- Computer/Systems Architecture
- Databases/Information Systems
- Graphics/Human Computer Interfaces
- Numerical Analysis
- Scientific Computing
- Programming Languages/Compilers
- OS/Networks
- Software Engineering
- Theory/Algorithms

24] Earth Sciences
- Biogeochemistry
- Cosmochemistry
- Environmental Sciences
- Geology
- Geochemistry
- Geophysics & Seismology
- Glaciology
- Mineral Physics
- Paleobiology
- Paleontology
- Soil Science
- Tectonics & Structure
- Vulcanology

Physical Sciences (Continued)

25] Climate Sciences
- Atmospheric Sciences
- Climate
- Fresh Water Studies
- Meteorology
- Oceanography

26] Physics
- Astronomy/Astrophysics
- Atomic/Molecular/Optical Physics
- Biological & Chemical Physics
- Condensed Matter Physics
- Fields Engineering Physics
- Elementary Particles Physics
- String Theory/Relativity/Gravity
- Cosmology/ Nuclear Physics
- Non-linear/Fluid Dynamics
- Optics/Plasma/Beam Physics
- Quantum Physics

Engineering

27] Aerospace Engineering
- Aeronautical Vehicles
- Space Vehicles
- Systems Engineering
- Design Optimization
- Aerodynamics/Fluid Mechanics
- Astrodynamics
- Structures & Materials
- Propulsion & Power
- Navigation & Guidance
- Control & Dynamics
- Multi-Vehicle Systems
- Air Traffic Control

28] Biomedical Engineering & Bioengineering
- Biological Engineering
- Bioelectrical & neuro-engineering
- Bioimaging & bio-optics
- Biomaterials
- Biomechanics & Bio-transport
- Biomedical instrumentation
- Molecular engineering
- Systems engineering

29] Chemical Engineering
- Biochemical Engineering
- Catalysis Engineering
- Complex Fluids
- Membrane Science
- Petroleum Engineering
- Polymer Science
- Process Control & Systems
- Thermodynamics
- Transport Phenomena

30] Civil & Environmental Engineering
- Construction Engineering/management
- Environmental Engineering
- Geotechnical Engineering
- Structural Engineering

31] Computer Engineering
- Computer & Systems Architecture
- Digital Circuits
- Data Storage Systems
- Digital Communications & Networks
- Hardware Systems
- Robotics

32] Electrical Engineering
- Controls/Control Theory
- Electrical & Electronics
- Electromagnetics & photonics
- Electronic Devices & Semiconductor Manufacturing
- Nanotechnology Fabrication
- Power & Energy
- Signal Processing
- Systems & Communications
- VLSI & circuits: Embedded/Hardware Systems

33] Materials Science
- Engineering Mechanics
- Dynamics
- Mechanics of Materials

34] Materials Engineering
- Biology & Biomimetic
- Ceramic
- Metallurgy
- Polymer & Organic
- Semiconductor & Optical
- Structural

35] Mechanical Engineering
- Acoustics, Dynamics, & Controls
- Applied Mechanics
- Biomechanical engineering
- CAD/CAM
- Electro-Mechn Systems
- Energy Systems
- Heat Transfer
- Manufacturing
- Ocean Engineering
- Tribology

36] Operations Research, Systems Engineering
- Ergonomics

37] Industrial Engineering
- Operational Research
- Systems Engineering

38] Emerging Fields:
- Computational Engineering
- Information Science
- Nanoscience & Nanotechnology
- Nuclear Engineering

Social Sciences

39] Anthropology
- Archaeological
- Biological & Physical
- Linguistic
- Social & Cultural

40] Architecture
- Architecture
- Landscape Architecture
- Real Estate Initiative
- Urban Planning/Design

41] Communication
- Advertising
- Broadcast & Video
- Critical/Cultural Studies
- Health Communication
- Intercultural Communication
- Journalism Studies
- Mass Communication
- Organizational Communication
- Public Relations

- Social Influence & Politics
- Speech & Rhetorical Studies
- Technology & Media

42] Economics
- Behavioral Economics
- Econometrics
- Economic History
- Economic Theory
- Growth & Development
- Industrial Organization
- Int'l Economics
- Labor Economics
- Macroeconomics
- Public Economics

43] Geography
- Environmental Geography
- Human Geography
- Nature & Society Relations
- Geographic Info Science

44] Linguistics
- Anthropological/Socio
- Applied
- Comparative/Historical
- Computational
- Discourse/Text
- Typological & Diversity

44] Linguistics
- Anthropological/Socio
- Applied
- Comparative/Historical
- Computational
- Discourse/Text
- Language Acquisition
- Morphology
- Phonetics/Phonology
- Psycholinguistics
- Neurolinguistics
- Semantics/Pragmatics
- Syntax

CURRICULUM

Social Sciences (continued)

45] Political Science
- American Politics
- Comparative Politics
- International Relations
- Models & Methods
- Political Theory
- Public Administration
- Public Affairs & Policy
- Urban Studies

46] Psychology
- Biological
- Clinical
- Cognitive
- Community / Social
- Developmental
- Health
- Industrial / Organizational
- Cognition & Perception
- Personality & Social Contexts

47] Sociology
- Demography & Ecology
- Family & Society
- Gender & Sexuality
- Inequality/ Stratification
- Medicine & Health
- Methodologies:
- Quantitative/Qualitative
- Comparative/Historical
- Place & Environment
- Political/Social Change
- Race & Ethnicity
- Regional Sociology
- Rural sociology
- Social Control, Law, Crime
- Social Psychology
- Sociology of Culture
- Theory, Knowledge & Science
- Work & Economy
- Criminology

Arts and Humanities

48] American Studies
- Film Studies
- Material Culture
- Popular Culture
- Ethnic Studies

49] Classics
- Ancient History (Greek & Roman through Late Antiquity)
- Ancient Philosophy
- Byzantine & Modern Greek
- Classical Archaeology & Art History
- Classical Literature & Philology
- Indo-European Linguistics & Philology

50] Fine Arts
- Art (Paint, Draw, Sculpture)
- Art Restoration
- Cinematography
- Dance
- Dance Therapy
- Design (Crafts, Interior & Fashion Design, Gold, Ceramics & Silversmith)
- Dramatic Arts
- Graphic Arts Technologies (Lithography Techn)
- Music Performance
- Photography
- Photography Techn

51] Foreign Language Literature
- French Linguistics/Literature
- German Linguistics/Literature
- Portuguese Linguistics
- Portuguese Literature
- Spanish Linguistics/Literature

52] Language & Literature
- English Literature (UK)
- Literature in English, Anglophone (not UK/ NA)
- English Literature (NA)
- Ethnic & Minority Literature
- Rhetoric/Composition

53] Language & Societies
- African
- East Asian
- European
- Latin American
- Near Eastern
- Slavic
- South/Southeast Asian

54] History
- African / Asian / European
- Islamic World/Near East
- Latin American
- United States
- Cultural/Diplomatic History
- History of Religion
- History of Science/Technology
- History of Medicine
- Intellectual / Social History
- Medieval History
- Legal/Military/Political History
- Gender/Women's History
- Feminist & Gender Studies

55] Art, Architecture & Archaeology
- American Art/Architecture
- Ancient, Medieval, Renaissance & Baroque Art & Architecture
- Asian Art & Architecture
- Contemporary Art/Architecture
- Theory & Criticism

56] Music (not performance)
- Composition
- Ethnomusicology
- Musicology
- Music Theory

57] Philosophy
- Continental Philosophy
- Epistemology
- Esthetics
- Ethics/Political Philosophy
- Feminist Philosophy
- History of Philosophy
- Logic & foundations of mathematics
- Metaphysics
- Philosophy of Language
- Philosophy of Mind
- Philosophy of Science

58] Religion
- Biblical Studies
- Comparative Methodologies
- Ethics
- History of Religions of Western Origin
- History of Religions of Eastern Origins
- Religious Thought/ Theology/Philosophy of Religion

59] Theatre & Performance Studies
- Theatre History
- Literature, Criticism & Theory
- Performance Studies
- Playwriting

60] Emerging Fields:
- Feminist, & Film Studies
- Ethnicity & Rhetoric

Medical Science

61] Dentistry
- Biologic & Materials Sciences
- Restoration & Endodontics
- Oral & Maxillofacial
- Surgery/Hospital Dentistry
- Orthodontics / Child Dentistry
- Periodontics & Oral Medicine

62] Human Medicine
- Anatomy
- Anesthesiology
- Biological Chemistry
- Biomedical Engineering
- Biophysics
- Cell & Developmental Biology
- Cellular & Molecular Biology
- Dermatology
- Emergency Medicine
- Family/Internal Medicine
- Human Genetics
- Immunology
- Hearing Research
- Microbiology/Immunology
- Neurology/Neuroscience
- Obstetrics/Gynecology
- Ophthalmology
- Otolaryngology
- Pathology
- Communicable Diseases
- Pharmacology
- Physical Medicine & Rehab
- Physiology
- Psychiatry
- Pulmonary & Critical Care
- Radiation Oncology
- Radiology
- Surgery

63] Nursing
- Community Care
- Home Health Care
- Gerontological Specialist
- Medical-Surgical Specialist
- Occupational Health Nurse
- Mental Health Nurse
- Adult Acute Care Nurse Practitioner
- Infant, Child, Adolescent, Pediatric Nurse
- Psychiatric-Mental Health Nurse
- Women's Health (post master)
- Certified Nurse-Midwife Program
- Nursing Business & Health Systems
- Nursing Management & Administration
- Nursing Informatics
- Nursing & Health Services Administration

64] Osteopathic Medicine
- Family Medicine
- Biochemistry & Molecular Biology
- Internal Medicine
- Microbiology & Molecular Genetics
- Manipulative Medicine
- Neurology & Ophthalmology
- Surgical Specialties
- Pharmacology & Toxicology
- Pediatrics Physiology
- Physical Medicine
- Rehab Psychiatry
- Radiology

65] Pharmacy
- Clinical Sciences
- Medicinal Chemistry
- Pharmaceutical Sciences
- Social & Administrative Sciences

66] Public Health
- Biostatistics
- Environmental Health Sciences
- Hazardous Substances
- Human Nutrition
- Industrial Hygiene
- Occupational & Environmental Epidemiology
- Occupational & Environmental Medicine
- Toxicology
- Epidemiology
- Hospital & Molecular Epidemiology
- Dental Public Health, International Health
- Health Behavior & Health Education
- Health Management & Policy
- Life Sciences & Society
- Public Health Genetics
- Reproductive & Women's Health

67] Veterinary Medicine
- Animal Clinical Sciences
- Microbiology & Molecular Genetics
- Pathobiology & Diagnostic Investigation
- Pharmacology & Toxicology
- Physiology
- Veterinary Tech Program

Government, Law, Policy, Business

68] Government
- International Development
- Public Admin in Int'l Develop
- Public Administration
- Public Policy
- Public Policy/Urban Planning
- Social Policy

69] Law
- Antitrust Law
- Commercial Law
- Constitutional Theory
- Corporate Law
- Criminal Law & Procedure
- Cyberlaw & Technology
- Employment & Labor Law
- Environmental Law
- Family & Children's Law
- Federal Law & Federalism
- Financial Institutions
- Gender & the Law
- Health Law
- Intellectual Property
- Int'l, Comparative Law
- Intellectual Property
- Human Rights Law
- Jurisprudence
- Law & Economics
- Legal History
- Legal Profession, Ethics,
- Litigation
- Local Government Law
- Negotiation & Mediation
- Public Interest Law
- Race & Race Relations
- Regulatory & Taxation

70] Public Policy
- Business Administration
- Law & Public Policy
- Public Health & Public Policy
- Russian & East European Studies & Public Policy
- Higher Ed & Public Policy
- Environment & Public Policy
- Social Work & Public Policy
- Urban & Regional Planning

71] Business
- Accounting & Taxation
- Business/Gvrmt/Int'l Economy
- Entrepreneurial Management
- Finance & Banking
- Investments & Securities
- Hotel & Restaurant
- Labor & Industrial Relations
- General Management
- Marketing & Advertising
- Operations Research (MIS)
- Negotiation, Firms, Markets
- Organizational Behavior
- Personnel Management
- Purchasing & Supply Chain
- Statistics & Economics
- Strategy & Technology
- Operations Management

72] Agriculture & Natural Resources

- Agribusiness Management
- Agricultural Markets & Analysis
- Agricultural & Extension Education
- Animal Science
- Animal Science - Environmental Toxicology
- Biosystems Engineering
- Building Construction Management
- Community, Agriculture, Recreation, & Resource
- Crop & Soil Sciences
- Ecology, Biology & Behavior
- Entomology
- Environmental Design
- Environmental Economics
- Environmental Toxicology
- Finance & Production Economics
- Fisheries & Wildlife
- Food Science
- Forestry
- Gender, Justice & Environmental Change
- Horticulture
- Human Nutrition
- Interior Design
- Intn'l Agricultural Development
- Packaging
- Park, Recreation & Tourism Resources
- Plant Breeding & Genetic
- Plant Pathology
- Professional Integrated Pest Management
- Resource Development-Urban Studies Law
- Urban & Regional Planning

73] Education

Administration
- Supervision
- Curriculum & Instruction
- Institutional Management & Cafeteria Management

Education, General
- Pre-elementary Education (Kindergarten)
- Elementary Education, General
- Secondary Education, General
- Junior High and High School Education

Educational Theory
- Counseling & Guidance
- Educational Testing, Evaluation & Measurement
- Family Relations & Child Development
- History & Philosophy

- Media Specialist
- Psychology
- Statistics & Research

Higher Education, General
- Jr. College Education
- Adult & Continuing Education

Jr. High & High School:
- Art
- Business & Commerce
- Consumer Economics & Home Management
- English
- Foods & Nutrition
- Industrial, Technical & Vocational Education
- Language: French, Spanish, Latin & Other
- Health Education
- Home Economics
- Mathematics
- Music
- Physical Ed
- Reading
- Social Studies
- Science

Special Education:
- Deaf & Blind
- Gifted & Disadvantaged
- Retarded & Remedial
- Speech Correction
- Emotionally Disturbed
- Physical Disturbed

Technology and Support
- Library Science
- Education Technologies
- Food Service & Home Economics Technologies
- Library Technologies

74] Military Officer Training

- Air Force ROTC
- Army ROTC
- Marine ROTC

75] Seminary

Admin. & Counseling
- Human Development & Psychology
- International Education Office
- International Education Policy
- Language & Literacy
- Mind/Brain/Behavior Initiative
- Risk & Prevention

Biblical Studies:
- Old Testament
- New Testament

Education in Religion
- Christian Education
- Arts in Education
- Education Management
- Field Experience Program
- Higher Education
- Learning & Teaching
- Religion/Secondary Learning
- School Leadership
- Teacher Education
- Technology in Education
- Women's Studies in Religion

History: Church & Religions
- Ecumenics
- Christianity and Society

Practical Theology
- Congregational Ministry
- Pastoral Care and Specialized Ministries
- Preaching and Worship
- Speech Communication

Theology
- Philosophy / Doctrine
- Christian Ethics

Because I tried not to tell my grandchildren or you what to think but how I think and learn, I resisted summarizing my opinion on important issues (except God) until now. Philosophy that attempts to provide insights for humanity without a concept of God goes nowhere useful. I am for protecting the environment, feeding the poor, big business (regulated properly), privatized national healthcare (like Germany), the UN, legal immigration, better education, a capitalistic democracy and much less government. Women and men citizens whatever their color or culture are entitled to the same individual rights and responsibilities. I am against monopolies, more government, most political and environmental activism, lobbyists, judicial activism, atheism disguised as humanism, and riots disguised as protests. Military action is the only viable response to governments harboring terrorists or drug lords. I believe in God; for millennia, religion has guided morality, ethics and law and has been used to justify many evils. Grandchildren are the future.

www.ingramcontent.com/pod-product-compliance
Lightning Source LLC
Chambersburg PA
CBHW071858290426
44110CB00013B/1194